HISTORY

OF THE

AMERICAN WAR OF 1812

J. Kennedy s.

The brave Brigadier General

ZEBULON M. PIKE,

*Who gloriously fell in his Country
cause April 27th 1813*

AT YORK, IN UPPER CANADA.

HISTORY

OF THE

AMERICAN WAR OF 1812,

FROM

THE COMMENCEMENT,

UNTIL

THE FINAL TERMINATION THEREOF,

ON THE

MEMORABLE EIGHTH OF JANUARY, 1815,

AT

NEW ORLEANS.

*EMBELLISHED WITH A STRIKING LIKENESS OF GENERAL PIKE,
AND SIX OTHER ENGRAVINGS.*

SECOND EDITION.

PUBLISHED BY WM. M'CARTY.

BOOKS FOR LIBRARIES PRESS
FREEPORT, NEW YORK

First Published 1816
Reprinted 1970

STANDARD BOOK NUMBER:
8369-5469-6

LIBRARY OF CONGRESS CATALOG CARD NUMBER:
75-126242

PRINTED IN THE UNITED STATES OF AMERICA

CONTENTS.

iv CONTENTS.

CONTENTS. v

DIRECTIONS TO THE BINDER.

HISTORY

OF THE

AMERICAN WAR.

DURING the last thirty years the United States has been increasing in population and wealth in a ratio unparalleled in history. Within that period, its numbers have been more than doubled, while its forests have been rapidly changing into cultivated fields, and flourishing towns and villages rising, as if by magic, in the midst of the wilderness. These blessings, however, have not been entirely unalloyed. The rapid increase of wealth had introduced luxury, with its accompanying evils, and had, especially in the larger cities, considerably sullied our republican simplicity of manners. Our extensive commerce, too, had embroiled us with several of the European powers, and finally involved us in war; while the thirst for speculation which it had excited in almost every class, has undoubtedly had a demoralizing tendency, thought not perhaps in the degree attributed to it by some politicians, who have placed solely to that account the want of public spirit and nationality, which has been charged to this country. The late war, whatever other evils it may have introduced, has certainly checked this evil. It has raised the character of the nation in the eyes of foreign powers, and erected an altar of national glory on which all local prejudices have been sacrificed, and politicians of every party have joined hand in hand to celebrate the triumphs of our country.

A formal declaration of war against Great Britain, was passed by congress on the 18th of June; 1812, which was proclaimed by the president on the following day. At this time the whole naval force of the United States amounted only to seven frigates, and a few sloops of war and other smaller vessels. The land forces were next to nothing. An army of 35,000 men, it is true, were authorized by congress, and the president was empowered to call out 100,000 militia; but the latter species of force, though strong in defensive operation, in offensive is perhaps worse than nothing, and in a free country like this, where a comfortable subsistance is so readily procured, the

B

embodying of a large regular force is far from being the work of a day. Besides, some time is necessary to change the habits of men from civil to military; men brought up to ease and indolence cannot at once execute the duties and meet the perils of war. Considerable difficulties were experienced likewise in finding officers fitted for command. Many of the revolutionary characters were dead, and those who survived were almost too old for active service. In this state of things, can it be a subject of wonder that the raw forces of the United, States, headed by officers who had never seen service, and accompanied by rash militia, without subordination, should experience some disasters in the commencement of their career? These disasters, however, have thrown no disgrace on the American name. On the contrary, the conduct of the American armies has reflected honour on their country, and all their reverses have been occasioned either by the rashness of undisciplined bravery, or by the misconduct or inexperience of their leaders.

From the disadvantages under which the army laboured, the little navy of America was entirely free. The previous embarrassments of commerce rendered it easy for our naval officers to supply themselves with a sufficient number of seamen, and with men too who had all their lives been engaged in similar pursuits, and under the most rigorous discipline; for we apprehend that but little difference exists as to discipline and general habits between a merchantman and a ship of war.

At the time of the declaration of war, general Hull, governor of the territory of Michigan, was on his march through the Indian country in the state of Ohio, with an army of about 2000 men, destined for Detroit. In the preceding month of April the governor of Ohio had been ordered by the president to call out 1200 militia. This requisition was principally filled up by volunteers who rendezvoused at Dayton on the 29th of April, and were shortly after placed under the command of general Hull. In the beginning of June the detachment advanced to Urbanna, where, on the tenth, they were joined by the 4th regiment of United States infantry. The following day they commenced their march through the wilderness.

From Urbanna to the rapids of the Miami of the Lakes, the country belongs to the Indians, and is entirely destitute of roads. From the rapids to Detroit, along Lake Erie and Detroit river, are various settlements, principally of French Canadians. By the treaty of Greenville, concluded by general Wayne with the Indians in 1795, a number of tracts, generally six miles square, were ceded to the United States, which form chains of posts joining the lakes with the Ohio by the course of the navigable rivers and the portages connecting them. By the treaty a free passage both by land and water was to be allowed to the people of the United States, along these chains of posts. Forts or block-houses have been erected and garrisoned in most of these ceded tracts since the declaration of war, but at the time that the country was traversed by general Hull's detachment, no civilized being was to be seen between Urbanna and the Rapids, a distance of at least 120 miles.

Towards the end of June the army arrived at the rapids, where a beautiful and romantic country suddenly opened to their view, enlivened by the signs of cultivation, and by the dwellings of their countrymen. Here a beam of joy animated every countenance, and gave fresh energy and fortitude to those who had undergone with difficulty the fatigues of a march at once gloomy and oppressive. On men who had just emerged from a dreary wilderness, unincumbered by a single hut reared by the hand of civilization, occupied by nought but Indians and beasts of prey, the change of scenery had a wonderful effect.

After stopping here one day for refreshment, the army recommenced their march, having previously loaded a small schooner with the hospital stores and officers' baggage, which was dispatched to Detroit by water, under a guard of a lieutenant and thirty men. Before they reached Detroit the army were informed of the capture of the schooner, and of the declaration of war. On the morning of the 5th of July, they arrived at Spring Wells, opposite Sandwich, within a few miles of Detroit, where they encamped.

As general Hull had received, before his taking command of the army, discretionary powers to act offensively in case of war, the invasion of Canada was now determined on, and the utmost diligence was used in preparation for that event. The arms of the troops were repaired, a part of the ordinance found in the fort at Detroit was mounted, and every exertion was used by the officers to impress on the minds of the soldiery the necessity of strict discipline and obedience to orders.

On the 12th of July the army crossed into Canada, with the exception of a small part of one company of militia, that refused to pass the river. They encamped at Sandwich, a little below Detroit, where a proclamation was issued by general Hull. The inhabitants fled in the utmost consternation on the approach of the army, but on receiving the proclamation, many of them returned to their homes.

On the 14th a company of militia and a rifle corps, under

colonel M'Arthur, were detached to reconnoitre the country. They penetrated to M'Gregor's mills, upon the river La Tranche, or Thames, a short distance from the field of battle where the British army was captured fifteen months afterwards by general Harrison. On the 17th, they returned to camp, having collected a great quantity of provisions, and a number of blankets, besides a considerable quantity of ammunition and other military stores.

That part of Upper Canada traversed by the detachment is described by one of the volunteers that composed it as extremely fertile and beautiful. The fields of wheat and Indian corn were remarkably fine; but as every male capable of bearing arms had been drafted for the defence of the province, vast quantities of the wheat remained ungathered.

On the 16th, another reconnoitering party of 280 men, under colonel Cass, was dispatched in an opposite direction, towards Fort Malden, where the British and Indians had concentrated their forces.

Malden, or Amherstburgh, is situated near the junction of Detroit river with lake Erie, about thirteen miles south from the camp of general Hull at Sandwich. The road lies along the river, and crosses two creeks, and the river Aux Canards, the latter about four miles from Malden. Cass's detachment found the British advanced posts in possession of a bridge over the Aux Canards. After examining their position, the colonel posted a company of riflemen near the bridge, and forded the river about five miles above with the remainder of his force with the intention of surprising the British post. For that purpose the riflemen were instructed to commence firing, in order to divert the attention of the enemy, as soon as they should perceive their companions on the opposite side of the river. Unfortunately, however, being entirely destitute of guides, the detachment marched too near the bank of the river, and found their progress checked by a creek, which obliged them to make a circuit of two or three miles. This gave the enemy time to make their arrangements, and prepare for their defence. On being attacked, however, they retreated to Malden, and left the bridge in possession of the detachment; but as colonel Cass had received no orders to keep possession of any post, but had been sent merely to reconnoitre, this bridge, which formed the principal obstruction between the American camp and Malden, was abandoned, and the detachment returned to camp.

Meanwhile the main body of the Americans remained inactive at Sandwich. Not a single cannon or mortar was on wheels suitable for the attack of Malden; nor was it until the 7th of August that two 24 pounders and three howitzers were prepared. Previous to that day, however, a great change had taken place in the prospects of the Americans. The news of the surprise and capture of the island and fort of Michillimackinac* by a combined force of British and Indians, which took place on the 17th of July, and reached the army on the 28th. The surrender of this post is stated by general Hull to have " opened the northern hive of Indians," and to have induced those who had hitherto been friendly to pass over to the British.

The policy observed by the British and American government ments towards the Indians was of a diametrically opposite complexion. The American government did every thing in its power to civilize those unfortunate tribes who live within their limits, and to introduce among them the practice of agriculture and the mechanic arts, with a view to wean them from the hunter state, a state which is becoming daily more precarious and unprofitable from the increase of the population of the country, and which renders them extremely dangerous neighbours. The policy of the British, on the contrary, is to keep them in their hunter state, by which they not only supply a lucrative branch of trade, but furnish a powerful weapon in war, It is not to be wondered at, then, that the Indians, who delight in warfare, and all of whose habits are averse from the pursuits of civilized life, should cling to the British, and should view the Americans, from their rapid increase of population and strength, with jealously and dislike. From this cause Canada has ever been a thorn in the side of the United States. While in possession of the French, by whom it was originally settled, the most powerful efforts were made by the British and provincial troops to gain possession of the country.

In the French war of 1756, after three wholly disastrous campaigns, and one of mingled disaster and success, the Americans, assisted by powerful British aid, at last succeeded in,

---

* Michillimackinac, or Makina, is a small island situated in, he entrance of the strait between lakes Huron and Michigan. The fort is the most northern military post in the United States. Here a great fair was annually held, previous to the war, which, was principally frequented by the Indian traders, and the merchants of Montreal, for the purpose of exchanging the peltries, of the uncivilized regions for the manufactures of Great Britain.

uniting Canada to the British dominions, and thereby restoring peace to their harrassed frontiers. The same complaints against the possessors of Canada for exciting the Indians to hostility were urged in those days, that have been repeated against their successors the British, and by none was the use of this weapon more reprobated than by those who lately employed it. Such is the different lights in which a subject appears when it operates for or against us!

By the fall of Michillimackinac, the junction of the Indians, and the reinforcements, both of militia and regulars, which the inactivity of the Americans enabled the British to collect for the defence of Malden, it soon became evident that no effective measures towards the reduction of Canada could be undertaken by this army.

Several skirmishes happened between reconnoitering parties of the Americans and the Indians and British advanced posts towards the end of July and in the beginning of August, in which both sides claimed the victory. Most of these skirmishes took place near the river Aux Canards. By these parties it was discovered that the bridge over that river had been taken up by the British, except the sleepers; that a battery was erected at one end of it; and that the Queen Charlotte, which carried eighteen 24 pounders, lay in the Detroit river, at the mouth of the Aux Canards, about a mile from the bridge, with a gun-boat cruizing round her.

In the mean time the Indians had crossed the Detroit, and cut off the communication of the American army with the state of Ohio, on which they depended for supplies. As a small reinforcement of volunteers, with a quantity of provisions for the army, was daily expected by this route, a corps of 200 men was detached on the 4th of August to open the communication. This detachment fell into an ambuscade which was formed by the Indians at Brownstown, where they were totally defeated, and returned to camp without effecting the object of their expedition. About the same time an express arrived from general Hall, the American commander on the Niagara frontier, stating that there was no prospect of a co-operation from that quarter.

It being indispensably necessary to open the communication with Ohio, general Hull resolved to suspend the operations against Malden, and to concentrate the main force of the army at Detroit. Unwilling, however, to abandon the inhabitants of Upper Canada, many of whom had accepted his protection under the proclamation, he established a fortress on the banks of the river, a little above Sandwich, where he left a garrison of 300 men. The remainder of the army recrossed the river and encamped at Detroit, on the evening of the 7th and the morning of the 8th of August.

In pursuance of the object of opening the communication 600 men were immediately detached under lieutenant-colonel Miller. This detachment consisted principally of the regular troops, and a corps of artillerists, with one six pounder and a howitzer, a small body of cavalry, and detachments from the Ohio and Michigan volunteers. They marched from Detroit on the 8th of August, and on the 9th, about 4 P. M. the van guard was fired upon by an extensive line of British and Indians, at the lower part of Maguago, about 14 miles from Detroit. The van guard maintained their position in a most gallant manner, under a very heavy fire, until the line was formed, when the whole except the rear guard, was brought into action. The enemy were formed behind a temporary breast work of logs, the Indians extending in a thick wood on their left. The Americans advanced till within a small distance of the enemy, where they made a general discharge, and then proceeded with charged bayonets. The enemy maintained their position till forced at the point of the bayonet, when they commenced a retreat. They were pursued in the most vigorous manner, about two miles, when the pursuit was discontinued on account of the fatigue of the troops, the approach of evening, and the necessity of returning to take care of the wounded.— The Indians in this battle were under the command of Tecumseh, and are said to have fought with great obstinacy.

The British regulars and volunteers in this action are stated in general Hull's despatch to have amounted to 400, with a larger number of Indians: the Americans were 600 in number. The American loss was 18 killed and 64 wounded: the loss of the British was not ascertained. Four of their regulars were made prisoners, who stated that the commander, major Muir, and two subalterns, were wounded, and that 15 were killed and wounded of the 41st regiment; and as the militia and volunteers were in the severest part of the action, their loss must have been much greater. About 40 Indians were found dead on the field; and Tecumseh, their leader, was slightly wounded; the number of wounded Indians was not ascertained.

Nothing, however, but honour was gained by this victory. The communication was opened no farther than the points of their bayonets extended; and the necessary care of the sick and wounded, and a severe storm of rain, rendered their return to camp indispensably necessary. Boats had been sent from Detroit to transport the wounded thither by water; but the attempt was found impracticable. The boats being descried from Malden, the Hunter and Queen Charlotte were despatched in pursuit, and they were forced to convey the wounded from the boats into the woods, and there leave them until waggons could be procured from Detroit.

It was now determined entirely to abandon Canada, and accordingly the fort at Sandwich was evacuated and destroyed.

Suspicions of treachery in the general, which had begun to arise immediately after the return of the army to Detroit, had now become very prevalent among the troops. A letter was written to governor Meigs, of Ohio, by five of the principal officers, begging him instantly to make every effort to open the communication, and informing him of their fears and suspicions.

On the 14th of August another attempt was made to penetrate to the river Raisin, where it was understood the detachment from Ohio had arrived with the provisions. Colonels M'Arthur and Cass selected 400 of the most effective men, and set off by an upper route through the woods. The same day the British began to erect batteries opposite Detroit.

On the 15th, general Brock despatched two officers with a flag of truce, from Sandwich, which had previously been taken possession of by the British, requiring the surrender of Fort Detroit to the arms of his Britannic majesty, and threatening that the Indians would be beyond his controul the moment the contest commenced. General Hull, in his answer, replied, that he was ready to meet any force which might be at his disposal, and any consequences which might result from his exertion of it. On the return of the flag of truce, the British commenced a fire upon Detroit from their batteries, which was vigorously returned from the American fort. The British continued to fire and throw shells till 10 o'clock that night, and at break of day the firing was renewed on both sides.

During the night the ships of war had moved up the river nearly as high as Detroit, and the British and Indians landed under cover of their guns, and were advancing towards the fort, when general Hull ordered a white flag to be hoisted, and the firing to be discontinued. The firing from the opposite side was immediately stopt, and a parley was held, when articles of capitulation were agreed upon, by which fort Detroit, with all the troops, regulars as well as militia, with all the public stores, arms, and every thing else of a public nature, were surrendered to the British. The militia and volunteers were to be permitted to go home, on condition of not serving again till exchanged. The detachment with the provisions at the river Raisin, and that under colonel M'Arthur, which had been sent to meet it, were included in the surrender. It was stipulated that private persons and property of every description should be respected.

Shortly after this capitulation took place, colonel M'Arthur's detachment returned to Detroit, their attempt to penetrate to the river Raisin having proved equally unsuccessful with the former ones. When they arrived within a mile of that place, they learnt its surrender, on which a council was held, when it was determined to send an officer to the fort with a flag of truce. In the evening he returned with two British officers, who informed them that they were prisoners of war. The detachment then marched to Detroit, where they stacked their arms on the citadel.

The day following the surrender of the army, a British officer arrived at the river Raisin and delivered to captain Brush, the commander of the detachment from Ohio, copies of the capitulation, and of a letter from colonel M'Arthur, stating that his force was included in the surrender. At first these papers were considered forgeries, and the officer and his party were put into confinement; but their truth being confirmed by several soldiers who had made their escape from the garrison at Detroit; a council of the officers was held to consider what was proper to be done. This council decided that general Hull had no right to capitulate for them, and that they were not bound by his acts; and they accordingly concluded instantly to return to Ohio, and to carry with them all the public property that was possible. It was determined, however, that it would be improper to destroy those public stores that could not be carried off, as there were a number of American families who had taken refuge in the fort, and some soldiers who were too sick to be removed, had to be left behind. It was likewise conceived, that the destruction of the stores might induce the enemy to deal more rigidly with the garrison at Detroit, These resolutions of the council were immediately carried into effect, and the detachment returned to the settlements.

Twenty-five pieces of iron and 8 of brass ordnance fell into the hands of the British at Detroit, several of the latter being pieces which had been surrendered by Burgoyne on the same day, 35 years before, viz. the 16th of August, 1777. Twenty-five hundred muskets and rifles, and a considerable quantity of ammunition likewise fell into their hands.

The reasons stated by general Hull for this unfortunate surrender, were the great inferiority of his force to that of the enemy, joined to the numerous band of Indians, who were daily increasing in number; the hazardous situation in which the detachment under colonels M'Arthur and Cass was placed; and the impossibility of furnishing his army with the necessary supplies of provisions, military stores, clothing; and comforts for the sick, on pack horses, through a wilderness of 200 miles, filled with hostile savages. The contest, he observes, could not have been sustained more than a day for the want of powder, and but a very few days for the want of provisions. " A large portion," continues he, " of the brave and gallant officers and men I commanded, would cheerfully have contested until the last cartridge had been expended, and the bayonets worn to the sockets. I could not consent to the useless sacrifice of such brave men, when I knew it was impossible for me to sustain my situation."

The disasters accompanying this expedition did not end here. On the change of prospects in general Hull's army in Canada, a messenger was despatched to Chicago, or fort Dearborn, situated near the south-west corner of lake Michigan, with orders to captain Heald to evacute that post, and proceed with his command, which consisted of 66 men, to Detroit, leaving it to his discretion to dispose of the public property as he thought proper. The neighbouring Indians, hearing that the goods in the factory were to be given to them, crowded into the fort from all quarters. On the 13th of August, captain Wells arrived from fort Wayne with 30 Miamies, whom he had brought by request of general Hull, for the purpose of escorting the garrison to Detroit. The following day all the goods in the foctory store were delivered to the Indians. The surplus arms and ammunition, however, and the spirituous liquors were destroyed, lest the Indians should make a bad use of them if put into their possession.

On the 15th the garrison commenced their march for Detroit, a part of the Miamies being detached in front, and the remainder in the rear, as guards, under the direction of captain Wells. Their course lay along the beach of lake Michigan, the lake on their left, and a high sand bank on their right, distant about 100 yards. They had not proceeded two miles before they were fired on by the Indians from behind the bank, and an action immediately commenced; but the Miamies giving the garrison no assistance, in fifteen minutes thirty-eight soldiers, two women, and twelve children were killed, and the Indians had gained possession of all their horses, provisions and baggage. The remainder were surrounded and made prisoners. They were then carried back to the fort, and distributed among the different tribes. Next morning the Indians burnt the fort, and carried off their prisoners. The number of Indian warriors in the action was between four and five hundred; their loss about fifteen. Captain Heald and his lady were carried to the mouth of the river St. Joseph, and being both badly wounded, were permitted to reside there with an Indian trader, whence they took an opportunity of going to Michillimackinac, where the captain surrendered himself to the British as a prisoner of war. A lieutenant, twenty-five non-commissioned officers and soldiers, and eleven women and children, were prisoners when the captain separated from them.

By the disastrous issue of this unfortunate expedition of general Hull, besides the loss of men and arms at Detroit, a weak frontier of vast extent was exposed to the brutality of Indian warfare, which continued for twelve months to harass the western settlements, and the territory of Michigan was occupied as a British province.

From the disastrous scenes which followed the first efforts of our arms in the north-west, we turn with pleasure to record the glorious events that have taken place on the ocean. There our gallant tars, strong in spirit, though weak in number, in despite of the thousand ships of the self-styled mistress of the ocean, have triumphantly borne the flag of America through every sea, from the rude and inclement shores of Greenland, to the rich and temperate regions of Chili and Peru. The enemy, with his immense disparity of force, has to boast of but few triumphs over us, whilst we can claim more than we have ships.

But the courage of our tars, though it has achieved victories which have thrown a halo of glory around our little navy, forms by no means the most conspicuous or lovely trait in their character. Their modesty and disinterestedness, their humanity and liberality to the conquered, have been such as uniformly to extort the grateful acknowledgments of the enemy that they have thus doubly vanquished, and have convinced the world, that the character of bravery which they have acquired, does not rest merely on the exertion of physical strength and technical skill.

Nor has the naval glory of America suffered by the few reverses that have taken place. On no occasion has its honour been in the slightest degree tarnished; it has been equally sustained in defeat as in victory; and the clouds of adversity have served but to display its character in a new light, and to shew that it is adequate to every emergency.

These remarks do not solely apply to national vessels. The commanders and crews of our privateers have not been out-

shone either in courage or magnanimity, as has been amply
proved by their valorous deeds, and by the numerous public
testimonies which have been borne to their worth by the un-
flattering tongue of those who have suffered by their enter
prize.*

---

* *We are favoured with the following anecdote by a gentleman who was present when the circumstance related took place,
he having been captured by the British squadron in a merchant
vessel which sailed from England before the knowledge of the
war.*

*In July 1812, the privateer Dolphin, captain Endicot, of Sa-
lem, was captured by a British squadron under commodore
Broke, and the captain and crew were put on board the Eolus,
lord James Townsend. Endicot, during the short space of
time that had elapsed from the declaration of war to his capture, had taken fifteen vessels, and by his enterprize, activity,
and courage, had excited a considerable degree of asperity
against him in the minds of the officers of the squadron, who
had almost daily heard of his exploits. On the arrival of the
crew on board the Eolus, they were treated with much haughti-
ness, and suffered some indignities. Captain Endicot, in particular, was treated with such haughty reserve, that for several
days not a word was exchanged with him.*

*This treatment, however, was but of short duration. On
board the Dolphin the British found more of their own countrymen prisoners than there were men in the privateer, and on examining them, they were equally surprised and mortified to hear
the conduct of the Americans spoken of in the highest terms of
approbation, to find that every thing had been done to render
their situation comfortable, and that all on board had shared
equally in every luxury that the vessel afforded. It was also
discovered that in a former cruize Endicot had captured off
Nova Scotia a vessel in which there was an old woman passen-
ger, who had 800 dollars in cash on board, and who appeared in
great distress at the prospect of losing her property. Endicot
had with difficulty soothed her, as she could hardly be persuaded
that her little all was not irrecoverably gone. The crew, on
hearing of the woman's fears, unanimously declared that not a
cent of it should be touched. In the warmth of her gratitude
for this liberality, she made the circumstance publicly known
through the newspapers on her arrival in the United States.*

*The British officers ashamed now of their past conduct, and
mortified at being outdone in magnanimity by a privateersman,*

A few days previous to the declaration of war, the frigates United States and Congress, and the brig Argus, received orders to rendezvous off Sandy Hook. On their arrival there on the 21st of June, they were joined by the brig Hornet and the President, from New York, and the same day commodore Rodgers, who commanded the squadron, having received official intelligence of the declaration of war, they put to sea in search of a British convoy which had sailed from Jamaica in the preceding month. The following night information was received of the convoy from an American brig, which had passed them four days before, and the squadron crowded all sail in pursuit.

Next morning, however, their course was altered by the appearance of the British frigate Belvidera, to which they immediately gave chase. The pursuit continued from six in the morning until past four in the afternoon, when the commodore's ship, the President, having got within gun-shot, commenced a fire with the bow chase guns, at the spars and rigging of the Belvidera, in hopes of crippling the one or the other so far as to enable them to get along side. The Belvidera returned the fire of the President with her stern guns, and the firing was kept up without intermission for about ten minutes, when one of the President's chase guns burst, by which unfortunate accident sixteen men were killed and wounded; among the wounded was commodore Rodgers, who had his leg fractured. By the bursting of the gun, and the explosion of the passing box, from which it was served with powder, both the main and forecastle decks were so much shattered as to prevent the use of a chase gun on that side for some time. Orders were therefore given to veer the ship, and a broadside was fired, in the hope of disabling the spars of the enemy. This, however, did not succeed; but considerable damage was done to the rigging and the stern. The utmost exertion was now used on board the President, by wetting the

---

changed their conduct towards Endicot, and invited him to mess in the gun room, where his frank, manly behaviour quickly secured him their highest respect. In speaking of privateers, he remarked to the British officers, that they were under the same regulations as national vessels, and that American privateering naturally differed from that of other nations, as it was generally considered in the United States as a national mode of carrying on the war, and hastening peace, by operating on the enemy in her most vulnerable point.

C

sails, &c. to gain ground of her opponent, but without success.
A constant firing was kept up on both sides, the President at
times giving broadsides, until about seven o'clock, when the
Belvidera, having cut away her anchors, started a number of
water casks, and thrown overboard her boats and every thing
that could be, spared, began to gain ground, and to get out of
the reach of the President's shot. The chase, however, was
continued with all the sail our squadron could set, until about
half past eleven, when it was given up as hopeless. Considerable injury was done to both vessels in this action. One of
the first shots fired by the President killed one man and wounded six; the captain was severely wounded in the thigh by the
breaking of the breeching of a carronade. On board the President there were three killed and nineteen wounded, the greater part by the bursting of the gun.

The squadron now resumed their course in pursuit of the
convoy from Jamaica, but did not receive further intelligence
of it until the 29th of June, when an American schooner was
spoken on the western edge of the banks of Newfoundland,
that had passed them two days before. On the 1st of July they
fell in with quantities of cocoa-nut shells, orange peels, &c.
which indicated that the convoy were not far distant. On the
9th they captured the British privateer Dolphin, which had
passed the convoy the preceding evening. The pursuit was
continued, but without success, until the 13th, the squadron
being then within eighteen or twenty hours sail of the British
channel.

From this they steered for the island of Madeira, and thence
passing the Azores stood for Newfoundland, and from the latter place by the way of cape Sable to Boston, where they arrived on the 31st of August.

During a great part of this cruize the weather was such as
to obscure every distant object: for several days the fog was so
thick as to prevent the vessels of the squadron from seeing
each other, even at cable's length asunder; in consequence of
which although they chased every vessel they saw, and brought
to every thing they chased, with the exception of four vessels,
they made only seven captures and one recapture. The
cruize, however, was not barren of benefit to the country, as
the knowledge of the squadron's being at sea obliged the enemy to concentrate a considerable portion of his most active
force, and thereby prevented his capturing a large amount of
American property that would otherwise have fallen a sacrifice. The vessels that escaped were, the Belvidera, another
British frigate, by night, and two American privateers.

The Constitution frigate, under the command of captain Hull, had received orders to join the squadron, and for that purpose sailed from Annapolis on the 5th of July. On the 17th, off 'Egg Harbour, four ships, apparently of war, were discovered from the mast-head to the northward, and in shore of the Constitution, and, in the belief that it was the American squadron' waiting her arrival, all sail was made in chase of them. At four in the afternoon another ship was seen from the mast-head, to the north-east, standing for the Constitution with all sail set, the wind at this time being very light, which course she continued till'sun-set, but was still too far off to distinguish signals. At ten in the evening, being then within six or eight miles of the strange sail, the private signal was made by the Constitution, and kept up nearly an hour; it not being answered, it was concluded that she and the ships in shore were enemy's vessels. Captain Hull immediately laid his vessel in the same course with the others, having determined to lie off till day-light to see what they were.

Next morning, about day-light, two frigates were seen from the Constitution, under her lee, one frigate four or five miles, and a line of battle ship, a frigate, a brig, and a schooner ten or twelve miles directly astern, all in chase, and coming up fast they having a fine breeze, and it being nearly calm where the Constitution was. After sunrise, finding there was but little chance for escape, being then within five miles of three heavy frigates, the Constitution was cleared for action, and two guns were run out at the cabin windows, and two at the ports on the quarter deck. At eight, four of the ships were nearly within gun-shot, some of them having six or eight boats ahead towing, with all their oars and sweeps out.

In this perilous situation, a new expedient was determined on, which was the happy-means of saving the vessel. Being in only twenty-four fathoms water, boats were sent out ahead with anchors, and the ship warped up to them, by which they soon began to get ahead of the enemy. They, however, adopted the same plan, and all the boats from the furthermost ships were sent to assist those nearest. For two days and nights were they chased by the squadron, sometimes with light winds, at others warping, and towing in a calm, seldom much beyond gun-shot distance. On the morning of the 20th only three of the squadron could be seen from the mast-head, the nearest about 12 miles distant, directly astern. Having now a light breeze, all hands were employed in wetting the sails from the royals down, and the enemy were soon left far behind. The Constitution, not being able to find the United States squadron, now bore away for Boston, where she shortly after arrived.

On the 2d of September the Constitution again put to sea, and on the 19th a vessel was discovered and chased, which at half-past 3 P. M. was made out to be a frigate. The ship was immediately cleared for action, and the chase, which proved to be the Guerriere, backed her main top-sail, waiting for her to come down. As soon as the Constitution was ready she bore down, with the intention of immediately coming to close action; but on approaching within gun-shot, the Guerriere gave a broadside, and filled away and wore, giving a broadside on the other tack, but without effect, her shot falling short. Both vessels continued to manœuvre for three quarters of an hour, the Guerriere for the purpose of gaining a raking position, the Constitution for the purpose of closing and avoiding being raked. At last they closed and kept up a heavy fire for sixteen minutes, when the mizen-mast of the Guerriere fell overboard, and brought the ship up in the wind, which enabled the Constitution to take a raking position, and to sweep her enemy's deck by her grape-shot and musquetry. The fire was kept up with equal warmth for fifteen minutes longer, when, by the falling of the Guerriere's main and fore-mast, she became an unmanageable wreck. On seeing this the Constitution ceased firing, but shortly after, perceiving the colours still flying, she took a raking position within pistol shot, when they were immediately hauled down.

Early next morning a sail was discovered, and all was got ready for action, but she shortly after stood off again At daylight the lieutenant on board the prize hailed the Constitution, and informed that she was in a sinking condition, and had four feet water in her hold. Accordingly the prisoners, were removed, and at 3 P. M. she was set on fire, and shortly after blew up.

Captain Hull in his official letter states, that all his crew fought with the utmost bravery: from the smallest boy in the ship to the oldest seaman, not a look of fear was seen. They all went into action giving three cheers, and requesting to be laid close along-side of the enemy. Their humanity was equal to their bravery. Captain Dacres, in his official letter, confesses their conduct to have been " that of a brave enemy the greatest care being taken to prevent the men losing the slightest article, and the greatest attention being paid to the wounded."

On board the Constitution there were seven killed and seven wounded; on board the Guerriere fifteen were killed, and six-

CONSTITUTION & GUERRIERE.

ty-three wounded, and twenty-four missing; the latter were stated by one of the officers to be away in prizes.

The Constitution rated 44 guns and carried 56; her complement of men is 450. The Guerriere rated 38 guns and carried 49, the odd gun shifting, which makes it equal to two; she had on board about 300 men.

Meantime the other vessels of our little navy were not idle. The Essex sailed from New York on the 3d of July, and shortly after fell in with a fleet of transports, under convoy of a frigate and two bomb ketches, from Jamaica for Halifax, with troops. The Essex kept at a distance until night, when she cut off a brig with 150 soldiers on board, which was ransomed for a bill of exchange on London for 14,000 dollars. The men were disarmed, an exchange receipt taken for them, and they severally took an oath not to serve till exchanged. Captain Porter, in his letter to the secretary of the navy, lamented that he had not with him a sloop of war, that the ships of the convoy might have been kept in play while he engaged the frigate. "Had this been the case," says he, "instead of taking only 200 prisoners, I have not a doubt that we should have made prisoners of the whole of the troops, as well as the frigates' and transports' crews, which would have exceeded 2000 men."

The following day the Essex captured the brig Lamprey, from Jamaica. Intelligence was received from her that the Thetis frigate, with specie and a large convoy for England, was to have sailed about the 26th of June, and that several running ships were on the departure. Every exertion was therefore made to get off St. Augustine in time to fall in with them, but without effect, as fresh gales prevailed from the south-west, which increased until the 19th of July, when, by the violence of the tempest, they were compelled to run before the wind.

On the 13th of August, the Essex captured the Alert sloop of war, after an action of eight minutes. The Alert, which was said to have been sent out for the purpose of taking the Hornet, ran down on the weather quarter of the Essex, and gave three cheers at the commencement of the action. When she struck her colours she had only three men wounded, but she had seven feet water in her hold, and was much cut to pieces. The Essex received not the slightest injury.

Being much embarrassed with his prisoners, who amounted including those of the Alert, to 500, captain Porter concluded an arrangement with the captain of the Alert, for despatching that vessel as a cartel to carry the prisoners to a British port. Her guns were accordingly thrown overboard, and she was entrusted to the command of a lieutenant of the Essex, with orders to proceed to St. John's, Newfoundland. The commander of the British naval forces at that place, in a letter to the American secretary of the navy, strongly protests against this practice of immediately despatching captured vessels as cartels; "nevertheless, as a proof of respect for the liberality with which the captain of the Essex has acted, in more than one instance, towards the British subjects who have fallen into his hands," and through a desire to fulfil the engagements entered into by a British officer, he consented to the proposed exchange. The Alert is now in the American service.

On the afternoon of the 30th of August, a British frigate was perceived standing for the Essex under a press of sail.—Porter was instantly prepared for action, and stood towards the frigate, and at the approach of night a light was hoisted for the purpose of preventing a separation. At nine a signal was made by the enemy consisting of two flashes and one blue light, apparently about four miles distant. The Essex continued to stand for the point where the signal was seen until midnight, when, not getting sight of the enemy, she hove too until daylight, on the presumption that the other had done the same, or at least would keep in the neighbourhood; but to the surprise and mortification of all on board, in the morning the coast was clear.

On the 4th of September, off the tail of St. George's bank, two ships of war were discovered to the southward, and a brig to the northward, the latter in chase of an American merchantman. The Essex gave chase to the brig, which attempted to pass her and join the other two, but was prevented, and compelled to stand to the north. She, however, escaped, the wind being light, by means of her sweeps. On the Essex showing her colours to the American vessel, the vessels to the southward fired signal guns, and made all sail in chase of her, and by 4 P. M. had gained her wake, and were coming up very fast. Calculating on escaping by some manœuvre in the night, captain Porter hoisted American colours and fired a gun to windward. The ships still continued to gain on him, and the largest being considerably to windward of the other, and only five miles astern, captain Porter determined to heave about as soon as it grew dark, and, in the event of not being able to pass him, to fire a broadside and lay him on board, a resolution that was received with three cheers when proposed to the crew.—At 20 minutes past seven she was accordingly hove about, but saw no more of the enemy; a circumstance which seems the more extraordinary, as a pistol was fired by accident on board

UNITED STATES & MACEDONIAN.

the Essex, at the moment when she must have been at the shortest distance from them. On the 7th of September the Essex arrived in the Delaware.

On the 8th of October, the President frigate, in company with the United States, Congress, and Argus, sailed from Boston on a cruize. On the 13th the United States and Argus parted company with the squadron in a gale of wind. On the 15th the President and Congress captured the British packet Swallow, having on board specie to the amount of nearly 200,000 dollars. On the 31st they captured a south sea ship, loaded with oil, one of two ships under convoy of the Galatea frigate, to which they gave chase, but lost her in a fog. During the remainder of this cruize they saw no other British vessel except the frigate Nymph, which escaped in the night. On the 31st of December they arrived at Boston, having been as far to the east as longitude 22 degrees, and to the south as latitude 17 degrees N., whence they ran down the trade wind to 50 degrees W., and on their return to the north passed within 120 miles of Bermuda.

The Argus, after parting from the squadron, proceeded to the coast of Brazil, sailed along the north coast from cape St. Roque to Surinam, thence to the windward of the West Indies, and thence in every direction between the Bermudas, Halifax, and the continent. After being out 96 days she arrived at New York, having made five prizes, valued at 200,000 dollars. During her cruize, she fell in with a British squadron, consisting of six sail, two of which were of the line, one of them a remarkable fast sailer. The favour of the moon enabling them to chase by nigh as well as by day, the chase was continued for three days, without intermission, and under various circumstances; but by unremitted exertions, the Argus was enabled to elude the pursuit. Pressed on all sides by the number of the enemy, and the baffling and unsettled state of the weather, she was at one time within musket shot of a 74, and at another nearly surrounded. While in this perilous situation she actually captured and manned one of her prizes.

The United States was still more fortunate. On the 25th of October, off the Western Islands, about two weeks after being separated from the squadron, she fell in with and captured, after an action of an hour and a half, the British frigate Macedonian, of the same class and strength with the Guerriere.— The Macedonian, being to windward, had the advantage of choosing her distance, which was so great that for the first half hour the United States could not use her carronades, and at no time were they within musket or grape shot. To this circum-

stance, and a heavy swell which prevailed, is ascribed the
great length of the action.   In this contest, the superiority of
the American gunnery was strikingly obvious.   On board the
Macedonian there were 36 killed ahd 68 wounded; she also lost
her mizen mast, fore and main-top-masts, and main yard, and
was much cut up in her hull. On board the United States there
were only five killed and seven wounded; the damage sustained by the ship was not so much as to render her return to port
necessary.

The United States, arrived off New London with her prize
on the 4th of December, and thence proceeded through the
sound for New York.

An equal degree of liberality was displayed by commodore
Decatur, as on a former occasion by captain Hull. All the property of the officers and men on board the Macedonian was
given up; that claimed by captain Carden included a band of
music and several casks of wine, which were valued at $800,
and paid for by the commodore.

While on this subject, we cannot forbear to mention an instance of generosity that occurred on this occasion among the
common seamen.   In the action with the Macedonian one of
the carpenter's crew was killed, and left three children at the
mercy of the world and of a worthless mother, who had abandoned them.   On the arrival of the two frigates at New York,
their grandfather went on board the United States to claim the
property and wages of his son, when an enquiry into the circumstances of the family took place, and a plan was agreed upon by the seamen for the relief of the orphans, by which $800
were instantly collected for their maintenance and education,
to be placed in the hands of suitable trustees for the purpose.

But of all the victories which have been achieved by single
vessels, perhaps the most brilliant is that which it has now become our most pleasing task to record.   At the time of the
declaration of war, the Wasp sloop of war commanded by
captain Jacob Jones, was on her passage from Europe, whither
she had carried despatches to our ministers in England and
France. She arrived in the Delaware a few weeks after that
event, and sailed again on a cruize on the 13th of October. On
the 16th she experienced a heavy gale, in which she lost her jib-
boom and two men. On the evening of the following day,
about eleven o'clock, in a clear moon-light evening, being then
in the track of vessels passing from Bermuda to Halifax, she
found herself near five strange sail, steering eastward. " As
some of them seemed to be ships of war, it was thought better
to get farther from them. The Wasp, therefore, hauled her

WASP & FROLIC

wind, and having reached a few miles to windward, so as to escape or fight as the occasion might require, followed the strange sail through the night. At day-break on Sunday morning, captain Jones found that they were six large merchant ships, under convoy of a sloop of war, which proved to be the Frolic, captain Whinyates, from Honduras to England, with a convoy, strongly armed and manned, having all forty or fifty men, and two of them mounting sixteen guns each. He determined, however, to attack them, and, as there was a heavy swell of the sea, and the weather boisterous, got down his top-gallant yards, close reefed the top-sails, and prepared for action. About 11 o'clock the Frolic showed Spanish colours; and the Wasp immediately displayed the American ensign and pendant. At 32 minutes past 11, the Wasp came down to windward, on her larboard side, within about sixty yards, and hailed. The enemy hauled down the Spanish colours, hoisted the British ensign, and opened a fire of cannon and musquetry—this the Wasp instantly returned; and coming near to the enemy, the action became close and without intermission. In four or five minutes the main-top-mast of the Wasp was shot away, and falling down with the main-top-sail yard across the larboard fore and fore-top-sail braces, rendered her head yards unmanageable during the rest of the action. In two or three minutes more her gaft and mizen-top-gallant-mast were shot away. Still she continued a close and constant fire. The sea was so rough that the muzzles of the Wasp's guns were frequently in the water. The Americans, therefore, fired as the ship's side was going down, so that their shot went either on the enemy's deck or below it, while the English fired as the vessel rose, and thus her balls chiefly touched the rigging, or were thrown away. The Wasp now shot ahead of the Frolic, raking her, and then resumed her position on her larboard bow. Her fire was now obviously attended with such success, and that of the Frolic so slackened, that captain Jones did not wish to board her, lest the roughness of the sea might endanger both vessels; but, in the course of a few minutes more, every brace of the Wasp was shot away, and her rigging so much torn to pieces, that he was afraid that his masts, being unsupported, would go by the board, and the Frolic be able to escape. He thought, therefore, the best chance of securing her was to board, and decide the contest at once. With this view he wore ship, and running down upon the enemy, the vessels struck each other; the Wasp's side rubbing along the Frolic's bow, so that her jib-boom came in between the main and mizen rigging of the Wasp, directly over the heads of captain Jones and the first lieutenant, Mr Biddle, who were, at that moment, standing together near the captain. The Frolic lay so fair for raking that they decided not to board until they had given a closing broadside. Whilst they were loading for this, so near were the two vessels, that the rammers of the Wasp were pushed against the Frolic's sides, and two of her guns went through the bow ports of the Frolic, and swept the whole length of her deck. At this moment Jack Lang,* a seaman of the Wasp, a gallant fellow, who had been once impressed by a British man of war, jumped on a gun with his cutlass, and was springing on board the Frolic; captian Jones wishing to fire again before boarding, called him down; but his impetuosity could not be restrained, and he was already on the bowsprit of the Frolic; when, seeing the ardour and enthusiasm of the Wasp's crew, lieutenant Biddle mounted on the hammock cloth to board. At this signal the crew followed, but lieutenant Biddle's feet got entangled in the rigging of the enemy's bowsprit, and midshipman Baker, in his ardour to get on board, laying hold of his coat, he fell back on the Wasp's deck. He sprang up, and as the next swell of the sea brought the Frolic nearer, he got on the bowsprit, where Lang and another seaman were already. He passed them on the forecastle, and was surprised at seeing not a single man alive on the Frolic's deck, except the seamen at the wheel and three officers. The deck was slippery with blood, and strewed with the bodies of the dead. As he went forward, the captain of the Frolic, with two other officers, who were standing on the quarter-deck, threw down their swords, and made an inclination of their bodies, denoting that they had surrrendered. At this moment the colours were still flying, as probably none of the seamen of the Frolic would dare to go into the rigging for fear of the musquetry of the Wasp. Lieutenant Biddle, therefore, jumped into the rigging himself, and hauled down the British ensign, and possession was taken of the Frolic, in forty-three minutes after the first fire. She was in a shocking condition; the birth-deck particularly was crowded with dead and wounded, and dying; there being but a small proportion of the Frolic's crew who had escaped. Captain Jones instantly sent on board his surgeon's mate, and all the blankets of the Frolic were brought

---

* " *John Lang is a native of New Brunswick in New-Jersey. We mention, with great pleasure, the name of this brave American seaman, as a proof, that conspicuous valour is confined to no rank in the naval service.*

from her slop-room for the comfort of the wounded. To increase this confusion both the Frolic's masts soon fell, covering the dead and every thing on deck, and she lay a complete wreck.

" It now appeared that the Frolic mounted sixteen thirty-two pound carronades, four twelve pounders on the main-deck, and two twelve pound carronades. She was therefore, superior to the Wasp, by exactly four twelve pounders. The number of men on board, as stated by the officers of the Frolic, was one hundred and ten—the number of seamen on board the Wasp was one hundred and two; but it could not be ascertained whether in this one hundred and ten were included marines and officers, for the Wasp had, beside her one hundred and two men, officers and marines, making the whole crew about one hundred and thirty-five. What is however decisive, as to their comparative force, is, that the officers of the Frolic acknowledged that they had as many men as they knew what to do with, and in fact the Wasp could have spared fifteen men. There was, therefore, on the most favourable view, at least an equality of men; and an inequality of four guns. The disparity of loss was much greater. The exact number of killed and wounded on board the Frolic could not be precisely determined; but from the observations of our officers, and the declarations of those of the Frolic, the number could not have been less than about thirty killed, including two officers, and of the wounded between forty and fifty; the captain and second lieutenant being of the number. The Wasp had five men killed and five slightly wounded.

" All hands were now employed in clearing the deck, burying the dead, and taking care of the wounded, when captain Jones sent orders to lieutenant Biddle to proceed to Charleston, or any southern port of the United States; and as there was a suspicious sail to windward, the Wasp would continue her cruize. The ships then parted. The suspicious sail was now coming down very fast. At first it was supposed that she was one of the convoy, who had all fled during the engagement, and the ship cleared for action; but the enemy, as she advanced, proved to be a seventy-four—the Poictiers, captain Beresford. She fired a shot over the Frolic; passed her; overtook the Wasp, the disabled state of whose rigging prevented her from escaping; and then returned to the Frolic, who could, of course, make no resistance. The Wasp and Frolic, were carried into Bermuda.

" It is not the least praise due to captain Jones, that his account of this gallant action is perfectly modest and unostenta-

tious. On his own share in the capture it is unnecessary to
add any thing. ' The courage and exertions of the officers and
crew,' he observes; ' fully answered my expectations and wishes.   Lieutenant Biddle's active conduct contributed much to
our success, by the exact attention paid to every department
during the engagement, and the animating example he afforded the crew by his intrepidity. Lieutenants Rodgers and Booth
and Mr. Rapp, showed, by the incessant fire from their divisions, that they were not to be surpassed in resolution or skill.
Mr. Knight, and every other officer, acted with a courage and
promptitude highly honourable. Lieutenant Claxton, who was
confined by sickness, left his bed a little previous to the engagement; and though too weak to be at his division, remained
upon deck, and showed by his composed manner of noting its
incidents, that we had lost by his illness the service of a brave
officer.' "*

     Meanwhile the utmost exertions were used on the lakes, in
order to retrieve the disasters occasioned by the surrender of
the force under general Hull. When that event took place,
there was only one vessel of war owned by government on
these waters, the brig Oneida, of 16 guns, on lake Ontario,
commanded by lieutenant Woolsey. In the beginning of October, commodore Chauncey arrived at Sackett's Harbour with
a body of seamen, for the purpose of taking the command, and
several schooners which had been employed as traders on the
lake were instantly purchased and fitted out as vessels of war,
and lieutenant Elliot was despatched to lake Erie to make arrangements there for building a naval force superior to that of
the enemy. Elliot had not been many days at Black Rock, before an opportunity offered for a display of the most determined courage.

     On the morning of the 8th of October, two armed British
vessels the brig Detroit, late the United States brig Adams,
and the brig Caledonia, came down the lake from Malden, and
anchored under the guns of fort Erie, which is situated nearly
opposite, and within a few miles of Black Rock, on the Niagara, near where it leaves the lake. Elliot instantly determined to make an attack, and if possible get possession of them;
and accordingly despatched an express to hasten the arrival of
some sailors who were hourly expected. The sailors arrived
about 12 o'clock, 50 in number. Though wearied with a
march of 500 miles, they were only allowed till midnight to re-

* *Port Folio.*

fresh themselves, when, being reinforced by 50 of the regular land forces, they put off from the mouth of Buffaloe creek in two boats, with lieutenant Elliot at their head. Having rowed into the lake above the vessels, they drifted down with the current, till they were hailed by a centinel on board one of them, when they instantly sprang to their oars, and closing in upon the vessels, they jumped on board, drove the British below, and in ten minutes from their getting along side, the prisoners were all secured, the topsails sheeted home, and the vessels under way. Unfortunately the wind was not sufficiently strong to carry them up against a strong current into the lake, and both ran aground. The Caledonia, however, was beached under the protection of one of the batteries at Black Rock, but the Detroit lay near the head of an island in the middle of Niagara river, exposed to the batteries and flying artillery of the enemy. The Americans returned their fire from the Detroit; but finding they could not bring the guns to bear with advantage, the prisoners were all got on shore, and the brig was deserted. In the course of the day several unsuccessful attempts were made by the British to board and destroy the military stores in the Detroit; but a considerable portion of them was secured by the Americans, after which she was set on fire and abandoned.

The Caledonia belonged to the N. W. Company, and was loaded with peltry, which was estimated at 150,000 dollars. The Detroit was a government vessel, which was captured at Detroit. She was laden with military stores, and had on board sixty men and thirty American prisoners. She mounted six guns. The Caledonia mounted two guns, and she had 12 men, and 10 prisoners on board. The loss of the Americans in this gallant exploit was only two killed and four wounded.

The force stationed on the Niagara frontier consisted of about 5000 men, of whom the majority were militia, under the command of general Van Rensselaer. The ardour of the troops having been very much excited by the successful issue of the enterprize of lieutenant Elliot, an invasion of Canada was determined on, and accordingly, on the morning of the 13th of October, the troops at Fort Niagara and Grand Niagara, having been marched to Lewistown the preceding evening, the soldiers began to embark at the dawn of day, under cover of a battery mounting two 18 pounders and two sixes.

To accomplish their landing on the opposite shore, they had only 12 boats, each capable of conveying 20 men. The movement being soon discovered by the enemy, a brisk fire of musquetry was poured from the whole line of the Canada shore,

D

aided by three batteries. In the face of this tremendous fire the first landing was affected by only 100 men, who were form- ed in a masterly manner by colonel Van Rensselaer, and soon succeeded in gaining the heights, and reinforcements arriv- ing, the forts were stormed, and the enemy driven down the hill in every direction. Having received a reinforcement of several hundred Indians, however, the British shortly after re- commenced a furious attack upon our troops, but they were quickly repulsed, and driven at the point of the bayonet.

At this interesting crisis, when the victory was already achieved by a handful of troops, the ardour of the militia, most of whom were still on the American side, suddenly abated. Either dismayed by the yells of the Indians, or by the appear- ance of reinforcements which were seen marching from Fort George, they began to raise constitutional objections against crossing the lines, and at last absolutely refused to embark. Finding it impracticable to obtain the necessary reinforce- ments, the general ordered a retreat; but unfortunately the boats were dispersed, and many of the boatmen had fled, panic struck. This little band of heroes were consequently aban- doned to their fate, and after a severe conflict with a very un- equal force, they were under the necessity of surrendering. The loss of the Americans in this battle is variously stated, but is believed not to have exceeded 1000 in killed, wounded, and prisoners, of whom perhaps more than one-half were re- gulars. The loss of the enemy is not known, but must have been considerable, as they were twice repulsed and driven down the heights. General Brock, who commanded, was kill- ed, and his aid-de-camp mortally wounded.

General Van Rensselaer shortly after this affair resigned his command, which devolved on general Smyth, who, towards the end of November, projected another expedition, which was to have sailed from Buffaloe, at the head of the Niagara river. This expedition failed from the same cause which brought about the disaster at Queenstown, the refusal of the militia to cross the lines.

Preparatory to the intended invasion, two parties were sent over, the one for the purpose of capturing a guard and destroy- ing a bridge, below fort Erie, the other to spike the cannon in the enemy's batteries and some light artillery in the neigh- bourhood. The first party made some prisoners, but failed to destroy the bridge. The second, after rendering unservice- able the light artillery, separated by some misapprehension, and a part of them returned with the boats, leaving behind four officers, and 60 men. This small body, however, advanced to the batteries, attacked and took two of them in succession, spiked the cannon, and took a number of prisoners. They then retreated down the Niagara, where they found two boats, on board of which thirty of the privates, three officers, and all the prisoners embarked, leaving behind a captain and 30 men, who were captured by the British before the boats could return.

Meanwhile, as soon as day began to appear, all the troops in the neighbourhood were marched to the place of embarkation. A part of the detachment which had passed to the opposite shore having now returned and excited apprehensions for the residue, about 350 men under colonel Winder put off in boats for their relief, and a part of this force had landed; when a superior force with a piece of artillery appeared. A retreat was then ordered, which was effected with a loss of six killed and twenty-two wounded.

The general embarkation now commenced; but there not being a greater number of boats than would hold 1500 men, a council of officers was held, at which it was determined, that as positive orders had been received not to cross with less than 3000 men, it was inexpedient to make the attempt until a sufficient number of boats could be procured for the whole number to embark at once; dependence being still placed on the volunteering of the militia, it was thought that the actual number of volunteers could not be determined without an embarkation. The boats were accordingly moved a short distance up the river, and the troops disembarked.

An additional number of boats being procured, another embarkation took place on the morning of the first of December, but still no attempt was made to cross. After remaining in the boats a few hours, the troops were ordered to be withdrawn, and huts to be built for their winter-quarters.

Nothing could exceed the mortification of the troops on this occasion, nor indeed the disgust felt generally throughout the country. Proclamations had been issued by general Smyth a short time previous, in which reflections had been cast on the conductors of the former enterprises against Canada, and the " men of New York" had been called on to join the army for a few weeks, and acquire glory and renown under his banners. A number of volunteers had been collected by this invitation, some of whom had come a considerable distance. Their mortification may easily be conceived!

General Smyth, in his official report, relies, for his justification, on the positive orders that he had received not to cross without 3000 men at once, and states that considerably less

than 2000 was the extent of the force which could be depended upon. If this were the case, Smyth was certainly fully justified in declining the invasion; but it is to be lamented that
measures for ascertaining the strength of the army could not
have been adopted without such a waste of public patriotism,
and such a degradation of the military character. Perhaps the
public mind was never so much distracted, nor public confidence so much shaken as on this occasion.

The intelligence of the surrender of the army at Detroit, and
of the exposure thereby of an extensive frontier to the ravages
of Indian warfare, excited the most lively sensibility throughout the western country. The army destined for the relief
and reinforcement of general Hull, had been ordered to rendezvous under general Harrison, at Louisville and Red Banks
early in August, and on the receipt of the intelligence of the
capitulation, volunteers poured in so fast from all parts of
Kentucky and Ohio, that it became more necessary to repress
than to excite the ardour of the citizens, and vast numbers
were discharged, and with difficulty prevailed on to return to
their homes.

The first operations of Harrison were directed to the relief
of the frontier posts. He arrived at Piqua on the 2d of September with about 2500 men, whence, after completing his arrangements and receiving his military stores, he marched on
the 5th for Fort Wayne, a post situated at the confluence of
the rivers St. Mary and St. Joseph, which after their junction
assume the name of the Miami of the Lake. This post had
been for some time invested by hostile Indians, but, on hearing of the approach of Harrison they precipitately retreated,
and the army arrived at the fort, without opposition, on the 12th
of September.

Not being able immediately to move on towards Detroit, on
account of the want of proper supplies, Harrison determined
to employ the intermediate time in breaking up the towns of
the hostile Indian tribes. For this purpose two expeditions
were organized, one of which was destined against the Miami
towns, situated upon the Wabash, a little below its confluence
with the Tippacanoe river, the other against the Potawatamie
villages, which stand on a river called St. Joseph, which falls
into lake Michigan. Both of these detachments were successful. Nine villages were burnt, and all the corn cut up and destroyed, in order that the want of provisions might force the
Indians to leave that part of the country.

A few days after the return of the troops from those expeditions, general Winchester arrived at Fort Wayne with addi-

tional reinforcements. Winchester had been originally destined to the command of this army by the president; Harrison, who was governor of the Indiana territory, had merely been appointed a major-general by brevet by the governor of Kentucky, and by him placed in the command pro tempore, on account of the urgency of the occasion. On the arrival of Winchester, Harrison accordingly relinquished the command, and set out for his own territory with a body of mounted men, for the purpose of breaking up the Indian settlements in that quarter. He had not proceeded far, however, before he received, by express a commission from the president, constituting him commander in chief of the north-western army, general Winchester to act as second in command. These counteracting measures are said to have been owing to the ignorance of the president, at the time of Winchester's appointment, of the brevet appointment of Harrison, and to the general expression of confidence in the latter by the Kentuckians having reached the seat of government shortly after. Fortunately the measure created neither jealousy nor dislike on either side.

General Harrison arrived at Fort Wayne, and resumed the command on the 23d of September. The day previous to his arrival general Winchester had marched for Fort Defiance with 2000 men consisting of four hundred regulars, a brigade of Kentucky militia, and a troop of horse.

In this part of the country, one of the greatest difficulties which an army has to surmount, is that which arises from the difficulty of transporting provisions and stores. At all seasons the rout is wet and miry. The country, though somewhat level, is broken by innumerable little runs, which are generally dry, except during or immediately after a heavy rain, when they are frequently impassible until the subsiding of the water, which is generally from twelve to twenty-four hours. Another of the difficulties of transportation arises from the nature of the soil, which, being generally a rich loam, free from stones and gravel, in many places a horse will mire for miles full leg deep every step.

To avoid the inconveniences and dangers of delay in traversing this wilderness, each soldier was furnished with provisions for six days, and general Harrison proceeded to Fort St. Mary's, in order to forward a detachment with supplies by the Au Glaise river, which affords a water conveyance for a considerable part of the way. This detachment was placed under the command of colonel Jennings.

The army being now in the centre of a country which presented every facility for the Indian mode of warfare, the utmost vigilance was necessary to prevent a surprise. The troops were formed into three divisions, viz. right and left wings and centre. Near the centre was the baggage, with a strong guard in front and rear. The wings marched about 60 or 100 yards distant from the centre. The front guard, which was generally about 300 strong, marched far enough in advance for their rear to be even with the front baggage guard, and were preceded by a company of spies, 40 in number, who were generally one or two miles in advance. The rear of the spies was covered by the horse.

So great were the obstructions occasioned by the underbrush, &c. on this march, that the army never advanced more than from six to ten miles a-day. They generally halted about three o'clock to lay out and fortify their encampment, which was done by forming round it a breastwork of logs and brush, of four or five feet in height. As soon as it was dark, small fires were kindled at the mouth of each tent, and large fires on the outside, about twenty paces from the breastwork.

On the 24th of September, being the third day of the march, the first trail was discovered; the number of Indians was supposed, however, to be only twelve or fifteen. They were pursued by the horse for six or eight miles, when, being pressed, they scattered, which rendered further pursuit impracticable. The following day, ensign Legett, of the regulars, and four volunteers, solicited and obtained permission to push on to Fort Defiance, then 25 miles distant, to discover the strength and situation of the enemy. These gallant youths, however, had too little experience of the Indian mode of warfare to conduct with success an enterprize so hazardous. They fell the same evening, being shot, tomahawked and scalped in the most barbarous manner, and in that condition were found by the spies on the 26th, about six miles in advance of the encampment for the night.

Early on the 27th the spies were sent out to bury the dead, supported by about 40 of the troop of horse. They had not advanced far before the flankers discovered a body of Indians in ambuscade on each side of a small Indian trail, on which they supposed the spies would march. Ballard, the commander, however, aware of the Indian stratagems, had placed his men in two divisions, and marched one on each side of the trail. Finding their plan frustrated, the Indians left the ambuscade, and made for an elevation a short distance ahead. While forming on this elevation they were fired on by the spies, which they. instantly returned, accompanied by a loud and terrific yell. The cavalry were then ordered to advance to the charge; but the Indians on their approach raised the retreat yell, and precipitately fled to the swamps and thickets. The pursuit was continued for two or three miles; the nature of the country, however, rendered it impossible to act with effect. In this skirmish only one American was slightly wounded in the ankle. The Indians were supposed to have suffered more severely, as several trails of blood were discernible. After interring the remains of their unfortunate brethren, the detachment returned and took their usual station in front of the army.

On the 28th, shortly after forming the line of march, four Indians were discovered and fired on by the spies, but without effect. A general engagement being now expected to take place, the order of battle was formed; but no enemy appearing, the line of march was recommenced, and the advanced part of the horse was ordered to push forward to ascertain whether or not a strong force of the enemy was at hand. In a short time a fresh trail of Indians was discovered. These indications of the near approach to the enemy determined the general to cross the river as soon as possible, and accordingly a tolerable ford being discovered by the troopers, the army passed over and encamped on the opposite shore. Here a fresh trail was perceived nearly equal to the one made by the army, which was supposed to be the trail made by Jenning's detachment, a supposition which was hailed with joy by the soldiers, whose provisions were now exhausted. Their joy, however, was but of short duration. A party of horse, who had been despatched down the trail, reported on their return that it had been made by a large force of the enemy, whose encampment they had discovered about three miles below, two miles above Fort Defiance, with fires burning, war poles erected, and the bloody flag displayed.

Late on the night of the 29th an express arrived from Jennings's regiment, stating that they were encamped on the Au Glaize, 40 miles above Fort Defiance, where Jennings had been ordered to erect a block-house. While engaged on this duty he had ascertained by his spies that fort Defiance was in possession of the British and Indians, and he had therefore thought it imprudent to proceed further without reinforcements.

Early on the morning of the 30th, captain Garrard and 30 of his troopers were ordered to proceed with all possible despatch to Jennings' block-house to escort a brigade of pack horses with provisions for the relief of the starving army. The detachment reached the block-house in the course of the following day, and, after resting a few hours, again set off as an escort to the provisions. They rejoined the army on the evening of the 2d of October, drenched with 36 hours incessant rain. This was a joyful evening to the soldiers. Provisions were now plenty, and the escort was accompanied by their beloved general Harrison, who resumed the command. During the absence of the detachment, the army had taken possession of Fort Defiance, the British and Indians having retreated down the river.

On the 4th of October, general Harrison, having left at Fort Defiance the force which constituted the left wing of the army under general Winchester, returned to the settlements to organize and bring up the centre and right wing. On the day of his departure, he ordered general Tupper, with the mounted troops under his command, consisting of nearly 1000 men; to proceed on an expedition to the Rapids. This expedition was never carried into effect. Its failure arose partly from the undisciplined state of the troops which had been selected for the enterprize, and partly from a disagreement which took place between their commander and general Winchester, who commanded at Fort Defiance. The inefficiency of raw militia was perhaps never more strikingly displayed than on this occasion.

General Tupper, after returning with his mounted volunteers to Urbanna, was despatched with the centre of the north-western army, consisting of a regiment of regulars, and the Ohio volunteers and militia, to Fort M'Arthur. The right wing, consisting of a brigade of Pennsylvania, and a brigade of Virginia militia, were stationed at Sandusky.

Shortly after his arrival at Fort M'Arthur, general Tupper organized another expedition for the purpose of proceeding to the rapids of the Miami. He left the fort on the 10th, with a force consisting of upwards of 600 men, the soldiers carrying provisions in their knapsacks for five days. On the evening of the 13th, being then about 13 miles from the rapids an officer was despatched to examine the situation of the enemy, by whom it was ascertained that the British and Indians still occupied the settlements and fort at the rapids; and that the boats and vessels lay a little below.

In consequence of this information the detachment halted until sunset, when they proceeded to a ford about two and an half miles above the rapids, whence scouts were again detached to observe more particularly the situation and force of the enemy. The necessary information being soon received, the troops were ordered to cross the river, in order to attack the enemy at the dawn of day. Unfortunately, however, it was impracticable for the troops to cross. Every expedient that could be devised was unavailing, and a number of men who were swept down the rapids, were with difficulty saved, with the loss of their muskets and ammunition.

In the morning, convinced that he was unable to get at the enemy, general Tupper ordered the spies to endeavour to decoy them over; and they accordingly proceeded down and discovered themselves. The stratagem, however, proved unsuccessful; for though a few Indians crossed the river, they were too cautious to be drawn within the lines. The main body was then marched down the Miami, opposite to the encampment of the enemy. They appeared in considerable disorder as the advanced guard opened from the woods. The British, who were in the vessels and boats, immediately slipped their cables and proceeded down the river. The Indian women were seen running off on the road leading to Detroit; the men commenced a fire at the detachment from their muskets and a four pounder.

General Tupper having observed a number of mounted Indians proceeding up the river, and fearful of the camp being surprised, ordered the detachment to return. When within about a mile of the encampment, some of the soldiers, pressed probably by hunger, the provisions being now entirely exhausted, fired upon a drove of hogs, contrary to orders, and pursued them nearly half a mile; others left the ranks, and entered a field to gather corn. At this moment a body of mounted Indians came upon them, killed four men, and then commenced an attack on the rear of the right flank. The column being instantly thrown back, commenced a brisk fire, which caused the Indians to give ground; but they quickly rallied, and passing along the van-guard, made a violent charge upon the rear of the left column. This column was also thrown briskly back, and every attempt made to break the lines being resisted, in 20 minutes the Indians were driven from the field. Conceiving, however, that the charge of the mounted men was merely intended to throw the troops into disorder to make room for an attack of the foot, general Tupper ordered the right column to move up into marching order, lest that attack should be made on the right flank. This column had scarcely regained their position, when information was received that the Indians were crossing the river in considerable numbers. Tupper immediately ordered the left column to resume their marching order, and proceeded to the head of the right column, where he found that a number of Indians had crossed on horseback, that some were still in the middle of the river, and about 200 on the opposite bank. A battalion was immediately ordered to advance and dislodge them. This attack was successful.   The Indians were forced to retire, and several of them were shot from their horses while crossing the river.

The horses rode by the Indians in this attack are stated to have been much superior to those they had been accustomed to use.   They were high and active; they were also supplied with pistols and holsters.   A number of Indians were shot from their horses; but they were with great dexterity thrown on again, and carried off the field.   Split Log led on several of the charges at the commencement of the attack, mounted on a well trained white horse, from which he sometimes fired, and at other times leaped from him behind a tree.   It was supposed that he was wounded in the action, as another warrior rode the same horse in some of the last charges.

After the retreat of the Indians the detachment were compelled to return with all speed to Fort M'Arthur, as their provisions were consumed, and they had to march 40 miles before there was a possibility of a supply.

On the 13th of December, general Tupper conducted another detachment to the rapids, consisting of between 1500 and 2000 men.   On the east side of the Miami, a few miles above the rapids, a body of the enemy was discovered, consisting of 300 British regulars, and 600 or 700 Indians.   Having ascertained the position of the enemy, Tupper ordered a small detachment to advance and commence an attack, and then to retreat.   This stratagem succeeded.   The enemy pursued with impetuosity until they were nearly surrounded, and on being charged, were repulsed on all quarters with considerable slaughter, and put to flight.   Fourteen or fifteen of the British, and seventy or eighty Indians were left on the field.   Many were likewise killed in swimming across the river, into which they precipitately plunged, that being their only means of escape.

While these operations were carried on, on the borders of lake Erie, several expeditions were set on foot against the Indian settlements in the Indiana and Illinois territories.   A portion of the Kentucky volunteers, under general Hopkins, and a corps of Kentucky rangers, commanded by colonel Russel, were particularly destined for this service.   This force having met at Vincennes, it was agreed that Hopkins should first proceed to the relief of fort Harrison, a post higher up the Wabash, which was at that time invested by the Indians, and should then proceed to the Peoria Indian towns on the river Illinois, where he was to be met by the rangers under Russel.   Another detachment, under captain Craig, was to join them at the same place.   This last detachment was to march up the Illinois river.

Captain Taylor, the commander at Fort Harrison, having received information of the approach of the hostile Indians a short time before they made their appearance, had used every precaution that the smallness of his garrison would admit of. The first hostile symptoms appeared on the evening of the 3d of September, when two young men, who had been employed a short distance from the fort, were shot and scalped, and were found in that condition the next morning by a small party that had been sent out to seek them. This circumstance caused them to redouble their vigilance, and the officers of the guard were directed to walk the round all night, in order if possible to prevent any surprize.

About 11 o'clock on the evening of the 4th, the garrison being alarmed by the firing of one of the centinels, every man instantly flew to his post. In a few minutes the cry of fire added to the alarm; when it was discovered that the lower blockhouse, in which had been deposited the property of the contractor, had been fired by the Indians. Such was the darkness of the night, that although the upper part of the building was occupied by a corporal's guard as an alarm post, yet the Indians succeeded in firing it undiscovered, and unfortunately, a few minutes after the discovery of the fire, it communicated to a quantity of whisky that had been deposited there, and immediately ascended to the roof, baffling every effort that was made to extinguish it. As the block-house adjoined the barracks, which constituted part of the fortifications, most of the men gave themselves up for lost; and indeed the raging of the fire, she yells of the Indians, and the cries of the women and children (who had taken refuge in the fort,) were sufficient to appal the stoutest heart. Happily the presence of mind of the commander never forsook him. He instantly stationed a part of his men on the roof of the barracks, with orders to tear off that part adjoining the block-house, while the remainder kept up a constant fire on the Indians from another block-house and two bastions. The roof was torn off under a shower of bullets from without, by which, however, only one man was killed and two wounded.

By this success the soldiers were inpired with firmness, and now used such exertions, that before day they had not only extinguished the fire, but raised a breast-work five or six feet high in the gap occasioned by the burning of the block-house, although the Indians continued to pour in a heavy fire of ball and showers of arrows during the whole time the attack lasted (which was seven hours), in every part of the parade.

On the first appearance of the fire, two of the soldiers had, in despair, jumped the pickets. One of them returned about an hour before day, and, running up towards the gate, begged for God's sake that it might be opened. On suspicion that this was an Indian stratagem, he was fired at. He then ran to the other bastion, where, his voice being known, he was directed to lie down till day-light behind an empty barrel that happened to be outside of the pickets. This poor fellow was shockingly wounded, and his companion cut to pieces by the Indians.

After keeping up a constant fire till six in the morning, which after day light was returned with considerable effect by the garrison, the Indians retreated out of reach of the guns. They then drove together all the horses and hogs in the neighbourhood, and shot them in sight of their owners. The whole of the horned cattle they succeeded in carrying off.

In this attack the Americans had but three killed, and three wounded, including the two that jumped the pickets. The Indian loss was supposed to be considerable, but as they always carry off both their dead and wounded, the amount could not be ascertained. At the moment of the attack there were only fifteen effective men in the garrison, the others being either sick or convalescent.

The Indians, disheartened by this failure, made no further attempt on the fort, but the garrison still remained in a perilous situation, as the greater part of their provisions had been destroyed by the fire, and the loss of their stock prevented future supplies. Captain Taylor therefore attempted to send, by night, two men in a canoe down the river to Vincennes, to make known his situation, but they were forced to return, the river being found too well guarded. The Indians had made a fire on the bank of the river, a short distance below the garrison, which gave them an opportunity of seeing any craft that might attempt to pass, with a canoe ready below to intercept it. A more fortunate attempt was made by land, and the garrison was immediately after relieved by the force under general Hopkins, consisting of nearly 4000 men.

After the relief of Fort Harrison, Hopkins began his preparations for his expedition against the Peoria towns. They commenced their march on the morning of the 15th of October, and continued it for four days in a direction nearly north. But here again the spirit of insubordination began to show itself. The general states in his official despatch, that having ordered a halt on the afternoon of the 4th day, in a fine piece of grass, for the purpose of refreshing the horses, he was addressed by one of his majors, in the most rude and dictatorial manner, requiring him instantly to resume his march, or his battalion would break from the army and return. Of the reply of the general to this modest request we are not informed. Next evening, however, an event took place which seems to have spread the spirit of discontent through the whole detachment. A violent gust of wind having arisen about sun-set, just as the troops had encamped, the Indians set fire to the prairie all around them, which drove furiously on the camp. They succeeded, however, in protecting themselves by firing the grass around the encampment.

Next morning, in consequence of the discontent that prevailed, the general called a council of his officers, to whom he stated his apprehensions, the expectations of the country, and the disgrace attending the failure of the expedition; and, on the other hand, the exhausted state of the horses, and the want of provisions. He then requested the commandants of each regiment to convene the whole of the officers belonging to it, and to take the sense of the army on the measures to be pursued; adding, that if 500 volunteers turned out he would put himself at their head, and proceed in quest of the Indian towns, and the rest of the army might return to fort Harrison. In less than an hour the report was made almost unanimously to return.— In vain did the general request that he might dictate the course for that day only. His authority was now at an end; and all the efforts of the officers were necessary to restore order in the ranks, and to conduct the retreat without danger from the surrounding though unseen foe.

Though this expedition returned almost without obtaining the sight of an enemy, yet it was not altogether unproductive of benefit. The Indians of the neighbouring towns, hearing of its approach, had marched the greater part of their warriors to meet it, leaving their villages in a defenceless condition. In this state they were found by colonel Russell, who had marched upon them in the expectation of meeting with Hopkins' army, and his detachment attacked and defeated those who had been left behind. Having driven them into a swamp, through which the rangers pursued them for three miles, up to their waists in mud and water, he returned and burnt their towns, and destroyed their corn. The number of warriors who advanced to meet Hopkins from those towns is stated to have amounted to 700; Russell's force consisted of not more than 400 men. A considerable number of Indians were killed in this attack. On the part of the Americans there were only four wounded, none of them mortally.

Craig's force was still smaller than that under Russell; it is

E

stated to have consisted of not more than 80 men. With this small body he marched up to the Illinois river, twenty miles above the town destroyed by Russell. Here he attacked an Indian settlement, which he totally destroyed, with all the improvements, and took 42 prisoners, one of them an Englishman, and a large collection of furs. He returned with his prisoners and booty without the loss of a man.

In the month of November another Indian expedition was undertaken by general Hopkins, with about 1250 men. This was directed against the towns of the Wabash, where the battle of Tippacanoe had been fought about twelve months before.— Having left fort Harrison on the 11th, accompanied with boats for the transportation of provisions, forage, and military stores, Hopkins arrived at the Prophet's town on the 19th without interruption. Early in the morning of that day, 300 men were detached to surprise the Winebago town on Ponce Passu creek, a short distance below the Prophet's. Having surrounded it about the break of day, they were surprised to find it evacuated. The party, accordingly, after destroying it, rejoined the main body at the Prophet's town.

For three days Hopkins' detachment was employed in achieving the complete destruction of the Prophet's town, and the large Kicapoo village adjoining, the former consisting of 40 and the latter of 160 cabins and huts. They likewise destroyed all their cultivated fields, fences, &c. and constructed works for the defence of the boats and of the encampment.

On the 21st a reconnoitering party were attacked by a body of Indians, and one of their number killed. The following day 60 horsemen were despatched to bury their comrade, and gain a better knowledge of the ground, but they unfortunately fell into an ambuscade, in which 18 of the party were killed, wounded or missing. This party, on their return, brought information of a large assemblage of the enemy, who, encouraged by the strength of their camp, appeared to be waiting an attack.— Every preparation was accordingly made to march early next morning, to engage the enemy. A violent fall of snow, however prevented the movement on the 23d; and the camp was found abandoned on the following day. The position which the Indians had thus abandoned is spoken of as having been remarkably strong. The Ponce Passu, a deep rapid creek, was in their rear, running in a semicircle; in front was a bluff, 100 feet high. almost perpendicular, and only to be penetrated by three steep ravines.

On the return of the troops to camp, the river was found so full of ice, as to alarm them for the return of the boats. Hopkins had intended to have spent one week more in endeavouring to find the Indian camps; but the shoeless, shirtless state of the troops, now clad in the remnants of their summer dress; a river full of ice; the hills covered with snow; and, above all, the uncertainty of finding an enemy; all these circumstances determined him to return. They accordingly set out on the 25th, and in a few days arrived at Fort Harrison, having completed a march of upwards of 100 miles into the Indian country, which is totally devoid of roads, and destroyed three of their principal towns, in the space of less than twenty days.

The last Indian expedition of which mention is made, in this quarter, is one which was commanded by colonel Campbell, consisting of 600 men, which marched from Greenville, (Ohio) against the towns on the Mississinewa, a branch of the Wabash.

On the 17th of December, after marching all night, Campbell arrived at one of the towns about day-break, which he instantly attacked, and the Indians were driven across the Mississinewa river, with the loss of 7 killed and 37 prisoners. Only one American was killed and one wounded in this skirmish.—After securing the prisoners a part of the detachment was despatched down the river, who returned the same day, having burned three villages without resistance. They then encamped on the ground where the first village stood.

The following morning a little before day-light, the camp was attacked by a body of Indians, supposed to be about 300. They commenced their attack on the right, with a horrid yell. After a desperate conflict of about three quarters of an hour, a charge was made by the cavalry, which forced the Indians to retreat, leaving 40 killed on the field. In this affair the Americans had eight killed, and twenty-five or thirty wounded.

Another attack was anticipated, as information was received that Tecumseh; with four or five hundred warriors was only fifteen miles from the scene of action; but reinforcements shortly after arriving from Greenville, they effected their retreat without molestation.

A small body of Georgia volunteers had been collected early in August, for an expedition against the Indians on our Southern border, where considerable depredations had been committed. Several unforeseen circumstances, however, prevented its being carried into effect, until the 24th of September, when the detachment, consisting of only 117 men, with twelve horses, marched from St. John's under the command of colonel Newnan, against the Lotchaway towns in East Florida. This small force carried with them only four days provisions.

The detachment left St. John's in the evening, marching in

Indian file, with a small party in front and in rear, the openness of the country rendering it unnecessary to employ men on the right and left. The encampment at nights, there being three companies, was in the form of a triangle, with the baggage in the centre; the men lying with their clothes on, their feet pointing outwards, and their firelocks in their arms. In case of an attack, the officers were instructed to bring up thier companies upon the right and left of the company fronting the enemy, and to follow the Indian mode of fighting until ordered to charge.

In case of meeting the enemy on the march, the first company, which consisted of riflemen, was instructed to file off to the right, the centre company to advance and form to the front in single rank, and the company in the rear to file off to the left; the whole then to advance in the form of a crescent, and endeavour to encircle the enemy.

On the morning of the fourth day, when within a few miles of the Indian towns, the party in advance discovered a body of Indians marching along the path meeting them. The companies were immediately ordered to advance according to the previous instructions, which appeared exactly suited to the situation in which the enemy was found, and Newnan placed himself at the head of the centre company. The Indians were now seen falling back and making preparations for battle, by unslinging their packs, trimming their rifles, and forming; and the Americans continued to advance, taking advantage of the trees in their progress, until within musket shot of the enemy, when many of the Indians began to fire. The charge being now ordered, the enemy were forced precipitately to retire, and take refuge in a swamp. Unfortunately the riflemen in filing to the right, inadvertently took too great a circuit, by which means a small swamp was interposed between them and the Indians, which rendered the victory less decisive than it would have been had the whole charged together before the Indians dispersed. The action, including the skirmishing on the flanks, lasted two hours and a half, the Indians having frequently attempted to outflank and get in rear of the detachment, but were always repulsed, by the companies extending to the right and left. The detachment had one killed and nine wounded in this affair. The loss of the Indians was more considerable. Among the killed was their king Payne.

The Americans remained on the ground to watch the motions of the Indians, who were now seen near the swamp, painting themselves, and in consultation, which indicated an intention of renewing the combat. Accordingly half an hour before sun-set, having obtained a considerable reinforcement of negroes and Indians from their towns, they commenced the most horrid yells, imitating the cries and noise of almost every animal of the forest, their chiefs advancing in front in a stooping serpentine manner, and making the most wild and frantic gestures, until they approached within two hundred yards, when they commenced firing. The soldiers remained perfectly still and steady behind logs and trees, until the enemy had approached somewhat nearer, when a brisk and well directed fire soon drove them back to their original ground. The action lasted until eight o'clock, when the enemy were completely repulsed. Two men were killed and one wounded; the enemy carried off several of their men before it was dark, after which all firing was at the spot from whence the flash arose. After thus fighting all day, the detachment had to work throughout the whole of the night, and by day-light had completed a tolerable breast-work of logs and earth with port-holes.

As soon as it was dark, one of the officers was despatched to St. Jonh's for reinforcements and provisions, and six of the men took the liberty to accompany him, taking with them some of the best hórses.

For two days succeeding the battle, nothing was seen nor heard of the enemy; but on the evening of the third day they commenced firing at their works at long distance, and renewed it every day for five or six days, but without effect.

Seven or eight days having elapsed since the express had left them, hunger was staring them in the face, and they were now reduced to the necessity of eating one of the horses, they had no surgeon to dress the wounded, and apprehensions were entertained that the enemy would receive reinforcements from Augustine, or the Makasukie Indians. Expecting relief, however, every hour, Newnan was unwilling to leave the breast-work while a horse was left to eat; but one of the captains declared that he was determined to set off with his company; and many of the men, giving up all hopes of relief, talked of deserting in the night rather than perish or fall a sacrifice to the merciless negroes and Indians, whom they were taught to believe would surround them in great numbers in a few days.

In this trying situation, the few remaining horses being shot down, and the number of sick daily increasing, Newnan reluctantly consented to leave the works, and directed the litters to be prepared to carry the wounded. About nine in the evening they commenced their distressing march, carrying five wounded men in litters, and supporting two or three more; and had not proceeded more than eight miles, when the men became

E 2

perfectly exhausted from hunger and fatigue, and were unable to carry the wounded any farther.

This hasty retreat was peculiarly unfortunate; for they had not left the breast-work more than two hours when twenty-five horsemen with provisions, arrived to their relief, on a different road from the one they had taken, but, finding the place deserted they returned to St. John's, two men that had been despatched on the path the horsemen came, by some means or other missing them. They again constructed a plan of defence, and a sergeant-major with one private was despatched to Picalata, to learn what had had occasioned the delay of the supplies.

Here once more the spirit of insubordination began to display itself, and at three o'clock in the afternoon Newnan was compelled again to order the march. They had scarcely marched five miles, however, before the front of the detachment discovered the heads of several Indians on both sides of the path, from among some trees that had been laid prostrate by a hurricane; at the same instant the enemy fired upon the advanced party, and shot down four of them, one of whom died on the spot, and two survived but a few days. The moment the firing was heard, the detachment was ordered to charge, and the Indians were completely defeated in 15 minutes, many dropping their guns, and all running off without attempting to rally.— Four of them were left dead on the field. The detachment lay on the battle ground all night, and next day marched five miles, when they again threw up breast-works between two 'ponds, living upon gophers, alligators, and palmetto stocks, until the arrival of the provisions and horses, when they were enabled to proceed to St. John's. The number of Indians in the first engagement was from 75 to 100. In the second engagement their number, (including negroes, who are their best soldiers) was double that of the Americans; and in the third engagement there appeared to be 50, which was nearly equal to their force, after deducting the sick and wounded. The number of killed and wounded among the Indians must have been at least fifty.

Another expedition of volunteers was sent against those Indians from the state of Tennessee in the month of February, 1813, by whom they were defeated in three engagements, and 38 killed, a number wounded, and seven taken prisoners. The detachment then burnt their settlements to the number of 386 houses, destroyed several thousand bushels of corn, and took 400 horses, and about the same number of cattle. The Indians entirely disappeared before the detachment left the settlement. In the three engagements the Americans lost only one killed and seven wounded.

We have never seen the real value of the militia, and at the same time their total inadequacy in their present state, more strikingly exemplified than in the official narratives of those Indian expeditions. The *materiel*, the stamina of the militia, cannot be surpassed; but as to all other military requisites they are totally worthless. When we see them encountering fatigue, cold and hunger, without a murmur, and displaying in battle the most undaunted bravery and resolution, we cannot but lament that all those valuable qualities should be rendered of none effect by the total want of subordination and discipline, without which, zeal, numbers, and courage avail nothing.

It rests with the national legislature to apply the remedy to this evil. The constitution has clothed them with the power, and it is to be hoped they will no longer refuse to make use of it. The system ought either to be abolished altogether, as a most extravagant waste of time or money, or it ought to be made (and it is surely capable of being made so) a powerful and certain means of national defence, by a proper system of national instruction.

On the arrival of the Constitution frigate at Boston, after the capture of the Guerriere, captain Hull received permission to remain on shore for the settlement of his affairs, and commodore Bainbridge was appointed to command in his room. After undergoing the necessary repairs, she sailed on a cruize to the East Indies, towards the end of October, accompanied by the Hornet sloop of war, commanded by captain Lawrence; but in running down the coast of the Brazils, they found the Bonne Citoyenne, a British ship of war, loaded with specie, lying in the port of St. Salvador. The Bonne Citoyenne was a larger vessel, and had a greater force both in guns and men than the Hornet; but so eager was captain Lawrence to engage her, that he sent, through the American consul at St. Salvador, a challenge to her commander, captain Greene, pledging his honour that neither the Constitution, nor any other American vessel should interfere. This pledge was confirmed by commodore Bainbridge, who, to show his sincerity, left the Hornet before St. Salvador, and sailed on another cruize. The commander of the Bonne Citoyenne, however, did not see fit to accept of the challenge, but suffered himself to be blockaded by the Hornet.

On the 29th of December, a few days after leaving St. Salvador, about ten leagues from the coast of Brazil, at nine in the morning, Bainbridge discovered two strange sail, one of which stood in for the land, the other off shore towards the Constitution. At half past eleven, the private signal for the day be-

ing made, and not answered, it was concluded she was an enemy. The American ensign was hoisted at twelve, and shortly
after the enemy hoisted her colours. About half past one,
the vessel being perceived to be a British frigate, Bainbridge
tacked ship, and stood towards her, when she immediately bore
down with the intention of raking, which was avoided by wearing. At two, the enemy being then within a half a mile of the
Constitution, and to windward, and having hauled down her colours except the union, Bainbridge ordered a gun to be fired
ahead of her to make her show her colours, which was followed by a broadside; on which the enemy hoisted her colours, and
immediately returned the fire.

A general action now commenced with round and grape-
shot, the British frigate keeping at a much greater distance
than the commodore wished, but he could not bring her to
closer action without exposing his ship to being raked. A
number of manœuvres were now made by both vessels to obtain a raking position, during which the wheel of the Constitution was shot entirely away. Bainbridge now determined to
close with the enemy, notwithstanding the danger of being raked, and accordingly set the fore and mainsail, and luffed up
close to her.

About 4 o'clock, the fire of the enemy being completely silenced, and her colours in the main rigging being down, it
was supposed she had struck, and the Constitution shot ahead
to repair the rigging, leaving the enemy a complete wreck. It
was shortly after, however, discovered that the colours were
still flying; and accordingly, after repairing some of the damage,
the Constitution took a position across the enemy's bows, in
order to rake her, but this she prudently avoided by striking
her flag.

Bainbridge now sent his first lieutenant on board the prize,
which proved to be the Java, a frigate of the same rate as the
Guerriere and Macedonian, but with a much larger complement of men, having had upwards of 400 on board at the commencement of the action, 100 of them being supernumeraries
intended for the British ships of war in the East Indies. There
was also on board lieutenant-general Hislop, appointed to the
command of Bombay, major Walker and captain Wood of his
staff, and captain Marshall, master and commander in the
British navy, going to the East Indies to take command of a
sloop of war there. The commander was captain Lambert, a
very distinguished officer, who was mortally wounded in the
action.

The action lasted an hour and fifty-five minutes, in which

time the Java was completely dismasted, not having a spar of any kind standing. She had been fitted out in the most complete manner, and had copper on board for a 74 and two brigs building at Bombay; but the great distance from our coast, and the disabled state of the vessel, forbidding every idea of attempting to take her to the United States, after removing the prisoners and their baggage, she was set on fire, and soon after blew up.

The loss on board the Constitution was 9 killed and 25 wounded. The loss on board the Java could not be exactly ascertained, as the officers were extremely cautious in speaking of the number of her crew. Commodore Bainbridge states it at 60 killed and 101 wounded certainly; by a letter written on board the Constitution by one of the officers of the Java, and accidentally found, the number was stated to be 60 killed and 170 wounded.

After blowing up the Java, Bainbridge returned to St. Salvador, where he landed all the prisoners on their parole, to the number of 361, exclusive of nine Portuguese seamen, who were liberated and given up to the governor of St. Salvador, and three passengers, private characters, whom the commodore did not consider prisoners of war.

On account of the destruction of the boats of both vessels in the action, nothing was taken from on board the Java except the prisoners and their baggage, the whole of which was given up to them. Among other valuable articles given up was a chest of plate, which had been presented to general Hislop by the colonel of Demarara. Commodore Bainbridge received the public acknowledgements of the governor of St. Salvador, as well as of his prisoners, for the kind treatment and beneficence which he displayed on this occasion.

The Constitution again left St. Salvador on the 6th of January, and arrived at Boston about the middle of February.

Meanwhile the Hornet blockaded the Bonne Citoyenne, until the 24th of January, when the Montague, a 74 gun ship, hove in sight and chased her into the harbour; but night coming on, she wore and stood out to the southward. Knowing that she had left Rio Janeiro for the express purpose of relieving the Bonne Citoyenne and the packet which Lawrence had also blockaded for 14 days, and obliged her to send her mail to Rio Janeiro in a Portuguese smack, he judged it most prudent to shift his cruising ground, and accordingly shaped his course towards Pernambuco. On the 4th of February he captured the English brig Resolution, of 10 guns, laden with provisions and about $23,000 in specie; but as she sailed dull, and he could

not spare hands to man her, he took out the money and crew,
and set her on fire. He then ran down the coast for Moran-
ham, and cruised there a short time, and thence ran off Surinam. After cruising off that coast from the 15th to the 22d of
February, without meeting a vessel he stood for Demarara.
Next morning he discovered a brig to leeward, which he chased so near the shore that he was obliged to haul off for want of
a pilot. Previous to giving up the chase, however, he discov-
erèd a vessel at anchor without the bar of Demarara river, with
the English colours flying, apparently a brig of war. In beating around Carabona bank, in order to get at her, at half past
three in the afternoon, he discovered another sail on his weather quarter, edging down for him. At 20 minutes past 4 she
hoisted English colours, when she was discovered to be a large
man of war brig. The Hornet was immediately cleared for
action; and kept close to the wind, in order, if possible, to get
the weather guage. At 5 minutes past 10, finding he could
weather the enemy, Lawrence hoisted American colours, tacked, and shortly after exchanged broadsides with the British
ship, within half pistol shot. Observing the enemy in the act
of wearing, Lawrence now bore up, received his starboard
broadside, ran him close on board on the starboard quarter,
and kept up such a heavy and well directed fire, that in less
than 15 minutes the British struck their colours, and hoisted
an ensign, union down, from their fore rigging, as a signal of
distress.

Lieutenant Shubrick* was immediately sent on board the
prize, which proved to be the British brig Peacock, commanded by captain William Peake, who fell in the latter part of the
action. Shubrick, on getting on board, found that a number
of her crew were killed and wounded, and that she was sinking fast, being literally cut to pieces, and having six feet water
in her hold. Both vessels were immediately brought to anchor, and the Hornet's boats despatched to bring off the wounded; but although her guns were thrown overboard, the shot
holes that could be got at plugged and every exertion made
by pumping and bailing to keep her afloat until the prisoners
could be removed, all proved ineffectual, and she sunk in five
and a half fathoms water, carrying down 13 of her crew, and
three sailors belonging to the Hornet, who were nobly risking
their lives for the safety of the vanquished foe. A lieutenant

* Lieutenant Shubrick has had the good fortune to be in the
actions with the Guerriere, Java, and Peacock.

and other officers and men of the Hornet employed in removing the prisoners, with difficulty saved themselves, by jumping into a boat that was lying on her booms as she went down. Four of the 13 of the crew of the Peacock, mentioned as being in her when she went down, were so fortunate as to gain the fore-top, and were afterwards taken off by the boats. Previous to her going down, four of her men took to her stern boat, that had been much damaged during the action, and it is hoped reached the shore in safety; but from the heavy sea running at the time, the shattered state of the boat, and the difficulty of landing on the coast, it is more than probable that they were lost.

The exact number of killed on board the Peacock could not be ascertained from her officers. Captain Peake and four men were found dead on board by the Americans; the master, one midshipman, carpenter, captain's clerk, and 29 seamen were wounded, most of them severely, three of whom died of their wounds after being removed. On board the Hornet there was only one killed and two wounded by the enemy, but two men were severely burnt by the explosion of a cartridge during the action, one of whom survived but a few days. Her rigging and sails were much cut, a shot passed through the foremast, and the bowsprit was slightly injured; her hull received little or no damage.

The Peacock was deservedly styled one of the finest vessels of her class in the British navy. Her tonnage was supposed to be about equal to that of the Hornet. Her beam was greater by five inches; but her extreme length not so great by four feet. She mounted sixteen 24 pound carronades, two long nines, one twelve pound carronade on her top-gallant forecastle as a shifting gun, and one four, or six pounder and two swivels mounted aft. Her crew consisted of 134 men, four of whom were absent in a prize.

During the engagement, the L'Espiegle, the brig that Lawrence had been endeavouring to reach before the Peacock appeared, which mounted 16 thirty-two pound carronades, and two long nines, lay about six miles distant, and could plainly see the whole of the action. Apprehensions were entertained, that she would beat out to the assistance of her consort, and therefore such exertions were made in repairing damages, that by nine o'clock the boats were stowed away, a new set of sails bent, and the ship completely ready for action. She, however, declined coming out, and at two in the morning the Hornet got under way.

The morning after the action, Lawrence found that he had

277 souls on board, and therefore, as his own crew had been on two-thirds allowance of provisions for some time, and his supply of water was but scant, he determined to make the best of his way to the United States. He arrived at Holmes' Hole on the 19th of March, and a few days after proceeded down the sound to New York.

The kindness and hospitality shown by captain Lawrence and his officers to his unfortunate prisoners, was such as to penetrate them with the most lively gratitude, which the officers expressed shortly after their arrival by a public letter of thanks. "So much," say they, "was done to alleviate the distressing and uncomfortable situation in which we were placed when received on board the sloop you command, that we cannot better express our feelings than by saying ' We ceased to consider ourselves prisoners;' and every thing that friendship could dictate was adopted by you and the officers of the Hordet, to remedy the inconvenience we would otherwise have experienced from the unadvoidable loss of the whole of our property and clothes by the sudden sinking of the Peacock."

Nor was the crew of the Hornet a whit behind their superiors in that noble generosity which ever accompanies true bravery. As the sailors of the Peacock had lost every thing except what they had on their backs when she went down, our American tars united to relieve them, and made every English sailor a present of two shirts, a blue jacket, and a pair of trowsers.

The frigate Chesapeake, commanded by captain Evans; sailed from Boston about the middle of November on a cruize. From Boston she ran down by Madeira, the Canary, and Cape de Verd Islands; thence to the equator, between longitude 25° and 15° W., where she cruized six weeks. She then sailed along the coast of South America, and passed within fifteen leagues of Surinam. Thence she passed through the windward islands to the coast of the United States; near the capes of Virginia, and thence along the coast to Boston, where she arrived on the 10th of April, after a cruize of 115 days. During this cruize she took an American brig, sailing under an English license, and three British vessels, one of which she burnt after taking out the crew and cargo. On the first of January, off the Western Islands, she discovered two large sail bearing down on her, apparently ships of war, and lay too until near enough to ascertain that they were a 74 and a frigate, when she made all sail and escaped. Off the capes of Virginia, about ten days before her arrival, she gave chase to a sloop of war, and continued chasing for two days, when it escaped in the night.

The Chesapeake continued in Boston harbour until the first of June, the day of her unfortunate recontre with the Shannon. Captain Lawrence, of the Hornet, had a short time previous been appointed to command the Chesapeake, and hardly had he arrived at Boston, when the Shannon, commanded by captain Broke, appeared off the harbour, with the avowed purpose of seeking a combat with her.

" Stung with the repeated disasters of the British frigates, this officer resolved to make an effort to retrieve them; and when he deemed his ship perfectly prepared for that purpose, sent a formal challenge to captain Lawrence.

" ' As the Chesapeake,' his letter began, ' appears now ready for sea, I request you will do me the favour to meet the Shannon, with her, ship to ship, to try the fortune of our respective flags. To an officer of your character, it requires some apology for proceeding to further particulars. Be assured, sir, that it is not from any doubt I entertain of your wishing to close with my proposal, but merely to provide an answer to any objection that might be made, and very reasonably, upon the chance of our receiving unfair support.' After observing that commodore Rodgers had not accepted several verbal challenges which he had given, captain Broke then proceeds to state very minutely the force of the Shannon, and offers to send all British ships out of reach, so that they might have a fair combat, at any place within a certain range along the coast of New England which he specified; if more agreeable, he offers to sail together, and to warn the Chesapeake, by means of private signals, of the approach of British ships of war, till they reach some solitary spot—or to sail with a flag of truce to any place out of the reach of British aid, so that the flag should be hauled down when it was deemed fair to begin hostilities. ' I entreat you, sir,' he concludes, ' not to imagine that I am urged by mere personal vanity to the wish of meeting the Chesapeake, or that I depend only upon your personal ambition for your acceding to this invitation. We have both nobler motives. You will feel it as a compliment, if I say that the result of our meeting may be the most grateful service I can render to my country; and I doubt not that you, equally confident of success, will feel convinced that it is only by repeated triumphs in even combats, that your little navy can now hope to console your country for the loss of that trade it can no longer protect.'

" The style of this letter, with the exception of the puerile bravado about commodore Rodgers, is frank and manly; and if the force of the Shannon were correctly stated, would be such a challenge as might well be sent from a brave seamen to

F

a gallant adversary. We, however, are but too well satisfied, that captain Broke studiously underrated the number of his guns and crew; or that, after his challenge, he must have received additions to both. That the Shannon had more guns than the number stated by her commander, we learn from the testimony of the surviving officers of the Chesapeake; who also assert, that she had three hundred and seventy-six men; that she had an officer and sixteen men from the Belle Poule; and that the hats of some of her seamen were marked 'Tenedos.' Such as it was, however, this letter, most unfortunately, never reached captain Lawrence. If he had received it; if he had been thus warned to prepare his ship; if he had had an opportunity of selecting his officers, and disciplining his crew; if, in short, he had been able to place the Chesapeake on any thing like equal terms with the Shannon, the combat might have been more bloody—there might have been such an engagement as has not yet been seen between single ships on the ocean; though we cannot suffer ourselves to doubt the result of it. But he knew nothing of this challenge—he saw only the Shannon riding before him in defiance; he remembered the spirit with which he himself overawed a superior; and he could not brook for a moment, that an enemy, which seemed to be his equal, should insult his flag. Although, therefore, the Chesapeake was comparatively an inferior ship—although his first lieutenant was sick on shore—although three of his lieutenants had recently left her; and of the four who remained, two were only midshipmen, acting as lieutenants—although part of his crew were new hands, and all of them had lost some of their discipline by staying in port—yet, as he would have gone to sea in that situation had no enemy appeared, he felt himself bound not to delay sailing on that account, and throwing himself, therefore, on his courage and his fortune, he determined at once to attack the enemy. It was on the morning of the 1st of June, 1813, that the Chesapeake sailed out of the harbour of Boston to meet the Shannon. As soon as she got under weigh, captain Lawrence called the crew together, and having hoisted the white flag, with the motto of 'free trade and sailors' rights,' made a short address. His speech, however, was received with no enthusiasm—on the contrary, signs of dissatisfaction were evident; particularly from a boatswain's mate, a Portuguese, who seemed to be at the head of the malecontents; and complaints were muttered, that they had not yet received their prize-money. Such expressions, at the eve of an action, were but ill-bodings of the result of it; but captain Lawrence, ignorant as he was of the characters of his sailors, and unwilling at such a moment to damp their spirits by harshness, preserved his accustomed calmness, and had prize-checks, at once, given by the purser to those who had not received them. Whilst this scene was passing, the Shannon, observing the Chesapeake coming out, bore away, The Chesapeake followed her till four o'clock in the afternoon, when she hauled up and fired a gun, on which the Shannon hove too. They manœuvred for some time, till, at about a quarter before six, they approached within pistol shot and exchanged broadsides.

" These broadsides were both bloody; but the fire of the Shannon was most fortunate in the destruction of officers. The fourth lieutenant, Mr. Ballard, was mortally wounded—the sailing-master was killed, and captain Lawrence received a musket ball in his leg, which caused great pain, and profuse bleeding, but he leaned on the companion way, and continued to order and to animate his crew. A second, and a third broadside was exchanged, with evident advantage on the part of the Chesapeake; but unfortunately, among those now wounded on board of her was the first lieutenant, Mr. Ludlow, who was carried below—three men were successively shot from the helm, in about twelve minutes from the commencement of the action; and, as tne hands were shifting, a shot disabled her foresail, so that she would no longer answer her helm, and her anchor caught in one of the after ports of the Shannon, which enabled the latter to rake her upper deck. As soon as Lawrence perceived that she was falling to leeward, and that by the Shannon's filling she would fall on board, he called his boarders, and was giving orders about the foresail, when he received a musket ball in his body. The bugleman, who should have called the boarders, did not do his duty; and, at this moment commodore Broke, whose ship had suffered so much that he was preparing to repel boarding, perceiving, from this accident how the deck of the Chesapeake was swept, jumped on board with about twenty men. They would have been instantly repelled; but the captain, the first lieutenant, the sailing master, the boatswain, the lieutenant of marines, the only acting lieutenant on the spar-deck, were all killed or disabled. At the call of the boarders, lieutenant Cox ran on deck, but just in time to receive his falling commander, and bear him below.— Lieutenant Budd, the second lieutenant, led up the boarders, but only fifteen or twenty would follow him, and with these he defended the ship till he was wounded and disabled. Lieutenant Ludlow, wounded as he was, hurried upon deck, where he soon received a mortal cut from a sabre. The marines who were engaged fought with desparate courage; but they were

few in number; too many of them having followed the Portuguese boatswain's mate, who exclaimed it is said, as he skulked below, ' so much for not paying men their prize-money.'—
Meanwhile the Shannon threw on board sixty additional men, who soon succeeded in overpowering the seamen of the Chesapeake, who had now no officers to lead or rally them, and took possession of the ship; which was not however, surrendered by any signal of submission, but became the enemy's only because they were able to overwhelm all who were in a condition to resist.

" As captain Lawrence was carried below, he perceived the melancholy condition of the Chesapeake, but cried out, ' Dont give up the ship.' He was taken down into the ward-room, and, as he lay in excruciating pain, perceiving that the noise above had ceased, he ordered the surgeon to go on deck, and tell the officers to fight on to the last, and never strike the colours. ' They shall wave,' said he, ' while I live.' But it was too late to resist or struggle longer; the enemy had already possession of the ship. As captain Lawrence's wounds would not allow of his removal, he continued in the ward-room, surrounded by his wounded officers, and, after lingering in great pain for four days, during which his sufferings were too acute to permit him to speak, or perhaps, to think of the sad events he had just witnessed, or do more than ask for what his situation required, he died on the 5th of June. His body was wraped in the colours of the Chesapeake, and laid on the quarter deck, until they arrived at Halifax, where he was buried with the highest military and naval honours; the British officers forgetting in their admiration of his character, that he had been but lately their enemy. His pall was supported by the oldest captains in the navy then at Halifax, and no demonstratoin of respectful attention was omitted to honour the remains of a brave, but unfortunate stranger.

" In this sanguinary engagement the Chesapeake lost her commander and forty-seven men killed, and ninety-seven wounded, of whom fourteen afterwards died. Among these were lieutenant Ludlow, first lieutenant of the ship, and lieutenant Ballard, the fourth lieutenant both excellent officers.

" On the part of the Shannon, captain Broke was dangerously wounded, though he has since recovered; the first lieutenant, the purser, captain's clerk, and twenty-three seamen killed, and fifty seven persons wounded, besides captain Broke.

" The capture of the Chesapeake is to be ascribed wholly to the extraordinary loss of officers (a loss without any precedent, as far as we can recollect, in naval history); and to her falling

accidentally on board the Shannon. During the three broadsides, while the officers of the Chesapeake, were living, and
she was kept clear of the enemy, the superiority was manifestly with the Americans. The Chesapeake had received scarcely any damage while the Shannon had several shot between
wind and water, and could with difficulty be kept afloat during
the succeeding night. It was only when accident threw the
Chesapeake on board the Shannon, when her officers were unable to lead on the boarders, that captain Broke himself, contrary, we believe, to the regulations of the British navy, left
his own ship, and was able, by superior numbers, to overpower
the distracted crew of the Chesapeake.

"We have heard many accounts, which we are very reluctantly compelled to believe, of improper conduct by the British
after the capture, and of brutal violence offered to the crew of
the Chesapeake. As, however some allowances are due to
the exasperated passions of the moment, something too to the
confusion of a bloody and doubtful struggle, we are unwilling
to prolong the rememberance of imputations which may be dis-
proved, and perhaps have been exaggerated.

"But we should wrong the memory of captain Lawrence,
we should be unjust to the officers of the American navy, with
whose glory all the aspiring ambition of the country is so closely blended, if we omitted any opportunity of giving the last
and fairest lustre to their fame, by contrasting their conduct
with that of the enemy, or if we forbore, from any misplaced
delicacy towards our adversaries, to report circumstances
connected with the fate of the Chesapeake, which throw a broad
and dazzling light on the generous magnanimity of our countrymen."

Our readers cannot have failed to observe the liberality
which was extended to the officers and crews of the Guerriere,
Macedonian, and Java, and the still more striking instance of
the Peacock. "When the Chesapeake was taken by the Shannon, the key of captain Lawrence's store-room was demanded
of the purser. It was given; but the purser observed at the
same time, that in the captures of the Guerriere, Macedonian,
and Java, the most scrupulous regard was paid to the private
property of the British officers; that captain Lawrence had
laid in stores for a long cruize; and that the value of them
would be a great object to his widow and family, for whose use
he was desirous, if possible, of preserving them. This request
was not merely declined; it was haughtily and superciliously
refused.

"However we may mourn the sufferings of that day, the loss

of the Chesapeake has not, in our estimation, varied the relative standing of the marine of the two countries; nor does it abate, in the slightest degree, any of the loftiness of our naval pretensions. The contest was wholly unequal in ships, in guns, in crews, in officers, in every thing.

" The Shannon was a better ship; she had not upon her the curse of that ill-omined name, the Chesapeake. The Shannon was a stronger ship; she mounted twenty-eight eighteen pounders on the main deck, twenty-two thirty-two pound carronades, and two long brass nines or twelves, on the spar-deck, and a large carronade amidships, *in all fifty-two guns*, besides this last heavy carronade; while the Chesapeake mounted twenty-eight eighteen pounders on the main deck, and twenty thirty-two pound carronades, and one eighteen pounder, chase gun, on the spar-deck, *in all forty-nine guns.*

" The Shannon had a better crew. Besides her cómplement, she had seamen from two other ships. That crew, too, had been long at sea; long in the ship; were known; were tried; and as commodore Broke sent a challenge, were, of course, men on whom, if they were not picked for the occasion, he knew he could confide. The Chesapeake had on the contrary, in part, a new crew, unknown to their officers, not yet knowing their places or the ship. The ship had not been more than a few hours at sea, and the landsmen and the landswomen had been dismissed from her on the very day of the engagement. The officers, too, although we should be the last to detract from their merits, and although the manner in which they fought their ship does them the highest honour, the officers were young and few in number, and had as yet hardly any opportunity of disciplining or knowing their seamen; yet under all these disadvantages, the great damage sustained by the Shannon, and the great loss of her crew, all which took place before the boarding, warrant completely the opinion, that, but for the accidental loss of officers, the victory would have been with the Chesapeake."*

The brig Argus, commanded by lieutenant Allen, sailed from New York about the middle of May, having on board Mr. Crawford, our minister for France. She arrived at L'Orient on the 12th of June, and shortly after sailed on a cruize.

On the 14th of August, being then in St. George's channel, where she had made a number of captures, she was discovered by the Pelican sloop of war, which had been despatched in search

---

* *Port Folio.*

óf her. As soon as Allen discovered the Pelican he shortened sail; and the two vessels got alongside about half past five in the morning, when an action commenced, which was kept up with spirit on both sides for three quarters of an hour, when, lieutenant Allen being mortally wounded, and nearly forty others killed and wounded on board the Argus, she struck her flag. On board the Pelican there were only two killed and five wounded.

As the American account of this action has not been received, owing probably to the death of the commander, and as the British account is unusually barren, we are not able to state any of the particulars. That the Pelican was much superior in force, however, there is little room to doubt. She is rated at two guns more than the Argus; and it is stated in a London paper, that in the year 1797, she beat off a French 44 gun frigate, after an action of two hours. There is a circumstance mentioned in a Cork paper, too, which is totally kept out of view in the official account, and which, if true, takes away all the honour of the victory, small as it is, from the enemy. " As the action closed," says the Cork paper, " his majesty's ship Leonidas, captain Seymour, fell in with them." In Steele's List, the Leonidas is rated as a 38 gun frigate. That a sloop of war should surrender to a vessel of superior force, when a 38 gun frigate was close aboard of them, is a circumstance surely not to be wondered at.

A few days after the action, lieutenant Allen died of his wounds, and was buried at Plymouth with the honours of war.

Previous to her capture, the Argus had taken 19 vessels, most of them in St. George's Channel.

In recording the loss of the Chesapeake and Argus we have had to lament the still greater loss of their gallant commanders. We have now to record an event, at the remembrance of which tears for our loss mingle with exultations for our success.

On the first of September, the United States brig Enterprize, commanded by lieutenant William Burrows, sailed from Portsmouth on a cruize. On the morning of the 3d, Burrows discovered a schooner, which was chased into Portland harbour, where the Enterprize was brought to anchor. Having received information of several privateers being off Manhagan, he weighed anchor and swept out the following morning, and stood for that place. Next day a large brig of war was discovered, to which chase was immediately given. The enemy fired several guns, and stood for the Enterprize, with four ensigns hoisted. After manœuvering and reconnoitering for

some time, for the purpose of discovering the force of the enemy, Burrows, about three in the afternoon shortened sail, tacked and ran down, with the intention of bringing her to close
action.   At 20 minutes after three the firing commenced from
both vessels, within half pistol shot.   The action continued
for about a quarter of an hour, when the Enterprize ranged
ahead of the enemy, rounded too, and raked her.   Shortly after
the main-top-mast and top-sail yard of the enemy came down
The foresail of the Enterprize was then set, and she took a
position on the starboard bow of the enemy, and continued to
rake her,' until, about 40 minutes after the commencement of
the action, the enemy ceased firing, and cried for quarters;
their colours being nailed to the masts, could not be hauled
down.

The prize proved to be the British brig Boxer, of 14 guns.
The number of her crew could not be ascertained, but 64 prisoners were taken, including 17 wounded.   Captain Hull, in a
letter to commodore Bainbridge, describing the state of the
Boxer when brought into port, says that there was every reason to believe that there were 100 men on board.   On board
the Enterprize there was only one killed and thirteen wounded,
two of whom died of their wounds.

Lieutenant Burrows fell in the commencement of the action,
he, however, refused to be carried below, but, raising his head,
requested that the flag might never be struck.   When the
sword of the vanquished enemy was presented to the dying
conqueror, he clasped his hands and said, " I am satified; I
die contented;" and then, and not till then, would he consent
to be carried below, where every attention was paid to save his
life, but in vain.   A few hours after the victory he breathed
his last.—Captain Blythe, the commander of the Boxer, also
fell in the commencement of the action, having received a
cannon shot through the body.   His remains, in company with
those of Burrows, were brought to Portland, where the two
commanders were interred, side by side, with military honours.

The Boxer was so much damaged in her sails, rigging,
spars, hull, &c. as to render it difficult to carry her into port.
The Enterprize received but trifling injury.   On an examination of the prize, she was adjudged wholly to be the captors,
agreeably to law, as a vessel of superior force.

On the 23d of April, the President frigate, commanded by
commodore Rodgers, sailed from Boston.   On the 30th he took
his departure from President road, in company with the Congress, commanded by captain Smith.   On the 3d of May, while
in chase of a British brig of war, near the shoal of George's

Bank, they passed to windward of three sail, two of which, from their appearance, and from information previously received, where supposed to be the La Hogue, 74, the Nymph frigate, and a merchant brig. After getting clear of George's Bank they continued along east southwardly, in the direction of the southern edge of the Gulf Stream, until the 8th of May, when the President parted company with the Congress, the latter being in chase of a vessel, which proved to be an American merchantman. After parting company, Rodgers shaped his course, as near as the wind would permit, to intercept the enemy's West India commerce passing to the southward of the Grand Bank. Not meeting with any thing in this direction except American vessels from Lisbon and Cadiz, he next pursued a route to the northward, so as to cross the tracks of the West India, Halifax, Quebec, and St. John's trade. Not meeting any thing in this route, however, after reaching the latitude of 38 degrees N., he steered to the S. E. towards the Azores, off which, in different directions, he continued until the 6th of June, without meeting a single enemy's vessel. At this time, falling in with an American ship bound to Cadiz, and receiving information that she had, four days before, passed an enemy's convoy from the West Indies, bound to England, Rodgers crowded sail to the N. E., and, although disappointed in falling in with the convoy, nevertheless made four captures between the 9th and 13th of June.

Being now in the latitude of 46° N., and longitude 28° W., Rodgers shaped a course that afforded a prospect of falling in with vessels bound to Newfoundland from St. George's Channel, by the way of Cape Clear, as well as others that might pass north about to the northward of Ireland; to his astonishment, however, in all his route, he did not meet with a single vessel, until he made the Sheetland Islands, and even off there nothing but Danish vessels, trading to England, under British licences. A considerable portion of their provisions and water being now expended, it became necessary to replenish these, previous to determining what course to pursue next; accordingly, for this purpose, they put into North Bergen on the 27th June; but were not able to obtain any thing but water, there being an unusual scarcity of bread in every part of Norway, and at the time not more in Bergen than a bare sufficiency for its inhabitants for four or five weeks. After replenishing his water, Rodgers stretched over towards the Orkney islands, and thence towards the North Cape, for the purpose of intercepting a convoy of twenty-five or thirty sail, which it was said would leave Archangel about the middle of July, under the protection of two brigs or two sloops of war. In this object, however, he was disappointed by a line of battle ship and frigate making their appearance off the North Cape on the 19th of July, just as he was in momentary expectation of meeting the convoy. On discovering the ships of war, Rodgers stood towards them to ascertain their character, when he hauled by the wind on the opposite tack to avoid them; but, owing to faint, variable winds, calms, and entire day-light, the sun in that latitude, at that season, appearing at mignight several degrees above the horizon, they were enabled to continue the chase upwards of eighty hours; during which time, owing to the different changes of the wind, they were brought quite as near as was desirable.

Disappointed in meeting with the convoy, Rodgers now steered to gain the direction of the trade passing out of and into the Irish channel. In this position, between the 25th of July and 2d of August, he made three captures, when finding that the enemy had a superior force in that vicinity, he made a circuit round Ireland, and then steered for the banks of Newfoundland, near which he made two more captures, and by the latter one learned that a 74 and a frigate were on the eastern part of the bank only a few miles to the westward; he, however, did not fall in with them.

On the 23d of September, to the southward of Nantucket shoals, Rodgers fell in with and captured in a very singular manner, the British schooner Highflyer, tender to admiral Warren. On approaching the schooner she hoisted a private signal, which was answered by the President, by a signal which fortunately proved to be the British one for that day, on seeing which the Highflyer immediately bore up, and was boarded by one of the officers of the President in a British uniform. By this stratagem commodore Rodgers gained possession of the British private signals, and admiral Warren's instructions by which was discovered the number of British squadrons on the American coast, with their force and relative positions. He was thus enabled to avoid them, and on the 26th of September arrived safely at Newport, Rhode-Island.

During the cruise, the President captured twelve British vessels, three of which were ransomed and despatched to England as cartels, with 216 prisoners on parole. The British government, however, refused to sanction the terms of exchange entered into and signed by their officers, assigning as the reason, that " such transactions are inconsistent with the established understanding between the two countries." The President, on her arrival, had fifty-five prisoners on board.

The Congress, after parting with the President, continued her cruise until the 12th of December, when she arrived at Portsmouth, N. H. She captured two British brigs of ten guns each, one of which was destroyed, and the other after being dismantled, was given up to the prisoners, who were discharged on parole, and furnished with provisions, &c. sufficient to carry them to the West Indies. She likewise captured a British ship laden with wine and potatoes, which was destroyed after the greater part of her cargo was taken out.

After parting with the President, the Congress ran to the southward; and, crossing the equator, put into Seara, on the Brazil coast. After watering, she beat against a strong wind and current, up to Fernando de Noronha, where she again watered; and then proceeded to the eastward, in hopes to fall in with some Indiamen. She cruised as far as 18° W. from 6° S. to 6° N. under easy sail, made the island of St. Pauls; but until her return to Fernando de Noronha, which was nearly three months, never saw a vessel. She then returned to Seara, where she took in a quantity of cassada, jerked beef, &c. and ran under two reefed topsails to latitude 44° N., passing near Halifax, where she captured a brig, who informed them of Boston being blockaded by a superior force. She accordingly made for Portsmouth, where she arrived, with her crew, 410 men, in perfect health, having lost but four on the cruise. When the men commenced on the jerked beef and cassada, it did not agree with them, and about fifty were sick—but they soon recovered. The Congress was in perfect order and wanted no repairs. She had on board about thirty prisoners on her arrival.

The Essex frigate sailed from the capes of the Delaware on the 25th of October, 1812; on a cruise to the Pacific ocean, Letters, however, dated July 2, 1813, were received at the navy department about the middle of December following, from her commander, captain Porter, at which time he was cruizing of the western coast of South America, with a fleet of nine armed vessels under his command, eight of which were British letters of marque, which he had captured and fitted out. The first of these vessels, which was a ship of two guns and twenty-one men, was captured on the 29th of April. Two others were then in sight, close together, about seven miles distant from the Essex; the one mounting ten guns, six and nine pounders; the other six eighteen pounders, four swivels, and six long blunderbusses, mounted on swivels. The wind being light and variable, and confiding greatly in the bravery and enterprize of his officers and men, and apprehensive of their escape, from the prevalence of fogs in that climate, Porter directed the boats of the Essex to be armed and manned, and divided into two divisions. Suitable signals were established, and each boat had her particular station pointed out for the attack, and every other previous arrangement was made to prevent confusion.

The boats, seven in number, rowed off in admirable order. Guns were fired from the enemy to terrify them; they rowed up, however, undismayed, under the muzzles of their guns, and took their stations for attacking the first ship, and no sooner was the American flag displayed, as the signal for boarding and the intention discovered by the enemy, than their colours were struck without a shot being fired. They then left a crew on board the prize, and took their stations for attacking the other vessel, when her flag was also struck, on the first call to surrender. Thus were two fine British ships, each pierced for twenty guns, worth near half a million of dollars, mounting between them sixteen guns, and manned with 55 men, well supplied with ammunition and small arms, surrendered without the slightest resistance, to seven small open boats, with fifty men, armed only with muskets, pistols, boarding axes, and cutlasses.

On the 26th of March, previous to the capture of any of the letters of marque, Porter fell in with the Peruvian corsair ship Nereyda, mounting fifteen guns, which had, a few days before captured two American whale ships, the crews of which, amounting in number to 24 men, were then detained prisoners on board. As they could assign no other motive for the capture than that they were the allies of Great Britain, and, as such, should capture all American vessels they could fall in with, Porter, to prevent in future such vexatious proceeding, threw all her armament into the sea, liberated the Americans, and dismissed the Nereyda. He then proceeded with all possible despatch for Lima, to intercept one of the detained vessels, which had parted company with the Nereyda only three days before, and was so fortunate as to arrive there, and recapture her on the 5th of April, at the moment she was entering the port.

Captain Porter describes his crew as enjoying remarkably good health and spirits, no symptoms of scurvy having appeared, although they had been at sea for eight months, with the exception of 23 days. The Essex was in prime order, with abundant supplies, and two of her consorts were fitted out with 20 guns each, and well manned. He mentioned that British letters of marque were numerous in those seas, and that the American whalers had derived much benefit from his cruise.

The bravery and enterprize of American seamen have not been less conspicuous on board of our privateers than in our national vessels. We shall here present an account of a few of the most conspicuous actions that have taken place.

In no one action fought during the present war, has there been more courage and gallantry displayed than in the attack made by the privateer Rolla on the British ship Rio Neuva.— The Rolla originally carried four twelve pound carronades in her waist, and one double fortified twelve mounted on a pivot. In a gale of wind off Madeira, the 4 twelve pounders were obliged to be thrown overboard, and only one gun remained; with this however, on the 14th of December, 1812, the Rolla attacked the Rio Neuva, mounting 18 guns, and 30 men, and took her after an action of twenty-five minutes. During the action, the men on board the Rolla, animated by the courage and conduct of captain Dooley and his officers, evinced a fixed determination to take the enemy or perish. When the ship struck, the Rolla had ranged up within pistol shot, and was preparing to board.

The privateer schooner Comet, captain Thomas Boyle, sailed from Cape Henry, on the 25th of November, 1812, on a cruize to the coast of South America. On the 12th of December, at one in the afternoon, she discovered four sail standing out of Pernambuco, and lay by to give them an opportunity of getting off shore, in order to cut them off. At three, they being then about six leagues from the land, she bore up and made all sail in chase of them; and at six having discovered one of them to be a very large man of war brig, all hands were called to quarters, the guns loaded with round and grape shot, the deck cleared, and all got ready for action. At seven, being then close to the chase, the Comet hoisted her colours, and sheered up to the man of war, which had hoisted Portuguese colours. The Portuguese then sent his boat on board the Comet, the officer of which informed captain Boyle, that the brig was a Portuguese national vessel, mounting 20 thirty-two pounders, and 165 men, and that the three others were English vessels under his protection, which he would not suffer to be molested; he also mentioned that the English vessels were armed and very strong. Boyle having shown him his commission, answered, that the brig had no right to protect English vessels on the high seas, and that he was determined to capture those vessels if he could; that he should be sorry if any thing disagreeable took place, but if it did he would not be the aggressor; but that he should certainly resist any attempt to prevent his capturing the vessels. The officer having now re-

G

turned on board the brig, Boyle hailed her, and distinctly stated his intention of immediately attacking the convoy, which consisted of a ship of 14 guns, and two brigs of 10 guns each, the whole force including the Portuguese, being 54 guns.

Boyle accordingly made all sail for the English vessels, which were close together, and about half past eight, the moon shining clear, he hailed the ship, ordering them to back the main-top-sails. Little or no answer being given, Boyle, having quick way at the time, shot a little ahead, saying that he should be along side again in a few minutes, when, if his orders were not obeyed, a broadside would be poured into him. After a few minutes he tacked, the man of war close after him. He then ran alongside the ship, one of the brigs being close to her, and opened his broadside upon them both, all the vessels at this time carrying a crowd of canvass. From his superior sailing, Boyle was frequently obliged to tack, by which he would have received considerable advantage, had he not been closely followed by the man of war, which now opened a heavy fire upon him; which was returned by the Comet. Having now the whole force to contend with, Boyle kept as close as possible to the English vessels, which frequently separated to give the man of war an opportunity of giving a broadside. The Comet continued the action, sometimes pouring her broadsides into the merchantmen, at others into the man of war, until eleven o'clock, when the ship surrendered, being all cut to pieces, and rendered unmanageable and directly after one of the brigs, which was also very much disabled. A boat was now despatched to take possession of the brig, but it was forced to return, being prevented from passing by the fire of the man of war; one of whose broadsides almost succeeded in sinking it. The Comet now directed the whole of her fire at the Portuguese, who soon sheered off, and was followed for a short distance by the Comet, which then returned, and made the third merchatman surrender, she also being cut to pieces.

Boyle now took possession of the Bowes, the brig that had first surrendered. He also spoke the ship, and ordered the captain to follow him, who answered, that his ship was in a sinking condition, having many shot holes between wind and water, and not a rope but what was cut away; but that he would, if posssible, follow his orders for his own safety. As soon as the Bowes was taken possession of, she received a passing broadside from the Portuguese. The moon having now set, it became very dark and squally, and the Comet was separated from all the vessels except the man of war, with whom for half an hour longer she continued occasionally to exchange broadsides. At day-light, however, the vessels being found to be still and in the neighbourhood, the Comet wore close to her prize. The man of war then stood down for them; on perceiving which Boyle immediately hove about, and stood for him, when he also tacked, and made signals for the convoy to make the first port. The two merchantmen accordingly put before the wind, accompanied by the Portuguese, by whose assistance and their own exertions, they succeeded with the utmost difficulty in regaining the harbour of Pernambuco, leaving the Bowes in possession of the Comet,

On the 11th of March, 1813, the General Armstrong, a privateer schooner, while cruizing off the mouth of Surinam river, discovered a sail, which was supposed to be a British letter of marque, and immediately bore down on her, with the intention of giving her two broadsides and then boarding. After giving her one broadside, and wearing and giving another, to their surprise they found they were along side of a frigate, pierced for 14 guns on the main deck, 6 on the quarter-deck, and 4 on the forecastle. The wind being light, the privateer lay for about ten minutes like a log in the water. During that time however, they shot away the frigate's fore-top-sail tie, his mizen gaff haulyards, which brought his colours down, and his mizen and main stay, when, thinking she had struck, they ceased firing; but being soon undeceived, they recommenced the action. The frigate lay for a few minutes apparently unmanageable, but soon getting way, opened such a heavy fire as would soon have sunk the schooner, had she not succeeded in making her escape by the assistance of her sweeps. In this action, which continued for 45 minutes, the privateer had six men killed and 16 wounded. All the haulyards of her head sails were shot away, the foremast and bowsprit one quarter cut through, all the fore and main shrouds but one cut away, both mainstays and running rigging cut to pieces, a great number of shot through the sails, and several between wind and water, which caused the vessel to leak, and a number in the hull. While they were getting away from the frigate, she kept up a well directed fire for the foremast and gaff of the schooner, but without effect.

On the 5th of August, 1813, the privateer Decatur, being on a cruize, discovered a ship and a schooner, the first of which proved to be the British packet Princess Charlotte, the other the British vessel of war, the Dominica. She immediately stood towards them, and soon found herself abreast of the schooner. Both vessels continued to manœuvre for two or three hours, the Dominica endeavouring to escape, and the

Decatur to board, during which time several broadsides were fired by the former, and a number of shot from the large gun of the latter. The Decatur at last succeeded in boarding the Dominica, a number of men passing into her stern from the bowsprit. The fire from the artillery and musquetry was now terrible, being well supported on both sides. The Dominica, however, not being able to disengage herself, dropped along side of the Decatur, and in this position was boarded by her whole crew. Fire arms now became useless, the crews fighting hand to hand with cutlasses, and throwing cold shot; when, the captain and principal officers of the Dominica being killed, and her deck covered with dead and wounded, the British colours were hauled down by the conquerors.

During the combat which lasted an hour, the Princess Charlotte remained a silent spectator of the scene, and as soon as it was over, she tacked about and stood to the southward. She had sailed from St. Thomas, bound to England, under convoy, to a certain latitude, of the Dominica.

The Decatur was armed with 6 twelve pound carronades, and one eighteen pounder on a pivot, with 103 men. Her loss in the action was three killed and sixteen wounded, one of whom afterwards died. The Dominica had 12 twelve pound carronades, two long sixes, one brass four pounder, and one thirty-two pound carronade on a pivot, with 83 men. She had 13 killed, and 47 wounded, five of whom afterwards died of their wounds. Perhaps this engagement has been the most bloody, and the loss in killed and wounded on the part of the enemy, in proportion to the number engaged, perhaps the greatest, of any action to be found in the records of naval warfare. The surviving officers of the Dominica attribute the loss of their vessel to the superior skill of the Decatur's crew in the use of musquetry, and the masterly manœuvering of that vessel, by which their carriage guns were rendered nearly useless.— The captain was a young man of not more than 25 years of age; he had been wounded early in the action by two musket balls in the left arm, but he fought till the last moment, refusing to surrender his vessel, although he was urged by the few survivors of his crew to do so; declaring his determination not to survive her loss.

The Decatur arrived at Charleston on the 20th of August with her prize. The surviving officers of the Dominica spoke in the highest terms of approbation of the humanity and attention displayed towards them by the officers and crew of the Decatur.

Towards the beginning of January, general Tupper having

in a manner paved the way by his expeditions, general Winchester proceeded down the Miami from Fort Defiance to the Rapids, with the force under his command. On his arrival there, he was strongly urged by the inhabitants of Frenchtown, on the river Raisin, to protect them from the violence and outrage of the horde of savages by whom they were surrounded, and to whose brutalities they were daily exposed. Yielding to the call of humanity, Winchester, on the 17th of January, by the unanimous advice of his officers, but, it appears, without consulting general Harrison, detached a body of about 750 men, under general Lewis, to their relief.

On the following day, when within three miles of Frenchtown, information was received that a body of British and Indians were encamped at that place, and that they had received notice of their approach. The troops were accordingly arranged and directed to prepare for action, and then proceeded within a quarter of a mile of the enemy, who immediately commenced a fire with a howitzer, from which, however, no injury was received. The line of battle being instantly formed, the whole detachment was ordered to advance across the river on the ice; in which they succeeded, though it was in many places extremely slippery. The left wing and centre were then ordered to possess themselves of the houses and picketing about which the enemy had collected, and where they had placed their cannon. This order was executed in a few minutes. Both battalions advanced amidst an incessant shower of bullets and succeeded in dislodging the enemy, neither the picketing nor the fencing over which they had to pass checking their progress.

The right wing fell in with the enemy at a considerable distance to the right, and pursued them a mile to the woods, where they made a stand with their howitzer and small arms, covored by a chain of enclosed lots and a group of houses, with a thick brushy wood full of fallen timber in their rear. Lewis now ordered the left and centre to possess themselves of the wood on the left, and to move up towards the main body of the enemy as fast as practicable, in order to divert their attention from the right. At the moment that the left and centre commenced their fire, the right advanced, and the enemy being soon driven from the fences and houses, both parties entered the wood together. The fight now became close, and extremely hot on the right wing, the enemy concentrating their forces on that side, in order to force the line. They were, however, still obliged to retreat, although slowly, the Americans being much fatigued, and were driven, in whole, not

G 2

less than two miles, every foot of the way under a continual charge.

The battle lasted from three in the afternoon till dark, when the detachment was drawn off in good order, and encamped at the place which the enemy had first occupied.

The force of the enemy in this affair has never been exactly ascertained; but from the best information, there were 80 to 100 British and 400 Indians. The number of their killed and wounded is likewise unknown, as they were enabled to carry off all but those left on the field where the battle commenced, which was about fifteen; but from the blood, the trails of bodies dragged off, and the reports of the people who lived near the place, the slaughter must have been great. One Indian and two of the Canadian militia were taken prisoners. A quantity of public stores was also taken. The loss of the Americans was twelve killed and fifty-five wounded.

On the 20th, general Winchester joined the detachment, with a reinforcement of 250 men.

Meanwhile colonel Proctor, who commanded at Detroit, hearing of the approach of the Americans advanced to meet the.h with a body of 1500 Indians and British, 300 of whom were regulars   On the night of the 21st he discovered the American detachment, and early next morning commenced an attack on their lines. The attack commenced at 6 in the morning, by a heavy fire of musquetry, assisted by six field pieces. The main body of the Americans were stationed within pickets on the left; a smaller force, unprotected, occupied the right, who gallantly sustained the shock for a quarter of an hour, when they began to give ground for the purpose of forming in a situation more favourable for their fire, and less exposed to that of the enemy.   At this moment Winchester arrived at the place of conflict, his quarters having been at the distance of three or four hundred yards from the camp, and his attention was immediately directed to rally the retreating party.   This retreat, however, being discovered by the enemy, the whole Indian force, together with a portion of the militia, bore down upon them with redoubled violence, and by the superiority of their numbers, and the severity of their fire, prevented their forming. After a short conflict, in which they suffered severely, all that survived, were made prisoners.

The left, who were stationed within the pickets, maintained their ground for several hours, and repulsed the British regulars, in three successive charges, with great slaughter. About 11 o'clock, however, Winchester was brought in as a prisoner to this part of the field, and perceiving that resistance was in vain, and influenced by the threat of their being abandoned to savage fury unless they instantly surrendered, he acceded to a capitulation, and sent a flag to the pickets to inform them they were prisoners.

General Harrison was at Lower Sandusky, when he received the intelligence of Lewis having advanced to the river Raisin, and fearing that he might be overpowered, he immediately set out for the Rapids, which he found that Winchester had just left with the reinforcement. When the news of Winchester's disaster reached Harrison, he was about three miles above the Rapids, with 360 men. He immediately ordered them to prepare to march, and set out with his staff to overtake a detachment of 300 men that had set out that morning for the river Raisin. He soon overtook them; but before the troops that he had left came up, it was ascertained that the defeat was complete, and it was the unanimous opinion of the officers that the detachment should return. A hundred and seventy of the most active men, however, were sent forward, with directions to proceed as far as possible to assist those who were fortunate enough to escape. These, however, were but few; the snow was so deep that the fugitives were entirely exhausted in running a few miles, those that did get off effected it by turning down to the lake, and secreting themselves. There were not more than 40 or 50 that got a mile from the scene of action, and the greater part of even these were overtaken.

Though the resistance on the part of the Americans was put an end to by the capitulation concluded by Winchester, we regret to say, that the most tragical events of this disastrous day are still to be recorded, events which affix an indelible stain on the arms of the British. After the battle the British returned to Malden with their prisoners, except about 50 or 60 wounded, who were not able to march. A few of the Indians remained behind, who, being joined next morning by about 50 more from Malden, immediately commenced a massacre of the wounded Americans, and afterwards set fire to the houses in which they had been left, and consumed their remains. The same day the Indians massacred a number of their prisoners, who had not been wounded, whose remains they would not suffer to be interred, but left them above ground, where they were torn to pieces and devoured by hogs. These horrid outrages are but too well substantiated, not only by the inhabitants of Frenchtown, but by some of the officers who had the good fortune to escape, by being purchased from the savages. Great indignities were likewise inflicted on a surgeon and his two companions, who, but a few days after the battle, had been de-

patched by Harrison with a flag of truce, to attend to the
wounded. One of them was killed by the Indians, and the
others robbed of the money with which they had been entrusted by the general, for the relief of the most pressing wants of
the wounded. After suffering many indignities, not only from
the Indians but from the British, under the flimsy pretext of
their using the flag only as a cover,* they were at length set
at liberty at Montreal, whither they had been carried and im-
prisoned.

On the 23d of January, the day after the surrender of Winchester, Harrison retreated to Carrying river, about midway
between Sandusky and the Miami. In the following month he
again advanced to the Rapids, where he constructed a fort,
which, in honour of the governor of Ohio, was named Fort
Meigs. This fort contains about nine acres of ground, nearly
in an octagon form. At each corner is a strong block-house,
with cannon planted so as to rake each line, and command every
elevated point near the fort. Between the block-houses are
strong picketings fifteen feet in height, against which a breast-
work of clay was thrown up on both sides, and in addition to
this, several long batteries were erected, which were well supplied with cannon.

The term of service of a large portion of the militia in Harrison's army having expired, 1200 men were called out by the
governor of Kentucky, and despatched under general Green
Clay to supply their place. They left Cincinnati, their place
of rendezvous, in the beginning of April, and arrived near
Fort Meigs on the 4th of May, which they learnt was besieged by a large force of British and Indians, under general Proctor.

Proctor had set out for Fort Meigs with 1000 British and
1200 Indians, about the middle of April, with the expectation
of capturing it before the arrival of Harrison's reinforcements
and supplies, but owing to incessant and heavy rains, he was
not able to open his batteries before the first of May. A brisk
firing was kept up on both sides until the fifth, when a small
party of general Clay's detachment arrived, with information

---

* General Harrison, in his official dispatch, states, that the
surgeon was furnished with a letter addressed to any British
officer he might meet, describing the character in which he went,
and the object for which he was sent, an open letter to general
Winchester, and written instructions to himself, all of which he
was directed to show to the first officer he met with.

of the rest being close at hand. Orders were immediately despatched to Clay, to proceed down the river in his boats, to land 800 men on the left bank of the river, who should immediately attack the enemy's batteries, and spike their cannon, and the remainder on the right bank, who would be aided by a sortie of the garrison. The plan was successfully executed, the cannon were spiked, but unfortunately, instead of returning acros the river to the fort, they pursued the flying enemy to the woods where they were surrounded, and the greatest portion taken prisoners. A great part of the baggage was also taken in the boats by the Indians.

Notwithstanding the unfortunate issue of this affair, however, Fort Meigs was relieved. Proctor, being deserted by the Indians, whom their chiefs could not prevent returning to their villages, as is their custom after any battle of consequence, with their prisoners and plunder, made a precipitate retreat on the 9th of May, having previously secured their ordnance on board a sloop.

No event of consequence took place on the New York frontier during the winter. The opposing armies being divided by a barrier of ice, not sufficiently strong to allow of the transportation of artillery, peace was only disturbed by a few petty incursions, which each party justified by the plea of retaliation.

On the 6th of February, captain Forsythe, the commanding officer at Ogdensburg, on the St. Lawrence, received information that several men who had deserted from the opposite shore, on the ice, had been taken on the American side by a party of British, and carried off and confined in the jail at Brockville.

In consequence of this intrusion, as it was deemed, Forsythe the same evening crossed over with about 200 militia and riflemen, for the purpose of retaking the prisoners, and capturing the military stores at Brockville. On approaching the Canada shore, a flanking company was detached above, and another below the town, to secure all the passes, to prevent information being communicated to the country. Before the main force reached the shore they were fired at by the centinels, but, instead of returning it, they rushed through the main street to the jail, which was instantly carried, the prisoners liberated, and then the magazine was secured. The troops in the town were completely surprised. One major, three captains, three lieutenants, one surgeon's mate, and forty-two privates, together with their arms, besides 130 rifles and muskets captured by the British at Detroit, and several casks of powder and fixed ammunition, were secured and brought off. Perfect order was observed by the officers and men, scrupulous respect paid to private property, and no injury was done to any individual.   Although a severe fire was kept up from the houses as the Americans advanced to the jail, there were none killed and but one wounded.

The following evening a party of 46 Indians, headed by a British officer, crossed over from Prescott, a village in Canada, a mile and a half above Ogdensburg, for the purpose of capturing a picket guard of nine men, belonging to Forsythe's company.   They succeeded in taking the centinel on post, and then attacked the guard, but were repulsed by their steady bravery, aided by their advantageous position.   The succeeding evening 15 or 20 American volunteers again crossed, and took a lieutenant and two men, together with 15 or 20 stand of arms.

On the morning of the 22d of February, the British crossed over in considerable force; and succeeded in capturing Ogdensburg.   Forsythe, with a force of less than half that of the British, effected his retreat to Black Lake in a masterly manner.   Considerable alarm for the safety of Sackett's Harbour was excited by this event, and immediate measures were taken for reinforcing it.   No attempts were made, however, at further conquest; the British shortly after retired across the St. Lawrence.

The ice having disappeared on Lake Ontario about the middle of April, the look-out boat Growler sailed from Sackett's Harbour on the 19th to reconnoitre the lake and immediate preparations were made for an embarkation of troops for the invasion of Canada.   The troops, to the number of 1700, under the command of general Dearborn, were embarked by the 23d, but the weather proving stormy, the fleet did not sail till the 25th.

On the morning of the 27th they arrived off York, the capital of Upper Canada, and left the fleet having taken a position to the south and westward of the principal fort, and as near the shore as possible; the debarkation of the troops commenced about 8, and was completed about 10 in the forenoon.   The place fixed on for landing was a clear field, the scite of the old French fort Tarento, but the wind blowing heavy from the eastward the boats fell to leeward, by which they were exposed to a galling fire from the enemy, who had taken a position in a thick wood, near where the troops were obliged to land.   This circumstance likewise prevented the fleet from covering the landing.   The cool intrepidity of the officers and men, however, overcame every obstacle.

The riflemen under Forsythe first landed, under a heavy fire from the enemy, who had collected all their force at this point, consisting of 700 regulars and militia, and 100 Indians, commanded by general Sheaffe in person. The contest was sharp and severe for about half an hour, when about 700 or 800 of the Americans having landed, commanded by general Pike, and the remainder of the troops pushing for the shore, the enemy retreated to their works, leaving a number of killed and wounded on the field. As soon as the troops were landed, the schooners were directed to take a position near the forts, in order that the attack upon them by the army and navy might be simultaneous.

Pike, having formed the troops on the ground originally intended for their landing, advanced to the batteries, which now opened their fire; which was returned from the schooners, that had beat up to a position within 600 yards of the principal fort. The troops were led in the most gallant manner by general Pike, who carried two redoubts, and was approaching the principal work, when the enemy, having previously laid a train, blew up his magazine, by which a great number of the troops were killed and wounded; and, among the former, the ever to be lamented general Pike. When the fall of Pike was made known to general Dearborn, he landed and took the command of the troops.

As soon as the magazine was blown up, the British set fire to their naval stores and a ship on the stocks; and then the regulars with Sheaffe at their head, made a precipitate retreat from the town. By two in the afternoon the American flag was substituted for the British, and by four the troops were in peaceable possession of York, a capitulation having been agreed on with the militia commanding officer, by which the town, stores, and nearly 300 militia were surrendered.

The total loss in killed on this occasion was, in battle 14 and by explosion 38; wounded in battle 32, by explosion 232.

The loss acknowledged by the British in their official account is: killed 62, wounded 34, wounded and prisoners 43, prisoners 10, and missing 7.

This loss of killed, wounded, and prisoners, however, must only include the regulars, as 300 militia were surrendered in the town.

The day after the capture of York was employed in burying the dead. The public buildings, barracks, &c. were then destroyed, together with the military stores that could not be brought away, and by the first of May the town was entirely evacuated, the militia prisoners parolled, and the troops embarked: but, owing to contrary winds, the fleet did not sail till

the 8th. On the afternoon of the same day they arrived at Four
Mile Creek, below Fort Niagara, where the troops and public
property were landed, and, on the 10th Chauncey again sailed
for Sackett's Harbour for reinforcements.   The day previous
to his departure, two schooners, with 100 picked men, sailed
for the head of the lake to seize a quantity of public stores.—
The stores were found to be guarded by about 80 regulars,
who were repulsed, the stores brought away, the public buildings burnt, and the expedition returned to Fort Niagara without loss.

Chauncey arrived at Sackett's Harbour on the 13th of May,
and having received 350 troops on board, again sailed on the
22d, and arrived near Fort Niagara, on the 25th, where the
troops ware landed.   A council was immediately held by general Dearborn, for the purpose of making arrangements for immediately passing to the opposite shore.   Next day Chauncey
reconnoitered the position for landing the troops, and at night
sounded the shore, and placed buoys to point out the stations
for the small vessels.   He then took on board of the Madison,
Oneida, and Lady of the Lake all the heavy artillery, and as
many troops as could be stowed.

On the 27th, at three in the morning, the signal was made
for the fleet to weigh, and before four the remainder of the
troops were embarked on board of boats, which were directed
to follow the fleet.   The schooners were judiciously placed in
positions to silence the enemy's batteries, and cover the landing of the troops, within musket shot of the shore.   In ten minutes after they opened on the batteries, they were completely silenced and abandoned.

The troops then advanced in three brigades, and landed near
a fort which had been silenced, at Two Mile creek.   Immediately on their landing, the enemy, who had been concealed in a
ravine, advanced in great force to the edge of the bank, in order
to charge them; but the schooners opened so well directed and
tremendous a fire of grape and cannister, that they were soon
obliged to retreat.   The troops formed as soon as they landed
and immediately ascended the bank, and charged and routed
the enemy in every direction, the schooners still keeping up a
constant and well-directed fire.   The British now re-entered
Fort George, and set fire to their magazines, after which they
moved off rapidly towards Queenstown, and were pursued
by the light troops for several miles.   The main body, however, having been under arms from one in the morning, were
too much exhausted for further pursuit.   They returned to
Fort George, of which they had quiet possession by twelve
o'clock.

On this occasion we find the first mention made of captain PERRY, the hero of lake Erie. He volunteered his services to commodore Chauncey, and rendered great assistance in arranging and superintending the debarkation of the troops. He was present at every point where he could be useful, under showers of musqetry, but fortunately escaped unhurt. The next day he was despatched to Black Rock, with fifty-five seamen, to prepare and take the command of the squadron fitting out there.

The loss of the Americans in capturing Fort George, was thirty-nine killed and 111 wounded. The British lost 108 killed and 278 prisoners, of whom 163 were wounded. The number of militia parolled by general Dearborn was 507.

The day after the capture of the fort, general Lewis marched with Chandler's and Winder's brigades, and the light artillery, dragoons and riflemen, in pursuit of the British, by the way of Queenstown. Information had been received that they had made a stand on the mountain, at a place called the Beaver Dam, where they had a depot of provisions and stores, and that they had been joined by 300 regulars from Kingston, and were calling in the militia. Dearborn, therefore was in hopes, that, confiding in the strength of his position, the enemy would await an action, by which an opportunity would be afforded to cut off his retreat. In this expectation, however, he was disappointed. The troops at Fort Erie blew up their magazine, and joined the main body at Beaver Dam, who then broke up and retreated along the mountains towards the head of lake Ontario. The same evening Fort Erie was taken possession of by a party from the opposite shore, and Lewis, finding that the enemy had made their escape, returned to Fort George.

Dearborn, still in hopes of being able to cut off the retreat of the enemy, on the 1st of June detached general Winder with his brigade, and one regiment from Boyd's brigade along the lake shore. On the 3d general Chandler followed with the remainder of Boyd's brigade. The British general, however, anticipated the blow, by attacking the American army before day on the morning of the 6th. Unfortunately, although the American loss was but small, and the enemy, whose force was very inferior, driven from the field, yet both the generals Chandler and Winder were taken prisoners. In this attack the Americans lost two generals and several other officers, but a greater number of prisoners were lost by the enemy.

Dearborn received the intelligence of this affair late in the same evening, and immediately despatched general Lewis to take the command of the troops. He arrived and took the command in the afternoon of the 7th. The British likewise

H

despatched a messenger to sir James Yeo, who was off York with the British fleet, with orders to co-operate in the attack on the Americans. Lewis found the army encamped at the Forty Mile Creek, on a plain of about a mile in width, ten miles in the rear of the ground where it had been attacked, its right flank resting on the lake, and its left on a creek which skirts the base of a perpendicular mountain of a considerable height.

Lewis had scarcely arrived at the camp before the hostile fleet hove in sight. It did not approach near enough before dark, however, to enable them to ascertain with certainty whether it was Yeo's or Chauncey's squadron. In this state of uncertainty, the army lay on their arms all night, and at break of day struck their tents, when the hostile fleet was discovered abreast of them, about a mile from the shore. About 6, it being a dead calm, the enemy towed in shore a large schooner, which on her approach, opened her fire on the boats which the army had employed for the transportation of their baggage and camp equipage, which then lay on the beach. As soon as her object was perceived, four pieces of artillery were sent down to the shore, and captain Totten of the engineers was ordered to construct a furnace for heating shot, which was prepared and in operation in less than 30 minutes, and the schooner was soon compelled to retire.

A party of Indians now made their appearance on the brow of the mountain, (which being perfectly bald, exhibited them to view,) and commenced a fire on the camp. They were quickly dislodged, however, by a small party under the command of lieutenant Eldridge. The Americans lost not a man by the attacks of the fleet and Indians.

Sir James L. Yeo now sent on shore an officer with a flag, demanding a surrender of the army, it being invested with savages in its rear, a fleet in its front, and a powerful army on its flank. To this demand general Lewis only answered, that " the message was too ridiculous to merit a reply."

Between 7 and 8 o'clock the four waggons that were with the army were loaded with the sick, and with ammunition; the camp equipage and baggage was put in the boats, and 700 men were detached to proceed in them for their protection. By some irregularity, however, the boats, induced probably by the stillness of the morning, put off before the detachment reached the shore, and they had not proceeded above three miles, when a breeze sprung up, which enabled an armed schooner to overhaul them. Some of the boats, however, kept on and escaped; the others were run to the shore and deserted, twelve of which were lost, principally loaded with baggage. At 10 o'clock the army was put in motion, and reached Fort George with the loss only of a few stragglers, who were picked up by the militia and Indians.

Shortly after this affair, the American troops concentrated at Fort George, having evacuated Fort Erie, and the remainder of the Niagara frontier.

On the evening of the 23d of June, Dearborn, despatched lieutenant-colonel Bœrstler, with 570 men, to Beaver Dam, a few miles beyond Queenstown, to attack and disperse a body of the enemy, who had collected there for the purpose of procuring provisions, and harrassing those of the inhabitants who were considered friendly to the United States. The force of the enemy was understood to be about 80 regulars, 150 or 200 militia, and from 50 to 60 Indians.

About 8 next morning, when within about two miles of Beaver Dam, Bœrstler was attacked from an ambuscade, but soon drove the enemy some distance into the woods. He then retired into a clear field, whence he immediately despatched an express for a reinforcement, stating that he would maintain his position till it arrived. Three hundred men were instantly marched to his relief. They were, however, too late; for on arriving at Queenstown they received authentic intelligence of the surrender of the whole detachment, and accordingly returned to camp.

The British account of this affair states that the detachment to which Bœrstler surrendered was but small, the Indians being the only force actually engaged; but that his position was surrounded by woods, which he was led to believe was occupied by a superior force.

While the American army was thus employed at Fort George, several enterprises were undertaken by the British. On the night of the 27th of May, a force of upwards of 1000 men, under sir George Prevost, were embarked at Kingston on board the British squadron, and in open boats, and immediately sailed for Sackett's Harbour. Next morning they were observed by lieutenant Chauncey, who commanded the small naval force remaining there, the principal part of the American squadron being engaged at Fort George, he immediately sailed into the harbour firing alarm guns. The alarm being immediately communicated, guns were likewise fired from the alarm posts, in order to bring in the militia, and instant measures were taken to resist the attack.

No attempt, however, was made to land on the 28th, the attention of the enemy being drawn off, at the moment when all was prepared for landing, by the appearance of a fleet of American barges passing from Oswego for Sackett's Harbour. The barges of the enemy were immediately despatched to cut them off, and succeeded in taking 12; the troops, however, had previously succeeded in landing and gaining the woods, and came into Sackett's Harbour the same evening. The remaining seven boats outsailed the enemy's barges, and got safe into port. It is presumed that the landing was now put off till next morning, under the expectation of cutting off more barges, as the fleet hauled their wind and stood into South Bay, and the armed barges were despatched, apparently in order to waylay them.

During the night a considerable militia force came in, and were stationed on the water side, near Horse Island, on which was placed a small body of Albany volunteers. The moment it was light, the enemy's squadron was perceived in line between Stony Point and Horse Island, and shortly after troops were landed on the latter, from thirty-three large boats, under cover of their gun-boats.

General Brown, who commanded the post, had directed that the volunteers should retreat across the neck which joins Horse Island to the main land, in case of the enemy landing there, which they accordingly did, and joined the militia under his command, amounting to between four and five hundred men. The enemy having landed and passed to the main land, were marching to the town, when they received the fire of the volunteers and militia, which somewhat checked their progress.— Unfortunately, however, the militia, totally unacquainted with military discipline, after giving the first fire, rose from their cover and fled to the woods. The handful of volunteers, thus losing their support, were likewise forced to retreat, but being joined by a few regulars from the town, succeeded in rallying a portion of the militia, and, by the aid of the fire from the fort, soon forced the enemy to withdraw to their ships. Unfortunately, the officer who was entrusted with the care of the navy barracks and store-houses, who had been instructed to fire them in case of the enemy proving victorious, mistaking the flight of the militia for a complete repulse, set them on fire, and they were totally consumed.

The American loss in this attack was twenty-one killed and eighty-four wounded, of the volunteers and regulars, and twenty-six missing. Of the militia there were twenty-five killed, wounded, and missing. Of the enemy, twenty-nine were found dead in the field, and twenty-two wounded, and thirty-five were made prisoners; in addition, many were killed in the boats while effecting their landing; a number were likewise carried off the field by the enemy, previous to the commencement of his retreat. In the British official account, their loss is stated as follows, viz: Killed forty-eight, wounded one hundred and ninety-five, wounded and missing, sixteen.

Commodore Chauncey returned to Sackett's Harbour on the 1st of June, from Fort George, where he was compelled to remain for near two months, until the new vessel, the General Pike, was ready for sea, as the enemy's fleet was now considerably superior in force.

Meanwhile the British lorded it over the lake. On the 16th of June their fleet appeared off the village of Sodus, where a quantity of provisions was deposited. The militia of the neighbourhood were instantly called to arms, and the following day arrived in considerable force. In the mean while, the enemy having disappeared, the provisions were removed from the warehouses on the water's edge to a small distance in the edge of the woods, and on the 19th the militia were discharged, excepting a small number as a guard. Before evening of the same day, however, the fleet again appeared. The alarm was instantly given, and expresses sent after the discharged militia, who immediately returned, but not in time to save the place.—The enemy having landed, and finding that the greater part of the provisions had been removed, set fire to all the valuable buildings in the place, which were consumed with their contents.

The next day the fleet appeared off Fort Oswego, and made several attempts to land troops, but each time returned on seeing the American troops ready to meet them on the shore.

Another attempt was made on Sackett's Harbour on the night of the 2d of July, by a considerable force in open boats, headed by sir James Yeo. This scheme being discovered by a deserter, commodore Chauncey as soon as possible got under way to intercept their retreat. The British, however, discovered the desertion; and decamped some time before the commodore could reach their place of landing.

On the morning of the 11th of July, 250 British regulars crossed the Niagara river, and landed a little below Black Rock. On moving towards that place, they were discovered by about 200 militia, who instantly fled. The enemy then set fire to the barracks, block-houses, &c. spiked several pieces of cannon, and took a quantity of flour and salt, and four small field pieces. While engaged in getting off the property, they were attacked by a force of 100 regulars, 130 militia and volunteers, and 20 or 30 Indians, who had come down from Buffaloe, who poured in upon them a successful fire, by which a considerable number were killed, nine of whom were left dead on the shore, besides a captain mortally wounded. Fifteen prisoners also were taken. They succeeded, however, in carrying off the property. The loss of the Americans was one killed and three wounded, two of whom afterwards died.

Nor were the British inactive upon Lake Erie. After their retreat from Fort Meigs in the beginning of May, several threatening movements were made from the lake at Fort Meigs, Lower Sandusky, Cleveland and Erie. No serious attempt was made, however, on any of these posts, until the first of August, when a combined force of the enemy, amounting to at least 500 regulars and seven or eight hundred Indians, under the immediate command of general Proctor, made its appearance before Lower Sandusky, As soon as the general had made such a disposition of his troops as would cut off the retreat of the garrison, he sent colonel Elliot, accompanied by major Chambers, with a flag, to demand the surrender of the fort, stating that he was anxious to spare the effusion of blood, which he should probably not have in his power to do, should he be reduced to the necessity of taking the place by storm.

The commander of the fort was major Croghan, a youth of 21 years of age. His answer was, that he was determined to defend the place to the last extremity, and that no force, however large, should induce him to surrender it. So soon as the flag returned, a brisk fire was opened upon the fort, from the gun-boats in the river, and from a five and a half inch howitzer on shore, which was kept up with little intermission throughout the night.

At an early hour the next morning, three sixes, which had been placed during the night within 250 yards of the pickets, began to play, but with little effect. About 4 in the afternoon, discovering that the fire from all the guns was concentrated against the north-western angle of the fort, Croghan became confident that the object was to make a breach, and attempt to storm the works at that point. He therefore ordered out as many men as could be employed for the purpose of strengthening that part, which was so effectually secured by means of bags of flour, sand, &c. that the picketing suffered little or no injury; notwithstanding which, about 500 of the enemy, having formed in close column, advanced to assault the works at the expected point, at the same time making two feints on other parts of the fort. The column which advanced against the north-western angle, consisting of about 350 men, was so completely enveloped in smoke, as not 'to be discovered until it had approached within 18 or 20 paces of the lines; but the men, being all at their posts and ready to receive it, commenced so heavy and galling a fire as to throw the column a little into confusion; being quickly rallied, however, it advanced to the outer works, and began to leap into the ditch. At that moment a fire of grape was opened from a six-pounder, which had been previously arranged so as to rake in that direction, which, together with the musquetry, threw them into such confusion, that they were compelled to retire precipitately to the woods.

During the assault, which lasted about half an hour, an incessant fire was kept up by the enemy's artillery, which consisted of five sixes and a howitzer, but without effect.

Before the attack was ended, the soldiers in the garrison supplied the wounded enemy in the ditch with water, by throwing over full canteens.

The whole number of men in the garrison was not more than 160. Their loss during the siege was one killed and seven wounded slightly. The loss of the enemy in killed, wounded, and prisoners, must have exceeded 150; one lieutenant-colonel, a lieutenant, and 50 rank and file were found in and about the ditch, dead or wounded. Those of the remainder who were not able to escape were taken off during the night by the Indians.

About 3 in the morning the enemy sailed down the river, leaving behind them a boat containing clothing and considerable military stores. Seventy stand of arms, and several brace of pistols, were afterwards collected near the works.

A few days after the assault, Proctor despatched a surgeon with a flag of truce, to assist in the care of the wounded, and with a request that such of the prisoners as were in a condition to be removed might be permitted to return to Malden, on *his* parole of honour that they should not serve until exchanged.

Harrison, in his reply, stated, that on his arrival at Fort Sandusky on the morning of the 3d, he found that major Croghan, conformably to those principles which are held sacred in the American army, had caused all the care to be taken of the wounded prisoners that his situation would permit; that his hospital surgeon was particularly charged to attend to them, and he was warranted in the belief that every thing which surgical skill could give was afforded. They have been liberally furnished too, he added, with every article necessary in their situation which the hospital stores could supply. Having referred to his government for orders respecting the disposition of the prisoners, he could not with propriety comply with the request for an immediate exchange. But he assured him, that as far as it depended upon him, the course of treatment which had been commenced towards them while in his possession would be continued.

It is impossible here to avoid contrasting the conduct of Proctor and Harrison, in two exactly parallel cases, the care of the wounded, and treatment of the surgeon sent for their relief after the battles of Frenchtown and Sandusky. In the one case the surgeon is treated with politeness, and only sent back because his aid is unnecessary, and the wounded are supplied with water by the garrison, even while the attack is carried on. The opposite conduct need not be repeated here. It has made too deep an impression to be so soon effaced.

On the 26th of December, 1812, an order in council was issued by the British government, declaring the Chesapeake and Delaware bays in a state of blockade, and on the 20th of March, all the ports south of Rhode Island were included. During the winter, intelligence had been repeatedly received by American prisoners from Bermuda, of the arrival of a British squadron at that place, well stored with bombs and Congreve rockets, and with a considerable body of troops on board, for the purpose of destroying some of our southern cities. The alarm, then, that was excited at Norfolk may be easily conceived, when intelligence was received of the approach of this squadron, which on the 4th of February was perceived in the Chesapeake, standing towards Hampton Roads, to the number of two 74's, three frigates, a brig, and a schooner. The frigate Constellation had come down the bay, and anchored in Hampton Roads the day before, and on the arrival of the first news of the near approach of the hostile squadron, it being then ebb-tide, was fast aground at Willoughby spit. Fortunately, however, the flood made, and the ship was afloat before the enemy hove in sight. She was immediately brought up Elizabeth river to Norfolk, and anchored between the two forts.

Every exertion was now made for the defence of the place, by calling out the militia, &c.; the recruits at the barracks were brought down to the fort, and the gun-boats stationed in the most favourable position to resist the expected attack. No attempt, however, was made upon the town. The squadron confined its operations to the capturing and destroying the bay craft, and forming an effectual blockade of the waters of the Chesapeake.

About the same time a British squadron entered the Delaware bay, which consisted of the Poictiers, 74, the frigate Belvidera, and several small vessels, and for some weeks were employed in fixing buoys, intercepting and capturing the outward and inward bound vessels, and burning the bay craft. On the 16th of March, sir J. P. Beresford, the commander of the squadron, transmitted a letter to Lewistown, a small fishing town near the mouth of the bay, addressed to the first magistrate, requesting him to send twenty live bullocks, with a proportionate quantity of vegetables and hay, on board the Poictiers, for the use of the squadron, which should be immediately paid for at the Philadelphia prices. The request was accompanied with a threat, that in case of a refusal, he should burn the town.

This demand was positively, though politely refused, as " a compliance would be an immediate violation of the laws, and an eternal stigma on the nation." To which Beresford answered, " that the demand he had made was, in his opinion, neither ungenerous, nor wanting in that magnanimity which one nation ought to observe to another with which it is at war. It is in my power," continues he, " to destroy your town, and the request I have made upon it, as the price of its security, is neither distressing nor unusual. I must, therefore, persist, and whatever sufferings may fall upon the inhabitants of Lewis, must be attributed to yourselves, by not complying with a request so easily acquiesced in."

Nothing further passed on the subject, till the 6th of April, when they renewed the demand, and fired several 32 pound shot into the town, previous to sending the flag on shore, to show that they were serious in their threats. In Beresford's letter on this occasion, he urges that no dishonour can be attached to complying with his demand, in consideration of his superior force. " I must, therefore," continues he, " consider your refusal to supply the squadron as most cruel on your part to the inhabitants. I grieve for the distress the women and children are reduced to by your conduct, and earnestly desire they may be instantly removed." To this letter merely a verbal reply was returned, that the commander, colonel Davis, was a gallant man, and had already taken care of the ladies. On the return of the flag, a cannonade was commenced from four launches with 24 and 18 pounders; two sloops, with 32 pounders and a mortar; a pilot boat, with six pounders; and a schooner with 12 twelve pounders, covered by the frigate Belvidera.

The town being seated on a considerable eminence, sustained little or no injury; the rockets passing over, and the bombs falling short. The fire from an eighteen pounder on shore, which was supplied by shot thrown by the enemy, silenced one of their most dangerous gun-boats. Above 600 shot were fired at the place, a great part of which was afterwards dug, by the boys, out of the sand, viz. 40 of 32lb. 96 of 18lb. 156 of 12's and 9's, with a large quantity of 6's and grape, besides shells and remains of rockets. Not a man was killed on the side of the Americans during this attack.

On the forenoon of the following day, a number of small boats approached the shore, apparently with the intention of landing; but, being gallantly met by the militia on the beach, they were recalled by a signal from the squadron.

In the Chesapeake the principal part of the squadron began to move up the bay about the beginning of April. On the 3d they anchored off the mouth of the Rappahannock, for the purpose of attacking the Dolphin, a privateer schooner of 10 guns, and three letters of marque bound for France, which had taken shelter in the river on the approach of the squadron.

Their tenders and launches, to the number of 17, being manned and sent up the river, a furious attack was made on the vessels, which unfortunately lay becalmed. Two of the letters of marque were speedily taken, they making but a slight resistance; the third was run ashore, and most of her crew escaped. The Dolphin bore the brunt of the action. The whole force of the enemy was soon directed to her, and she gallantly sustained the contest for two hours, when, at last, they succeeded in boarding her. Even then, however, she did not strike. The fight continued for some time on deck, until, overpowered by numbers, the Americans were forced to submit, the enemy having previously pulled down the colours.

A few days previous to this affair, a most unfortunate action took place here between the American privateer Fox and the United States' schooner Adeline and two gun-boats. The schooner and gun-boats were proceeding down the bay, under the command of lieutenant Sinclair, and at midnight made a harbour under Gwinn's island, near the mouth of the Rappahannock. After having anchored in a line across the channel, Sinclair was hailed by the Fox, and each taking the other to be an enemy, and consequently refusing to send a boat on board, Sinclair fired a musket ahead of the privateer, which she instantly returned with a broadside.

The schooner and gun-boats then opened their fire, and in fifteen minutes silenced the privateer. Being hailed, however, to know if she had struck, she renewed the action without answering, and in fifteen minutes more was again silenced. On being a second time hailed, she once more opened her fire, which she continued for half an hour and then cut her cable and escaped up the bay. On board the Fox the captain and five men were badly wounded, she had one shot in her hull, and her sails

&c. were very much cut. The damage on board the schooner, which bore the brunt of the action, was but small, only one man severely wounded, and the rigging a little cut.

The hostile squadron continuing to stand up the bay, on the 9th of April they reached Annapolis, and on the, 16th appeared off the mouth of the Patapsco, twelve of fourteen miles from Baltimore. Both Annapolis and Baltimore were threatened with an attack, but nothing was attempted, the enemy carefully keeping their vessels at a safe distance from the guns of the forts.

But though the fortified towns escaped the vengeance which had so long been threatened, it was not the case with the unprotected villages, which skirt the rivers that fall into the head of the bay. Four of these were laid in ashes by admiral Cockburn, who gallantly led the barges which ascended the rivers for this purpose. These plundering and burning expeditions will long render his name famous in the neighbourhood of the Chesapeake bay.

Having sufficiently signalized their prowess by the burning of Frenchtown, Havre-de-Grace,* Georgetown, and Fredericktown, and the farm-houses, mills, &c. adjoining, the squadron returned down the bay, destroying the oyster-boats, wood-shallops, and other river craft in their progress, and showing themselves, but at a convenient distance, at every fortification near the bay.

The squadron after returning down the bay, resumed their station in Hampton Roads, with the view of attacking Norfolk. Early on the morning of the 22d of June, they landed a large body of troops, from the accounts of deserters about 2500, on the west side of Elizabeth river, and marched them up towards Craney Island, the passage to which from the main land, is fordable at low water. Forty or fifty boats full of men, were then sent to effect a landing on the north side of the island, with whom the force on the main land was directed to co-operate.— The whole force on the island at the time of the attack was 487, riflemen, infantry, and artillery, and 150 seamen and marines, forty-three of whom were on the sick list.—With this handful

---

* The burning and plundering of Havre-de-Grace is perhaps the most signal of Cockburn's exploits. The houses being apart, had to be separately set on fire; and the labour bestowed in injuring the church must have been very considerable, every pane, of glass in the building having been broken by stones and brickbats.

of men was the landing of the enemy successfully opposed, and they were forced to retreat to their ships, with the loss of several boats by the fire of the artillery.

Foiled in their meditated attack on Norfolk by this repulse at the mouth of the harbour, the British again turned their attention to the easier task of laying waste unprotected villages, and that of Hampton, which lay nearly opposite, naturally presented itself. Here they landed a body of 2500 men, with but little opposition, there being only a small detachment of militia encamped near the town, who were soon foced to retreat under a heavy fire of artillery, musquetry, and Congreve rockets. The British now took possession of the village; and here a horrid scene of barbarity ensued, which was characterised by plunder, devastation, murder, and rape. The British troops shortly after retreated to their ships, when a correspondence took place by means of flags between general Taylor, the commandant at Norfolk, and sir Sidney Beckwith, quarter-master-general of the British forces, on the subject of these excesses. Sir Sidney attempted to justify them on the ground of inhumanity in some of the American troops on Craney Island, whom he charged with having waded into the river, and shot at their unresisting and yielding foe, who clung to the wreck of a boat which had been sunk by the fire of their guns. This imputation was promptly repelled, and a board of officers was immediately appointed to investigate the charge. From the evidence adduced it appeared, that in the action at Craney Island, two of the enemy's boats in front of their line were sunk by the fire of the batteries; the soldiers and sailors who were in those boats were consequently afloat, and in danger of drowning, and being in front of the boats that were uninjured, guns were necessarily fired in the direction of the men in the water, but with no intention whatever to do them further harm; but, on the contrary, orders were given to prevent this, by ceasing to fire grape, and only to fire round shot; it also was substantiated, that one of the enemy, who had apparently surrendered, advanced towards the shore, about one hundred yards, when he suddenly turned to his right and endervoured to make his escape to a body of the enemy who had landed above the island, and who were then in view; then, and not till then, was he fired upon to bring him back, which had the desired effect, and he was taken unhurt to the island. It further appeared, that the American troops exerted themselves in acts of hospitality and kindness to the unresisting and yielding foe.

But even if this charge had been founded on fact, it could not have justified the measures adopted by the British. The facts should surely have been first clearly ascertained and redress demanded, before any retaliation was resorted to; especially a retaliation so extravagant in its measure, applying not to the perpetrators of the alleged offence, nor to their comrades, but to the unresisting, innocent, and helpless.

During the remainder of the summer, hostile demonstrations were made by the British squadron in various points on the waters of the Chesapeake, particularly at Washington, Annapolis, and Baltimore, in which, if the aim of the enemy was merely to harass, they were certainly eminently successful. A part of the Chesapeake squadron, under admiral Cockburn, likewise appeared off Ocracock bar, North Carolina, where their barges destroyed two privateers, and landed a number of men at Portsmouth and Ocracock, who committed a number of wanton depredations.

The British squadron off New York confined themselves to keeping up a strict blockade. The American frigates United States and Macedonian, and the sloop of war Hornet, sailed from New York on a cruize in the beginning of May. Finding, however, that a much superior force lay off the Hook, they put back, and on the 25th passed through Hell-gate, with the intention of putting to sea through the sound. This intention was frustrated by the superior force of the enemy in that quarter, by which they were several times driven back, and on the first of June they were chased into New London by two 74's and a frigate, which immediately anchored off that place, and in a few days were joined by the force that had been blockading off the Hook. As the movements of the British indicated an intention of attacking New London, prompt measures were taken for its defence. Six hundred militia were called out, and to insure the safety of his squadron, commodore Decatur landed a number of his guns, which were mounted in a battery, and the vessels, thus lightened, proceeded up the river; where they were secure from any attempt of the larger vessels of the enemy.

New London is situated on the river Thames, about 7 miles from Long Island sound, and can be approached by ships of any draught of water. The channel, however, is narrow, and completely commanded by the surrounding heights, which were so strongly fortified, as to deter the sqadron from any hostile attempt. They contented themselves, therefore, with keeping up a blockade, and making a few predatory excursions on Long Island and the neighbouring continent.

An act was passed by congress in the winter of 1812—13, to encourage the destruction of the enemy's blockading vessels,

I

by a bounty of half the value of the vessel destroyed, if effected by any other means than by the armed or commissioned
vessels of the United States, in consequence of which several
abortive attempts were made. The two most remarkable were
those against the Ramilies, off New London, and against the
Plantagenet, off cape Henry, at the mouth of the Chesapeake
bay.

The attempt on the Ramilies was made on the 25th of June.
The schooner Eagle was loaded at New York with a number
of flour barrels filled with gun-powder, in one of which was
fixed a gun-lock, with a string to the trigger made fast to the
bottom of the vessel. Over these were placed a few barrels
of damaged flour. Thus prepared, she threw herself in the
way of the boats of the blockading squadron off New London,
and on their coming up to take possession of her, the crew
took to their boats, and made their escape. It was expected
that the schooner would be taken along side of the Ramilies to
unload; but the wind and tide being against them, and night
coming on, it was determined to unload as much of the flour
in the boats as could conveniently be done. When they came
to the barrel of powder in which the gun-lock was placed, and
hooked the tackle to hoist it on deck, it sprung the trigger,
and blew up the schooner and all on board and around her, and
in a few seconds not a vestige of them was to be seen.

The attempt on the Plantagenet was made in the month of
July, by means of a torpedo. On the night of the 18th, Mr.
Mix, of the United States navy, accompanied by two persons
who volunteered for the purpose, proceeded from Norfolk
down to the Plantagenet, in a large open boat, and from previous observations found no difficulty in ascertaining her position. When Mix had got to within 40 fathom of her, he dropped the torpedo over, in the very instant of doing which he
was hailed by one of the enemy's guard boats. The machine
was speedily taken into the boat again, and he made his way
off in safety. On the night of the 19th he made another attempt, and was again discovered ere he could accomplish his
purpose. On the night of the 20th he succeeded in getting
within 15 yards of the ship's bow, and directly under her jib-
boom. There he continued making his preparations for 15
minutes, when a centinel from the forecastle hailed "boat ahoy!"
and he had once more to decamp. The centinel not being answered, fired his musket, which was followed by a rapid discharge of small arms. Blue lights were made to find out the
boat, but failed; they then threw rockets in different directions,
which illuminated the water for a considerable width as far as

PERRY'S VICTORY

they were thrown, and succeeded in discovering the position of the nocturnal visitor; when the ship commenced a rapid fire of heavy guns, slipped her cables, and made some sail, while her boats were despatched in pursuit. The daring intruders, however, escaped unhurt. The visit was repeated on the nights of the 21st, 22d, and 23d, without success, as the ship, having taken the alarm, changed her position every night. On the night of the 24th, however, Mr. Mix succeeded in finding her out, and having taken his position within 100 yards distance, in a direction with her larboard bow, he dropped the fatal machine into the water just as the centinel was crying *all's well.* It was swept along with the tide, and would have completely effected its errand, it is said, had it not exploded a few seconds too soon. The scene was awfully sublime. It was like the concussion of an earthquake, attended with a sound louder and more terrific than the heaviest peal of thunder. A pyramid of water 50 feet in circumference was thrown up to the height of 30 or 40 feet; its appearance was a vivid red, tinged at the sides with a beautiful purple. On ascending to its greatest height, it burst at the top with a tremendous explosion, and fell in torrents on the deck of the ship, which rolled into the yawning chasm below, and had nearly upset. Impervious darkness again prevailed. The light occasioned by the explosion, though fleeting, enabled Mr. Mix and his companions to discover that the forechannel of the ship was blown off, and a boat which lay alongside with several men in her, was thrown up in the dreadful convulsion of the waters. Terrible, indeed, must have been the panic of the ship's crew, from the noise and confusion which appeared to our adventurers to prevail on board; and they are certain that nearly the whole ship's crew hastily betook themselves to the boats.

The following minute and interesting account of the naval conflict on lake Erie, was written by an eye-witness.—" Commodore Perry arrived at Erie in June, with five small vessels, from Black Rock. The Queen Charlotte and Lady Prevost, were cruising off Long Point to intercept him—he passed them in the night unperceived. The Lawrence and Niagara were then on the stocks—every exertion was made to expedite their building and equipment, and early in August they were ready to sail. But it was necessary to pass the bar at the entrance of the harbour, over which there was but six feet water, and the brigs drew nine. The British fleet appeared off the harbour, for the purpose of preventing ours from going to lake!— The means employed by our officers to take the brigs over the bar, were ingenious and deserve mention. Two large scows, fifty feet long, ten feet wide, and eight feet deep, were prepared—they were first filled with water and then floated along side one of the vessels in a parallel direction; they were then secured by means of large pieces of hewn timber placed athwart ship, with both ends projecting from the port holes across the scows; the space between the timbers and the boat, being secured by other pieces properly arranged; the water was then bailed from the scows, thereby giving them an astonishing lifting power. It was thus that the bar was passed, before the enemy had taken the proper steps to oppose it. One obstacle was surmounted, but the fleet was not in a condition to seek the enemy at Malden. There was not at this time more than half sailors enough to man the fleet. However, a number of Pennsylvania militia having volunteered their services, the commodore made a short cruize off Long Point, more perhaps, for the purpose of exercising his men than seeking an enemy.

" About the last of August commodore Perry left Erie, to cooperate with general Harrison in the reduction of Malden. He anchored off the mouth of Sandusky river, and had an interview with general Harrison, who furnished him with about seventy volunteers, principally Kentuckians, to serve as marines on board the fleet. Captain Dobbin, in the Ohio, was ordered to return to Erie for provisions. The Amelia had been left there for want of men to man her. Exclusive of these he had nine sail, mounting in all fifty-four guns. The British fleet at Malden, consisted of six sail, and mounted sixty-six guns,

" Commodore Perry appeared before Malden, offered battle, reconnoitered the enemy and retired to Put-in-Bay, thirty-five miles distant from his antagonist. Both parties remained a few days inactive; but their repose was that of the lion.

" On the morning of the 10th of September, at sunrise, the enemy were discovered bearing down from Malden for the evident purpose of attacking our squadron, then at anchor in Put-in-Bay. Not a moment was to be lost. Perry's squadron immediately got under way, and stood out to meet the British fleet, which at this time had the weather gage. At 10 A. M. the wind shifted from S. W. to S. E. which brought our squadron to windward. The wind was light, the day beautiful—not a cloud obscured the horizon. The line was formed at 11, and commodore Perry caused an elegant flag, which he had privately prepared, to be hoisted at the mast-head of the Lawrence; on this flag was painted, in characters legible to the whole fleet, the dying words of the immortal LAWRENCE:— " DON'T GIVE UP THE SHIP." Its effect is not to be describ-

ed—every heart was electrified. The crews cheered—the ex-
hilarating can was passed. Both fleets appeared eager for the
conflict, on the result of which so much depended. At 15 minutes before 12, the Detroit, the head-most ship of the enemy,
opened upon the Lawrence, which for ten minutes, was obliged to sustain a well directed and heavy fire from the enemy's
two large ships, without being able to return it with carronades, at five minutes before twelve the Lawrence opened upon
the enemy—the other vessels were ordered to support her,
but the wind was at this time too light to enable them to come
up. Every brace and bowline of the Lawrence being soon
shot away, she became unmanageable, and in this situation sustained the action upwards of two hours, within canister distance, until every gun was rendered useless, and but a small
part of her crew left unhurt upon deck.

"At half past two the wind increased and enabled the Niagara to come into close action—the gun-boats took a nearer position. Commodore Perry left his ship in charge of Lt. Yar-
nel, and went on board the Niagara. Just as he reached that
vessel, the flag of the Lawrence came down; the crisis had arrived. Captain Elliot at this moment anticipated the wishes
of the commodore, by volunteering his services to bring the
schooners into close action.

"At forty-five minutes past two the signal was made for
close action. The Niagara being very little injured, and her
crew fresh, the commodore determined to pass through the
enemy's line; he accordingly bore up and passed ahead of the
Detroit, Queen Charlotte and Lady Prevost, pouring a terrible raking fire into them from the starboard guns, and on the
Chippeway and Little Belt, from the larboard side, at half pistol shot distance. The small vessels at this time having got
within grape and canister distance, kept up a well directed
and destructive fire. The action now raged with the greatest
fury—the Queen Charlotte, having lost her commander and
several of her principal officers, in a moment of confusion got
foul of the Detroit—in this situation the enemy in their turn
had to sustain a tremendous fire without the power of returning it with much effect; the carnage was horrible—the flags of
the Detroit, Queen Charlotte and Lady Prevost, were struck
in rapid succession. The brig Hunter, and schooner Chippeway, were soon compelled to follow the example. The Little
Belt attempted to escape to Malden, but she was pursued by
two of the gun-boats and surrendered about three miles distant from the scene of action.

"The writer of this account, in company with five others,

arrived at the head of Put-in-Bay island, on the evening of the 9th, and had a view of the action, at the distance of only ten miles. The firing was incessant, for the space of three hours, and continued at short intervals forty-five minutes longer. In less than one hour after the battle began, most of the vessels of both fleets were enveloped in a cloud of smoak, which rendered the issue of the action uncertain, till the next morning; when we visited the fleet in the harbour on the opposite side of the island. The reader will easily judge of our solicitude to learn the result. There is no sentiment more painful than suspense, when it is excited by the uncertain issue of an event like this.

"If the wind had continued at S. W. it was the intention of admiral Barclay to have boarded our squadron; for this purpose he had taken on board of his fleet about 200 of the famous 41st regiment; they acted as marines and fought bravely, but nearly two thirds of them were either killed or wounded.

"The carnage on board the prizes was prodigious—they must have lost 200 in killed besides wounded. The sides of the Detroit and Queen Charlotte were shattered from bow to stern; there were scarcely room to place one's hand on their larboard sides without touching the impression of a shot—a great many balls, canister and grape, were found lodged in their bulwarks, which were too thick to be penetrated by our carronades unless within pistol shot distance. Their masts were so much shattered that they fell overboard soon after they got into the bay.

"The loss of the Americans was severe, particularly on board the Lawrence. When her flag was struck she had but nine men fit for duty remaining on deck. Her sides were completely riddled by the shot from the long guns of the British ships. Her deck, the morning after the conflict, when I first went on board, exhibited a scene that defies description— for it was literally covered with blood, which still adhered to the plank in clots—brains, hair and fragments of bones were still sticking to the rigging and sides. The surgeons were still busy with the wounded—enough! horror appalled my senses.

"Among the wounded were several brave fellows, each of whom had lost a leg or an arm—they appeared cheerful and expressed a hope that they had done their duty. Rome and Sparta would have been proud of these heroes.

"It would be invidious to particularize instances of individual merit, where every one so nobly performed his part. Of the nine seamen remaining unhurt at the time the Lawrence

struck her flag, five were immediately promoted for their un-
shaken firmness in such a trying situation. The most of these
had been in the actions with the Guerriere and Java.

" Every officer of the Lawrence, except the commodore and
his little brother, a promising youth, 13 years old, were either
killed or wounded.

" The efficacy of the gun-boats was fully proved in this action, and the sterns of all the prizes bear ample testimony of
the fact. They took raking positions and galled the enemy
severely. The Lady Prevost lost twelve men before either of
the brigs fired on her. Their fire was quick and precise. Let
us hear the enemy. The general order of Adjutant General
Baynes, contains the following words: " His [Perry's] numerous gun boats, [four] which had proved the greatest annoyance
during the action, were all uninjured."

" The undaunted bravery of admiral Barclay entitled him to
a better fate; to the loss of the day was superadded grievous
and dangerous wounds: he had before lost an arm; it was now
his hard fortune to lose the use of the other, by a shot which
carried away the blade of the right shoulder; a canister shot
made a violent contusion in his hip: his wounds were for some
days considered mortal. Every possible attention was paid to
his situation. When commodore Perry sailed for Buffaloe, he
was so far recovered that he took passage on board our fleet.
The fleet touched at Erie. The citizens saw the affecting
spectacle of Harrison and Perry leading the wounded British
Hero, still unable to walk without help, from the beach to their
lodgings.

" On board the Detroit, twenty-four hours after her surrender, were found snugly stowed away in the hold, two Indian
Chiefs, who had the courage to go on board at Malden, for the
purpose of acting as sharp shooters to kill our officers. One
had the courage to ascend into the round top and discharged
his piece, but the whizzing of shot, splinters, and bits of rigging, soon made the place too warm for him—he descended
faster than he went up; at the moment he reached the deck,
the fragments of a seaman's head struck his comrade's face,
and covered it with blood and brains. He vociferated the savage interjection " quoh!" and both sought safety below.

" The British officers had domesticated a bear at Malden.
Bruin accompanied his comrades to battle—was on the deck
of the Detroit during the engagement, and escaped unhurt.

" The killed of both fleets were thrown overboard as fast
as they fell. Several were washed ashore upon the island and
the main during the gales that succeeded the action.

" Commodore Perry treated the prisoners with humanity and indulgence; several Canadians, having wives at Malden, were permitted to visit their familics on parole.

" The British were superior in the *length* and *number* of their guns, as well as in the number of men.   The American fleet was manned with a motly set of beigns, Europeans, Africans, Americans from every part of the United States.   Full one fourth were *blacks*.   I saw one *Russian*, who could not speak a word of English.   They were brave—and who could be otherwise under the command of Perry?

" The day after the battle, the funeral obsequies of the American and British officers, who had fallen in the action, were performed, in an appropriate and affecting manner.   An opening on the margin of the bay, was selected for the interment of the bodies.   The crews of both fleets attended.   The weather was fine—the elements seemed to participate in the solemnities of the day, for every breeze was hushed, and not a wave ruffled the surface of the water.   The procession of boats— the neat appearance of the officers and men—the music—the slow and regular motion of the oars, striking in exact time with the notes of the solemn dirge—the mournful waving of the flags—the sound of the minute guns from the different ships in the harbour—the wild and solitary aspect of the place —the stillness of nature, gave to the scene an air of melancholy grandeur, better felt than described—all acknowledged its influence—all were sensibly affected.   What a contrast did it exhibit to the terrible conflict of the preceding day!   Then the people of the two squadrons were engaged in the deadly strife of arms.   Now they associated like brothers, to pay the last sad tribute of respect to the dead of both nations.

" Five officers were interred, two American and three British. Lt. Brooks and midshipman Laub of the Lawrence; captain Finnis and lieutenant Stokoe of the Queen Charlotte, and lieutenant Garland of the Detroit.   The graves are but a few paces from the beach, and the future traveller of either nation, will find no memento whereby he may distinguish the American from the British hero.

" The *marines* of our fleet were highly complimented by the eommodore, for their good conduct; although it was the first time the most of them had seen a square rigged vessel, being fresh from Harrison's army.   The Kentuckians proved, on this occasion, as has the commodore since, that they can fight on both elements."

As soon as the prisoners and wounded were landed, the fleet was employed in concentrating general Harrison's army, by transporting them from Portage River and Fort Meigs to Put-in-bay. This duty was completed about the 20th of September, and on the 22d about 1200 of the troops were landed by Perry on a small island about four leagues from Malden. On the following day they were again embarked, and landed in the afternoon a small distance below Malden, and in an hour after Harrison took possession of the town of Amherstberg, without opposition, general Proctor having previously burnt Fort Malden, the navy-yard, barracks, and public store-houses, and then retreated to Sandwich. Being followed by Harrison, he retired to a strong position on the right bank of the river Thames, near Moravian Town, about 80 miles from Detroit, leaving the Michigan territory in the possession of the Americans.

On the 2d of October general Harrison left Sandwich in pursuit of Proctor, with about 140 regulars, colonel Johnson's mounted regiment, and the Kentucky volunteers under the venerable governor Shelby, amounting, in the whole, to near 3500 men. Harrison was accompanied by commodore Perry, who volunteered as his aid-de-camp.

The army reached the river Thames, which falls into lake St. Clair, twenty-five miles above Detroit, the same evening, and next morning crossed by a bridge, which Proctor had neglected to destroy. Harrison put himself at the head of the mounted regiment, and pushed forward, in order, if possible, to save the bridges over three branches of the Thames, which ran between him and the British army. At the first of these they captured a lieutenant of dragoons and eleven privates, who had been despatched by Proctor to destroy it; and the second having been but imperfectly destroyed, was soon repaired, and the army passed over and encamped, on the evening of the 3d of October.

The baggage had thus far been brought in boats accompanied by gun-boats, to protect it, and if necessary to cover the passage of the army across the rivers: but the river above being narrow, with high woody banks, it became necessary to leave the baggage under a guard, and to trust to the bravery of the troops to effect a passage across the remaining stream. Next morning, about eight miles above their encampment, the army arrived at the third unfordable branch of the Thames, where they found that the bridge over its mouth, as well as one a mile above, had been taken up by the Indians. Here several hundred of the Indians attempted to dispute the passage of the troops, but the fire from two six-pounders soon drove them off, and in about two hours the bridge was repaired and the troops crossed, just in time to extinguish a house that had been set on fire containing a considerable number of muskets; which were fortunately saved. At the first farm above the bridge was found one of the enemy's vessels on fire, and here intelligence was received that they were but a few miles ahead.

The army halted for the night about four miles above the bridge, where they found two other vessels and a large distillery, filled with ordnance and other valuable stores to an immense amount, in flames. It was impossible to extinguish the fire, but two mounted twenty-four pounders were taken, and a large quantity of ball and shells of various sizes. Early on the morning of the 5th the troops were again put in motion, and in the afternoon the officer commanding the advance sent to inform general Harrison that his progress was stopped by the enemy, who were formed across the line of march.

Between the two armies, the road passed through an uncleared beech forest, pretty clear of underwood, near the banks of the river, parallel to which, at the distance of two or three hundred yards, extended a swamp several miles in length. Across this strip of land the British were drawn up; their left resting on the river, supported by artillery, their right on the swamp, covered by the Indians.

The American troops were now formed in order of battle. General Trotter's brigade formed the front line, his right upon the road, and his left upon the swamp, with general Desha's division, consisting of two brigades, formed *en potence**, upon his left. General King's brigade formed a second line, 150 yards in the rear of Trotter's; and Chiles' brigade a corps of reserve in the rear. Trotter's, King's and Chiles' brigades formed the command of major-general Henry. Each brigade averaged nearly 500 men. The crotchet formed by Desha's division was occupied by Shelby, the governor of Kentucky, a veteran of sixty-six years of age, who had distinguished himself in the revolutionary war at King's Mountain. The regular troops, who now amounted only to 120 men, occupied in columns of sections of four, the small space between the road and the river, for the purpose of seizing the enemy's artillery, and ten or twelve friendly Indians were directed to move under the bank. Harrison had directed Johnson's mounted infantry to

---

* *Troops are ranged* en potence *by breaking a straight line, and throwing a certain proportion of it either forward or backward, from the right or left, according to circumstances, for the purpose of securing that line.*—Duane's Military Dictionary.

form in two lines opposite to the enemy, and, when the infantry advanced to take ground to the left, and, forming upon that flank, to endeavour to turn the right of the Indians. It was perceived, however, that it would be impracticable for them to do any thing on horseback in that quarter, owing to the thickness of the woods and swampiness of the ground. A measure altogether novel was therefore determined on, which was crowned with the most signal success.—The American backwoodsmen ride better in the woods than any other people. A musket or rifle is no impediment to them, being accustomed to carry them on horseback from their earliest youth. A charge was determined on, and accordingly the regiment was drawn up in close column, with its right at the distance of fifty yards from the road, that it might in some measure be protected by the trees from the artillery, and the left upon the swamp.

The army moved on in this order but a short distance, when the mounted men received the fire of the British line, and were instantly ordered to charge. The horses in the front of the column recoiled from the fire; but on receiving a second fire, the column got into motion, and immediately, at full speed, broke through the enemy with irresistible force. In one minute the contest was over in front. The British officers seeing no hope of reducing their disordered ranks to order, the mounted infantry wheeling upon them, and pouring in a destructive fire, immediately surrendered. Only three of the Americans were wounded in this charge.

Upon the American left, however, the contest with the Indians was more severe. Colonel Johnson, who commanded on that flank of his regiment, received a most galling fire from them, which was returned with great effect. The Indians still further to the left advanced, and fell in with the front line of infantry, near its junction with the division *en potence*, and for a moment made an impression upon it. Governor Shelby, however, who, as already stated, was stationed near this point, brought up a regiment to its support. The enemy now received a severe fire in front, and a part of the mounted men having gained their rear, they immediately retreated with precipitation.

The moment had now arrived which was to prove whether the stigma which had been thrown on our Kentucky brethren was founded on truth or falsehood; when it was to be seen whether they were "a ferocious and mortal foe, using the same mode of warfare"* with the allies of Britain. The troops

---

* *General Brock's proclamation.*

who had now completely in their power the army under whose eyes had been acted the tragedy of the river Raisin, and that which was acted on the Miami after the defeat of colonel Dudley, were almost exclusively composed of Kentuckians, of men who had lost their brothers or friends in those shocking scenes.   Nor were even the instruments of vengeance wanting.   They were accompanied by the savages, that had perpetrated those deeds, who had just been suing for mercy, and would gladly have shown their claims to it, by re-acting upon the Thames the bloody scenes of the river Raisin.   But how did they avail themselves of the opportunity which now presented? Did they turn the tide of horrible warfare which had deluged their borders in the blood of wounded prisoners, and of helpless age and infancy, upon the heads of its abettors? No: to their honour and to the honour, of their country be it spoken, they did not.   The moment they were in their power all injuries were magnanimously forgotten, and the prisoners received the most honourable and delicate treatment from the hands of those whom they had stigmatised as savages, the employment of whom justified the use of the Indians.

Of the British troops, 12 were killed and 22 wounded in this action, and six hundred and one regulars were taken prisoners. General Proctor escaped by the fleetness of his horses, escorted by 40 dragoons and a number of mounted Indians. The Indians suffered the greatest loss.   Thirty-three were found dead on the ground, besides numbers who were killed in the retreat.   On the day of the action six pieces of brass artillery were taken, and two twenty-four pounders the day before. Several others were discovered in the river, which were expected to be saved.   Of the brass pieces, three were trophies of the revolutionary war, that were taken at Saratoga and York, and surrendered by general Hull.   The number of small arms captured by the Americans, or destroyed by the enemy, must have exceeded 5000; most of them had been taken by the British at Detroit, the river Raisin, and the Miami.   The loss of the Americans were seven killed and twenty-two wounded, five of whom have since died.

The American troops certainly deserved great praise for their conduct in this action; for, although they considerably outnumbered the British, it must be recollected that they were only militia, and that the British had chosen a position that effectually secured their flanks, and which it was impossible for the Americans to turn, or to present a line more extended than that of the enemy.

As soon as Harrison took possession of Amherstberg and

Sandwich, and re-occupied the territory of Michigan, several of the Indian tribes submitted and brought in hostages for their good behaviour, and while he was in pursuit of the British, five more tribes followed their example, and brought hostages to Detroit. They were received by general M'Arthur, whom Harrison had left in the command of that place, and it was agreed that hostilities should cease for the present, on condition that they should " take hold of the same tomahawk with the Americans, and strike all who are, or may be, enemies to the United States, whether British or Indians."

The army returned to Detroit shortly after the battle, where they embarked on board the fleet for Buffaloe, in order to join the army under general Wilkinson.

About the middle of September an expedition was sent from St. Louis, on the Mississippi, against the Indian settlements on the Peoria lake, on the river Illinois. It consisted of about 200 regulars of the 1st regiment of United States infantry, with a considerable body of rangers and mounted militia, under the command of brigadier-general Howard. The regulars ascended the Illinois in boats; the mounted troops proceeded up the Mississippi in two divisions, one on each side of the river, for a considerable distance, and then crossed the country to the Peoria lake. The different detachments had not proceeded far before it was discovered that the enemy were descending the Illinois to ravage the frontier; and a skirmish took place between a party of Indians and the detachment on the east side of the Mississippi, who, however, soon drove them before them. On the evening of the 28th of September, the two detachments that had marched up the Mississippi, and thence across to the Illinois, arrived within a few miles of the old village, and three men were sent forward to discover whether the regulars had arrived. During the night lieutenant-colonel Nicholson, who commanded the regulars, descended the Illinois to the encampment, and reported their arrival at Peoria, where they had commenced building a fort. He had been attacked by the Indians the day previous; but the enemy were soon dispersed by a well-directed discharge of musquetry, with the aid of a six pounder from two unfinished block-houses. In this attack none of the men were killed, and only one wounded.—It was evident that the assailants suffered considerably, but to what extent could not be ascertained.

On the 29th the mounted troops arrived at Peoria, and as soon as provisions could be drawn, were marched up the Illinois to the villages at the head of the lake, which was the

K

direction in which the enemy appeared to have retired from
Peoria. The villages, being found deserted, were destroyed,
and the troops returned to Peoria, where they remained till
the garrison was put in a state of defence. Two detachments
were then sent in pursuit of the enemy, one of which ascended
the Illinois above the mouth of the Vermillion river to the
Rapids; and within 17 miles of Chicago, on lake Michigan.
The other penetrated the country northwardly to within about
45 miles of Rock river. The latter discovered several encamp-
ments, which appeared to have been deserted about the time
of the army's arrival at Peoria, but neither of them were able
to come up with the enemy.

The mounted troops remained at Peoria from the 2d to the
15th of October, during which time they were actively
engaged, together with the United States Infantry, in erecting
Fort Clarke, which stands at the lower end of the Peoria lake,
completely commanding the Illinois river. This fort is one
of the strongest in the western country, and highly important
to the safety of the Indiana, Illinois, and Missouri territories.

The mounted troops moved from Peoria for the settlements,
on the 15th, leaving the regulars to garrison the fort. They
pursued generally a south course till the 21st, when they arrived at Camp Russell, where the mounted militia were discharged, and the rangers sent across the country to Vincennes
on the Wabash, where they safely arrived shortly after.

After the capture of Bœrstler's detachment, the army at
Fort George remained inactive, with the exception of a few
trifling skirmishes and attacks on out-posts, for the remainder
of the summer. Two circumstances are supposed to have
caused this inactivity. The first was the constant indisposi-
tion of general Dearborn, which prevented him from taking
any active part, and which continued till the 15th of July, when
he received orders to retire from the command of the army,
until his health should be re-established, and until further orders, the command devolving on brigadier-general Boyd. But
the principal cause of the inactivity of this army is presumed
to have been, the danger and indeed impracticability of undertaking great military movements before Chauncey had obtained the complete command of Lake Ontario. Before this
was achieved the army would always be liable to be surrounded, and to have its supplies cut off, and could not expect to be
successful even with a force considerably superior to that of
the enemy. The disaster at Detroit had taught a salutary les-
son on this subject.

Every exertion was accordingly made by commodore Chauncey for the attainment of this important object. After the capture of Fort George, however, commodore sir James Yeo, who commanded the British squadron, having added considerably to his force both of vessels and sailors, obliged Chauncey to remain in port until the new vessel the General Pike could be got ready, which was not completed until the middle of July. Before we enter upon the trial of skill which now ensued between Chauncey and Yeo, it may not be improper to take a view of his previous operations.

Commodore Chauncey arrived at Sackett's Harbour on the 6th of October, 1812, as commander of the United States forces on the lakes, at which time the only American vessel on these waters was the brig Oneida of 18 guns. He immediately purchased six merchant vessels, schooners, which were fitted out as gun-boats. His whole squadron mounted 40 guns of different calibres, with 450 men, including marines. The British force on Lake Ontario consisted at this time of the ship Royal George, of 26 guns and 260 men, ship Earl Moira, 18 guns and 200 men, and the schooners Prince Regent, 18 guns and 250 men, Duke of Gloucester, 14 guns and 80 men, Toronto, 14 guns and 80 men, Governor Simcoe, 12 guns and 70 men, and Seneca, 4 guns and 40 men, making a grand total of 108 guns and 890 men. Chauncey's squadron, especially the schooners, were poor vessels and dull sailers, but his men were much superior, a great part of the enemy's sailors at this time being Canadians.

On the 8th of November Chauncey sailed in the Oneida with his six schooners, in pursuit of the enemy, and on the same day fell with the Royal George, which he chased into the bay of Quanti, where he lost sight of her in the night. Next morning he again discovered her in Kingston channel, and immediately gave chase, and followed her into the harbour of Kingston, where he engaged her and the batteries for an hour and three quarters. Chauncey had made up his mind to board her notwithstanding she was protected by the batteries; but the wind blowing directly in, the pilots refused to take charge of the vessels, and it was therefore deemed imprudent to make the attempt at this time. He accordingly hauled off and beat up under a heavy fire from the enemy, to Four-mile point, where the squadron anchored. During the night it blew heavy, with squalls from the westward, and there being every appearance of a gale of wind, the pilot became alarmed, and Chauncey thought it most prudent to get into a place of more safety, and therefore reluctantly deferred renewing the attack until a more favourable opportunity.

The signal was made to weigh at 7 next morning, and the squadron beat out of a very narrow channel, under a heavy press of sail, to the open lake. At 10 they fell in with the Governor Simcoe, which escaped into Kingston harbour by running over a reef of rocks, under a heavy fire from three of the schooners, during which all her people ran below. It now coming on to blow very heavy, Chauncey bore up for Sackett's Harbour, and on his way thither captured two schooners one of which was burnt, after taking out her sails and rigging.

The Oneida, in this affair, had one man killed, and three slightly wounded, and a few shot through her sails. The schooners lost no men by the enemy's fire and received but little injury in their hulls and sails. One of their guns, however burst early in the action, which wounded her commander badly, and a midshipman and three men slightly. The Royal George received considerable injury in her hull and in men. as the gun vessels, with their long thirty-two pounders, were seen to strike her almost every shot, and it was observed that she was reinforced with men three different times during the action.

On the 12th Chauncey learnt that the Earl Moira was off the False Ducks, and immediately put off in a snow storm, in the hope of cutting her off from Kingston. In this he was disappointed, as she escaped into the harbour. A vessel under her convoy, however, was captured, in which was captain Brock, brother to the general. Chauncey now blockaded Kingston until the 7th of December, when he returned to Sackett's Harbour, being no longer able to keep the lake on account of the ice. During the winter the ship Madison, of 24 guns, was launched and fitted out.

The capture of York and Fort George have already been noticed in pages 78 and 80 of this volume. After these events nothing of importance occurred until the end of July, Chauncey being unable to keep the lake, owing to several new vessels being fitted out by the British, and the arrival of sir James Yeo, with a large body of seamen, to take command of the British squadron on Lake Ontario. It may be proper to mention, however, that the brig Duke of Gloucester was captured at York, and on the 18th of June lieutenant Chauncey, in the new schooner Lady of the Lake, captured the schooner Lady Murray, laden with provisions and ammunition, and sixteen officers and privates, besides the seamen.

About the middle of July, the General Pike being ready to sail, which brought the two squadrons nearly to a state of equality, Chauncey sailed from Sackett's Harbour, and, stretch-

ing over for the enemy's shore, thence stood up the lake. He
arrived off Niagara on the 27th. Here he was informed by
general Boyd, that the enemy had a considerable deposit of
provisions and stores at Burlington Bay, which he determined
to attempt to destroy, and for that purpose embarked a small
number of regulars. At six o'clock on the morning of the
28th, the fleet proceeded for the head of the lake, but owing
to light winds and calms, did not arrive there before the evening of the 29th. Two parties were immediately sent on shore,
who surprised and took some of the inhabitants, from whom
it was learned, that the enemy had received considerable reinforcements, and that his force in regulars was from six to eight
hundred men. The troops, marines, and a few sailors were,
however, landed next morning, but on reconnoitering the
enemy's position, he was found posted on a peninsula of very
high ground, strongly entrenched, and his camp defended by
about eight pieces of cannon. In this situation it was not
thought advisable to attack him with a force scarcely half his
numbers, and without artillery; more especially as they were
deficient in boats, not having a sufficient number to cross the
bay with all the troops at the same time. They accordingly
re-embarked in the course of the afternoon, and in the evening
weighed and stood for York, where they arrived on the afternoon of the 31st. The schooners ran into the inner harbour,
where the marines and troops were landed without opposition.
Several hundred barrels of flour and provisions were found in
the public storehouse, together with five pieces of cannon,
eleven boats, and a quantity of shot, shells, and other stores,
all of which were either destroyed or brought away. Next
morning, after burning the barracks and public storehouses,
the men were re-embarked, and the fleet sailed for Niagara,
where it arrived on the 3d of August.

   At day light of the 7th, the enemy's fleet being discovered
to windward, distant about five or six miles, Chauncey weighed
and stood towards them. The whole of this and the next day
was spent by the two squadrons in manœuvering to gain a
favourable position, in which Chauncey was much baffled by
the dull sailing of his schooners, two of which were lost in a
squall in the night, and every soul on board perished except
sixteen. In the evening of the 8th, it being very squally,
with the appearance of its continuing so during the night,
Chauncey ran in towards Niagara, and anchored outside of the
bar.

   The following morning (August 9th), Chauncey again
weighed and stood towards the enemy, when a trial of nautical
                              K 2

skill once more commenced between the two commanders, each entertaining too respectful an opinion of the other's force to come to an engagement without having the advantage of the wind. In the course of the day the wind frequently veered, which instantly changed the characters of the pursuers and the pursued. At length, towards midnight, Yeo, whose vessels sailed much better in squadron than those of Chauncey, succeeded in cutting off two of the American heavy-sailing schooners, which, added to Chauncey's loss in the squall, gave Yeo a considerable superiority of force over his opponent.—Chauncey, therefore, ordered two of his dullest sailing vessels to run into Niagara, and stood with the rest of his squadron towards Sackett's Harbour, where he arrived on the 13th.

Having victualled his squadron, which was roinforced with a new schooner, Chauncey shortly after sailed on a cruise, and on the 7th of September, at day-light, while lying in Niagara river, discovered the enemy's fleet close in with the shore.—The signal was instantly made to weigh, and the fleet stood out of the river after him. Yeo immediately made all sail to the northward, and Chauncey pursued for four days, but was prevented from closing with him by the heavy sailing of his schooners. On the fourth day while off Genesee river, Chauncey was favoured with a breeze, while Yeo lay becalmed until his opponent got within about three quarters of a mile of him, when he took the breeze. The squadrons now had a running fight for three hours and a half, when the British got out of gun-shot by their superior sailing. The next morning Yeo ran into Amherst bay, having been chased for five days without intermission. Amherst bay was so little known to the American pilots, and said to be so full of shoals, that they were not willing to take in the fleet; Chauncey, therefore, stationed his vessels off Duck Island, with the intention of blockading the enemy, and preventing them from getting out upon the lake.

In tne running fight which took place on the 11th, the British sustained considerable injury both in men and vessels. On board the American fleet not a man was hurt, and the vessels suffered no injury of any importance.

Chauncey continued his blockade until the 17th of September, when, the wind blowing heavy from the westward, and the enemy having run into Kingston, he left his station for Sackett's Harbour, where he arrived the same night. Next morning at day-light he again sailed, and on the 19th saw the enemy's fleet near the False ducks, but took no notice of him, as he wished him to follow up the lake. The squadron arrived in Niagara river on the 24th.

On the 26th, it was reported to Chauncey that the enemy's fleet was in York, when he immediately despatched the Lady of the Lake to ascertain the fact. She returned in the evening with the information that the enemy was in York bay. The squadron immediately weighed anchor, but, owing to a strong head wind, was not able to get out of the river till the evening of the 27th. Owing to the extreme darkness of the night a part of the squadron got separated, and did not join till next morning at eight, when the General Pike, Madison, and Sylph each took a schooner in tow, and made all sail for York, and soon after discovering the enemy's fleet under way in York bay, the squadron shaped their course for them, and prepared for action.

Yeo, perceiving that Chauncey intended to engage him in his position, tacked and stood out of the bay with the wind at east. Chauncey formed the line and ran down for his centre, and when he approached within about three miles of him, Yeo made all sail to the southward. Chauncey's squadron then wore in succession, and stood on the same tack with him, edging down gradually in order to close; and about twelve o'clock, Yeo, finding he must either risk an action, or suffer his two rear vessels to be cut off, tacked his squadron in succession, beginning at the van, hoisted his colours, and commenced a well-directed fire at the Pike, for the purpose of covering his rear, and attacking the rear of his opponent as he passed to leeward. Chauncey perceived his intention, and therefore, as soon as the Wolfe, the enemy's leading ship, passed the centre, and got abeam of the American squadron, he bore up in succession, preserving the line, for the centre of the British squadron. This manœuvre of Chauncey's not only covered his rear, but threw the enemy into confusion, and caused him immediately to bear away. Chauncey had now, however, closed so near as to make his guns to bear with effect, and in twenty minutes the main and mizen topmast and main yard of the Wolfe were shot away. Yeo immediately put before the wind, and set all sail upon his fore-mast; Chauncey made the signal for the fleet to make all sail; but the enemy, by keeping dead before the wind, which brought all the sail upon one mast, and prevented his feeling the loss of his main and mizen topmast, was enabled to outsail most of Chauncey's squadron. The chase was continued till near three o'clock, during the whole of which the Pike, with the Asp in tow, was within point-blank shot of the enemy, and sustained the whole of his fire. Captain Crane in the Madison, and lieutenant Brown in the Onei-da, used every exertion to close with the enemy; but the Madison having a heavy schooner in tow, and the Oneida sailing very dull before the wind, prevented those officers from closing near enough to do any execution with their carronades.—The Governor Tompkins kept in her station, until her fore-mast was so badly wounded as to oblige her to shorten sail.

Commodore Chauncey now reluctantly relinquished the pursuit. The reasons which induced this determination are thus stated in his letter to the secretary of the navy: " At the time I gave up the chase, this ship was making so much water, that it required all our pumps to keep her free (owing to our receiving several shot so much below the water edge, that we could not plug the holes from the outside); the Governor Tompkins with her fore-mast gone; and the squadron within about six miles of the head of the lake, it blowing a gale of wind from east, and increasing, with a heavy sea on, and every appearance of the equinox. I considered that if I chased the enemy to his anchorage at the head of the lake, I should be obliged to anchor also; and although we might succeed in driving him on shore, the probability was, that we should go on shore also—he amongst his friends, we amongst our enemies; and after the gale abated, if he could succeed in getting off one or two vessels out of the two fleets, it would give him as completely the command of the lake as if he had twenty vessels. Moreover he was covered at his anchorage by a part of his army, and several small batteries thrown up for the purpose. Therefore, if we could have rode out the gale, we should have been cut up by their shot from the shore: under all these circumstances, and taking into view the consequences resulting from the loss of our seperiority on the lakes at this time, I without hesitatiation relinquished the opportunity then presenting itself of acquiring individual reputation at the expense of my country."

The loss sustained by the Pike, the commodore's ship, was considerable, owing to her being so long exposed to the fire of the whole of the enemy's fleet; but her most serious loss was occasioned by the bursting of one of her guns, which killed and wounded twenty-two men, and tore up the top-gallant fore-castle, which rendered the gun upon that deck useless.—Four other guns were cracked in the muzzle, which rendered their use extremely doubtful. Her main-top-gallant mast was shot away in the early part of the action, and the bow-sprit, fore and main-mast wounded, rigging and sails much cut up, and a number of shot in her hull, several of which were between wind and water, and twenty-seven men killed and wounded, including those by the bursting of the gun. The

Madison received a few shot, but no person was hurt on board. The Governor Tompkins lost her fore-mast, and the Oneida had her main-top-mast badly wounded.

During the chase, one or two of the enemy's small vessels were completely within Chauncey's power, but in the engerness of his pursuit of the larger, he passed them unnoticed by which means they finally escaped.

Meanwhile general Wilkinson had arrived at Fort George, in order to take the command of the army. About the same time the secretary of war arrived at Sackett's Harbour, in order to be more conveniently situated for superintending military operations.

The wind still continuing unfavourable for an attack on the British squadron at the head of the lake, Chauncey ran off Niagara for the purpose of communicating with Wilkinson, to ascertain when he meant to move with the army to Sackett's Harbour. It was the general's opinion, that the public service would be best promoted by his watching the enemy's squadron, or, if possible, preventing its return to Kingston, while he moved with the army down the lake. Chauncey, therefore, having taken part of the troops on board his squadron, the remainder proceeding in boats to Sackett's Harbour, immediately proceeded in quest of the enemy. The following morning, October 2d, he discovered the British squadron standing towards him, and made all sail in chase; but as soon as the fleets approached so near as plainly to discern each other, Yeo put about, and stood towards the head of the lake. The chase continued until the 4th, little progress being made against the current, from the lightness or variableness of the wind, the British, however, evidently gaining ground of the American squadron. The morning of the 4th proving hazy, nothing could be seen of the enemy, and about noon it fell calm, when Chauncey ordered the Lady of the Lake to sweep up to Burlington bay, which was not far distant, to ascertain whether or not the squadron was there. In the evening she returned with information that the fleet was gone, there being nothing in the bay but two gun-boats.

It was now evident that Yeo, availing himself of the darkness of the preceding night, had either run for Kingston, or down the lake for the purpose of intercepting the flotilla with the army. Chauncey, therefore, immediately made all sail, and shaped his course for the Ducks, with a view of intercepting him, or his prizes, if he should have made any. The wind blowing a strong gale from the northward and westward, the fleet made a great run, and at three in the afternoon of the 5th, discovered seven sail near the False Ducks, to which, presuming they were the enemy's fleet, they instantly gave chase. In about an hour, however, they were discovered to be sloops and schooners, and were perceived to be separating on different tacks, on which the Sylph and the Lady of the Lake were dispatched after one part, and Chauncey in the Pike pursued the others. About five o'clock the enemy, finding that the Pike was fast gaining on him, took the people out of one of his gun vessels which sailed worse than the rest, and set her on fire. This, however, availed them but little, for, at sun-down, three of their vessels were forced to strike to the Pike, and soon after the Sylph captured another. A fifth ran into the Ducks, but the Sylph, which was left to watch her, took possession of her early next morning. A small schooner was the only vessel that escaped, owing to the darkness of the night.

The captured vessels were found to be gun-vessels, with troops from the head of the lake, but last from York, bound to Kingston. Two of them were the Julia and Growler, which Chauncey had lost in the action of the 9th of August. The prisoners taken amounted to nearly 300, principally belonging to the De Watteville, a German regiment. From them it was learnt that the British fleet, in the action of the 28th of September, at the head of the lake, was very much cut up in their hulls and spars, and had a great many killed and wounded, particulary on board of the Wolfe, and Royal George.

In adddition to the army in Ohio, and that on the Niagara frontier, a considerable body of troops was collected in the summer of 1812, upon lake Champlain; a number of vessels also were built to gain the command of those waters. In the campaign of that year, however, no important movement was made in this quarter. Towards the end of May, 1813, several of the British gun-boats having crossed the lines, for the purpose of capturing the craft upon the lake, two of the American armed sloops, the Eagle and Growler, sailed from Plattsburg on the 2d of June for their protection. They arrived within about a mile of the lines about dark, where they cast anchor for the night. Next morning, about day-break, they discovered three British gun-boats, to which they gave chase, but the wind being south, they unfortunately ran so far into the narrow channel that they found it difficult to return, and the Eagle, not being sufficiently strong for her weight of metal, became unmanageable, and at last went down; the water, however, being shoal, the crew were saved. The Growler, unwilling to abandon her companion, continued to fight until after the Eagle sunk when she was compelled to strike to superior force. The enemy had five gun-boats in the action, besides a considerable force in musquetry on both sides of the channel, which was so narrow as to place the sloops within their reach from both shores. An official account of this affair has not been published, but it is stated, on the authority of the enemy, that they had two killed, the Americans only one, but a considerable number of the latter were wounded. The British afterwards succeeded in raising the Eagle.

The loss of the sloops giving the British the superiority on the lake, on the 30th of July a considerable force crossed the lines in forty-four barges, protected by the Growler and Eagle, three row-gallies, and a gun boat, under the command of colonel Murray. The following day they appeared off Plattsburg, and a flag of truce was sent into the town to demand its surrender, with the assurance, that if no resistance was made, private property should be respected. There being no troops in the place, of course there was no resistance, and the enemy landed and burnt the public buildings, consisting of a blockhouse, barracks, arsenal, &c. when they again embarked.

On the 2d of August the enemy appeared off Burlington, on the other side of the lake, where the American army was stationed under general Hampton, and opened their fire from two sloops and a galley, which was returned from a battery in front of the town, the fire from which soon compelled them to make off. Several gun-boats and sloops lay under the battery, but were unable to pursue the enemy, having suffered severely in a gale a few days previous.

In the month of October, Hampton's army crossed the lake, and proceeded towards the Canada lines, which they crossed about the 20th or 21st. The army moved in two divisions, one on each side of the Chateaugay river, and on two different days drove in the British pickets, one of which they succeeded in capturing. Every precaution had been taken by the enemy to intercept the progress of the army. The roads were filled with trees, which they had previously felled in every direction; the bridges were destroyed, and the houses burnt or pulled down. Notwithstanding these impediments, however, they continued slowly to advance till the 26th, when the advanced guard was attacked on both sides of the river by a body of regulars, voltigeurs and Indians, posted in strong positions in a wood, flanked by the river and impassable swamps. The attack w sseveral times renewed and the enemy always driven behind their works. On the 27th one of the divisions forded the river, and the whole army returned within the American lines to Four Corners. The British claimed great merit from the splendid

victory, as they call it, which they assert was achieved by a
force of only 300 men, against Hampton's whole army, which
consisted of 3000 or 3500. From their own statement, however,
it would appear that their force was much larger than they represent it.   They state it to have consisted of.—

"Captains Levesque and Debartzch, with their flank companies of the 5th battalion incorporated militia, together with
about 200 of the Beuharnois division."

"Lietenant-colonel De Salaberry, with his voltigeurs, and
captain Ferguson's light company of the Canadian regiment."

Besides these, are mentioned, in the course of the action:—

"A *large body* of Indians under captain Lamothe."

"Lieutenant-colonel M'Donnell, of the Glengary light infantry, with a part of his light brigade.

These forces do not include the reinforcements which are
stated to have arrived the following day. And yet we are grave-
ly told, that, " though it may appear incredible, the whole force
engaged on our side did not exceed 300 men."*

But even allowing their forces to be as small as here represented, it by no means follows, either that a victory was gained,
or that Hampton's measures were baffled.   It does not appear
that it was the intention of the American general to push on by
this route to Montreal, for the reduction of which his small
force was utterly incompetent, independent of the natural impediments which this part of the country presented to an in-
vading army.   There is no reason to doubt, indeed, that this
movement was merely intended as a demonstration, to divert
and distract the attention of the enemy from the movements on
the St. Lawrence, and this end being completely attained, it
was not the general's intention to risk the loss of any part,
however small, of his army, by an attempt to force a position so
strong as the British represent this to have been.

General Wilkinson having transported his army in safety
from Fort George to Sackett's Harbour, in the beginning of
October, in a few days they were again moved to Grenadier
Island, with the intention of immediately proceeding down the
St. Lawrence against Montreal.   Considerable delay, however,
took place; owing to the uncommon severity of the weather,
and it was not until the 3d of November that he was enabled to
move.   On the evening of the 6th he reached Ogdensburg,

---

* *The statement here alluded to is not the official account. It
is a detailed account, apparently written by an officer who was
present at the affair.*

whence he wrote to general Hampton at Four corners (where he had established his head-quarters after his return from Canada,) ordering him to form a junction with him on the St. Lawrence, and recommending St. Regis as the most suitable place, where he expected to be on the 9th. " On the subject of provisions," continues Wilkinson, " I wish I could give a favourable information; our whole stock of bread may be computed at about fifteen days, and our meat at twenty. On speaking on this subject to the secretary of war, he informed me ample magazines were laid up on lake Champlain, and therefore I must request of you to order forward two or three month's supply by the safest route, in a direction to the proposed scene of action. I have submitted the state of provisions to my general officers, who unanimously agree that it should not prevent the progress of the expedition; and they also agree in opinion, if you are not in force to face the enemy, you should meet us at St. Regis or its vicinity."

A short distance above Ogdensburg, on the opposite side of the St. Lawrence, stands Prescot, a fortified post commanding the river. The lateness of the season not admitting of delay, Wilkinson determined to pass it in the night, in place of stopping to reduce it. This was effected on the night of the 6th, without other loss than two privates killed and three wounded. In the course of the 8th the cavalry was crossed from the American to the Canada shore, and a detachment of the infantry was landed, to prevent the enemy, who had previously lined the shore with musquetry, from harassing the boats in their passage down the river. A considerable body of the enemy from Kingston also, in concert with a heavy galley and a few gun-boats, hung on the rear of the Americans, and considerably retarded their progress.

On the morning of the 10th, general Brown advanced down the river, for the purpose of clearing its banks, as a rapid, eight miles long, was expected to be passed in the course of the day, in the passage of which, without this precaution, the army would be much exposed. About noon, the army was apprized by the report of artillery, that Brown was engaged some distance below, and about the same time the enemy were observed in their rear. Their galley and gun-boats having approached the flotilla, and opened their fire, Wilkinson ordered a battery of eighteen pounders to be planted, the shot from which soon compelled the vessels of the enemy to retire, together with their troops, after some firing between the advanced parties.

The day was now so far spent, that the pilots did not dare to enter the rapid, and therefore the flotilla fell down about two

L

miles, and came to for the night.   Early next morning every
thing was ready to move, but it was still deemed imprudent to
commit the flotilla to the rapid until the result of gen. Brown's
affair should be ascertained.   At half past 10, an officer arrived
with information that Brown had forced the' enemy to retire,
and that he would reach the foot of the rapid early in the day.
Orders were now given for the flotilla to sail; but at this moment the enemy's gun-boats appeared and began to fire, and information was received from general Boyd, that the enemy's
troops were advancing in column, on which Wilkinson sent him
orders to attack them.   This report was soon contradicted; but
their gun-boats continued to annoy the flotilla, and such a variety of reports of the movements and counter-movements of
the troops on shore was brought to Wilkinson, as convinced him
of their determination to hazard an attack, when it could be done
to advantage.   He therefore resolved to anticipate them; and
directions were accordingly sent to general Boyd to throw the
detachments under his command into three columns, to march
upon the enemy, outflank them if possible, and take their artillery.   The force under Boyd consisted of detachments from
the first, third, and fourth brigades, which were formed agreeably to orders, and placed respectively under colonel Coles,
general Covington, and general Swartwout.   A report was now
brought to Boyd from the rear guard, that a body of about 200
Baitish and Indians had advanced into the woods that skirted his
rear.   General Swartwout, with the fourth brigade, was immediately ordered to dislodge them; general Covington, with the
third brigade, being at the same time directed to be within supporting distance.   General Swartwout dashed into the woods,
and with the 21st infantry (a part of his brigade,) after a short
skirmish, drove them back to the position of their main body.
Here he was joined by general Covington.   The enemy had judiciously chosen his ground among the deep ravines which
every where intersected the extensive plain, and discharged a
heavy and galling fire upon the advanced columns of the Americans.   No opposition or obstacle, however, checked their ardour.   The enemy retired for more than a mile before their resolute and repeated charges.   During this time, the detachment of the first brigade under colonel Coles, whose greater
distance from the scene of action retarded its arrival, rapidly entered the field.   Being directed to attack the enemy's left flank,
this movement was promptly and bravely executed, amid a
shower of musquetry and sharpnel shells.   The fight now became more stationary, until the brigade first engaged, having
expended all their ammunition, were directed to retire to a

more defensible position to wait for a re-supply. This movement so disconnected the line, as to render it expedient for the first brigade likewise to retire.

The artillery, excepting two pieces attached to the rear division (which from the nature of the ground, and the circuitous route they had to take, were likewise much retarded in thier arrival), did not reach the ground until the line, for want of ammunition, had already begun to fall back. When they were arranged, their fire was sure and destructive. When the artillery was finally directed to retire, having to cross a deep, and, excepting in one place, to artillery, impassable ravine, one piece was unfortunately lost, by the fall of its gallant commander, lieutenant Smith, and most of his men.

The whole line was now re-formed on the borders of those woods from which the enemy had first been driven; when, night coming on, and the storm returning, Boyd, conceiving the object in view, which was to beat back the enemy that would retard the junction with the main body below, to have been accomplished, directed the troops to return to the ground near the flotilla; which movement was executed in good order, and without molestation from the enemy.

As the American force in this action, which took place in the neighbourhood of Williamsburgh, consisted of indefinite detachments taken from the boats, it is impossible to say with accuracy what was the number on the field; but it was supposed to be about 1600 or 1700 men. The force of the enemy was estimated at from 1200 to 2000, exclusive of militia. The British say their force did not exceed 800 rank and file, in which statement the militia and Indians are probably not included. The Americans had 102 killed, and 237 wounded, among the latter general Covington mortally. The British state their loss at 22 killed, 147 wounded, and 12 missing.— Both parties claim the victory in this battle: the British, because they captured a piece of cannon, and because the Americans retired from the battle ground; the Americans, because their object was fully attained, that of beating back the enemy, who was harassing them in their progress down the river: The British account states that they took upwards of 100 prisoners, of which no mention is made by the Americans.

At the time of this action general Wilkinson was confined to his bed, and emaciated almost to a skeleton, a disease with which he was assailed on the 2d of September, on his journey to Fort George, having with a few short intervals of convalescence, preyed on him ever since.

The Americans having resumed their position on the bank

of the St. Lawrence, the infantry, being much fatigued, were re-embarked, and proceeded down the river, without further annoyance from the enemy or their gun-boats, while the dragoons with five pieces of light artillery, marched down the Canada shore without molestation. The next morning the flotilla passed safely down the rapids, and joined general Brown, at Barnhart's near Cornwall, where he had been instructed to take post and wait their arrival.

At Barnhart's Wilkinson confidently expected to have heard of Hampton's arrival on the opposite shore, but immediately on his halting, colonel Atkinson waited on him with a letter from that officer, in which, to the surprise and mortification of Wilkinson, Hampton declined the junction, and informed him that he was marching towards lake Champlain, by way of co-operating in the proposed attack on Montreal. The reason assigned by Hampton for this measure, was the smallness of Wilkinson's stock of provisions, and the impossibility, from the difficulty of transportation at this season, of his bringing more than each man could have carried on his back. " When I reflected," says Hampton, " that in throwing myself upon your scanty means, I should be weakening you in your most vulnerable point, I did not hesitate to adopt the opinion, after consulting the general and principal officers, that by throwing myself back on my main depot, when all the means of transportation had gone, and falling upon the enemy's flank, and straining every effort to open a communication from Plattsburg to Coghnawaga, or any other point you may indicate on the St. Lawrence, I should more effectually contribute to your success, than by the junction at St. Regis. The way is in many places blockaded and abated, and the road impracticable for wheel carriages during winter—but by the employment of pack horses, if I am not overpowered, I hope to be able to prevent your starving. I have ascertained and witnessed that the plan of the enemy is to burn and consume every thing in our advance. My troops and other means will be described to you by colonel Atkinson. Besides the rawness and sickness, they have endured fatigues equal to a winter campaign, in the late snows and bad weather, and are sadly dispirited and fallen off; but upon this subject I must refer you to colonel Atkinson. With these means—what can be accomplished by human exertion, I will attempt—with a mind devoted to the general objects of the campaign."

Hampton's letter was immediately submitted to a council of war, composed of the general officers and the colonel commanding the elite, the chief engineer, and the adjutant-general, who unanimously gave it as their opinion, that " the attack on Montreal should be abandoned for the present season, and the army near Cornwall should be immediately crossed to the American shore for taking up winter quarters, and that this place afforded an eligible position for such quarters." This opinion was acquiesced in by Wilkinson, not, he states, from the want of provisions, because they could, in case of extremity, have lived on the enemy, but because the loss of the division under general Hampton weakened his force too sensibly to justify the attempt.

The army remained on the Canada shore until the next day, without seeing the enemy, and then crossed over and went into winter quarters at French Mills, near St. Regis, on the borders of Lower Canada.

Meanwhile general Harrison, having embarked at Detroit, with those of his troops whose term of service had not expired, or who were not considered necessary for the defence of the country he had overrun, arrived at Buffaloe towards the end of October, and immediately proceeded to Fort George.—— General Wilkinson having previously gone down the lake, and the fleet having not arrived for the transportation of Harrison's troops, arrangements were made by him and general M'Clure, whom he found in the command of Fort George, for an expedition against Burlington Heights, at the head of lake Ontario. Before the completion of these arrangements, however, commodore Chauncey arrived with orders immediately to bring down Harrison's troops for the defence of Sackett's Harbour. Commodore Chauncey was extremely pressing for the troops immediately to embark, stating that the navigation with small vessels was very dangerous at this season, and that should the troops not get down before the lake was frozen, the safety of the fleet at the harbour might be seriously endangered. The general therefore reluctantly relinquished the expedition, further delay in proceeding down the lake being considered impracticable. The troops were embarked about the middle of November, and shortly after arrived in safety at Sackett's Harbour.

After the departure of general Harrison, the force at Fort George, under General M'Clure, consisted almost exclusively of militia and volunteers, whose term of service was on the point of expiring. The contemplated expedition against Burlington Heights was once more undertaken, but the roads were found cut up in such a manner, and so obstructed by timber, that it was found impracticable to transport the artillery, and accordingly it was abandoned.

The abandonment of this expedition excited much dissatisfaction at Fort George, especially among the volunteers, many
of whom had made considerable sacrifices to join the army, in
the hope of being usefully and actively employed. Their term
of service now expiring, M'Clure used every effort to engage
them to remain for one or two months longer, but in vain. He
was left on the 10th of December with not more than sixty effective regulars to garrison Fort George. A council of officers
was then held, who were unanimously of opinion that the fort
should be immediately evacuated, the advance of the enemy,
who by some means had obtained information of the state of the
place, being within eight miles. Orders were accordingly given
to transport all the arms, ammunition, and public stores of every description across the river, which was principally effected
though the enemy approached so rapidly that ten of the soldiers
were made prisoners. The fort was blown up, and the town of
Newark, a handsome little place of about 200 houses, situated
a mile below the fort, was laid in ashes. " This act," general
M'Clure declares, " as distressing to the inhabitants as to my
feelings, was by an order of the secretary at war." " The inhabitants had twelve hours notice to remove their effects, and
such as chose to come across the river were provided with all
the necessaries of life." The only reason that we have seen
assigned for this outrage is by no means satisfactory: " that the
enemy might not have it in their power to quarter with their
Indian allies in the village, and maraud and murder our citizens," and we are much pleased to see that the act is almost
universally disapproved of.

On the 19th of December about 4 in the morning, the British
crossed the river a few miles above Fort Niagara, and succeeded in taking the place by storm about an hour before daybreak.
The fort appears to have been completely surprised. The men
were nearly all asleep in their tents, when the enemy rushed in
and commenced a dreadful slaughter. Such as escaped the
fury of the first onset, retired to the old mess-house, where they
kept up a fire on the enemy, until a want of ammunition compelled them to surrender. The disaster is attributed and with
too much appearance of probability, to gross neglect or treasonable connivance on the part of the commanding officer of the
fort, who is stated to have been absent at the time it took place,
notwithstanding the attack was expected, as appears from the
general orders issued by M'Clure a few days previous.

After the capture of the fort, the British with a large body
of Indians, proceeded up the river as far as Lewistown, and,
having driven off a detachment of militia stationed at Lewis-

town Heights, burnt that village and those of Youngstown and Manchester, and the Indian Tuscarora village. A number of the inoffensive inhabitants are said to have been butchered by the savages. On the 30th another detachment of the British and Indians crossed the Niagara, near Black Rock. They were met by the militia under general Hall; but overpowered by numbers, and the discipline of the enemy, the militia soon gave way and fled on every side, and every attempt to rally them was ineffectual. The enemy then set fire to Black Rock, when they proceeded to Buffaloe, which they likewise laid in ashes, thus completing the desolation of the whole of the Niagara frontier, as a retaliation for the burning of Newark.

Serious apprehensions were entertained for the safety of the fleet at Erie; the enemy, however, did not attempt to penetrate further at the moment, and a sufficient force was soon collected for its defence, which remained during the winter.

While active operations were thus carried on, on the north and northwestern frontier of the United States, the calamities of war began to extend to the southern portion. In the summer of 1813, the Creek nation commenced hostilities by an attack on Fort Mims, a post upon the Tensaw river. Before we enter on a narrative of the events of this war, however, it will be proper to notice another important event which took place in this quarter, in the month of April; namely, the surrender of Mobile to the arms of the United States.

By the treaty of St. Ildefonso, concluded on the 1st of October, 1800, between France and Spain, the latter, in consideration of certain stipulations in favour of the duke of Parma, ceded to the French republic " the colony or province of Louisiana, with the same extent that it now has in the hands of Spain, and that it had when France possessed it; and such as it should be after the treaties subsequently entered into between Spain and other states." By a treaty concluded at Paris, on the 30th of April, 1803, France ceded to the United States the territory she had acquired by the treaty of St. Ildefonso, "as fully and in the same manner as they have been acquired by the French republic." In virtue of the above-mentioned treaties, the United States claimed as the southern portion of Louisiana, all the country lying between the Sabine and Perdido rivers. The Spanish government, however, resisted this claim, and contended that its eastern boundary was the river Mississippi, and the lakes Maurepas and Pontchartrain. This country has accordingly been the subject of negociation for several years, between the American and Spanish governments, the latter still holding possession of the country. This negociation was put an end to by the troubles which took place in old Spain, in 1807; and a revolution breaking out in Florida, the United States, on the ground that Spain could no longer hold possession of the country, and that her rights would be jeopardized or lost by suffering it to pass into the hands of a third party (the revolutionists), on whom they could have no claim, took possession of the whole disputed country, in 1812, except the post of Mobile, a small fortified town of about 400 inhabitants, situated on the west side of Mobile bay, which continued to be held by a Spanish garrison until the 15th of April, 1813, when it was summoned to surrender to the arms of the United States, under general Wilkinson, which was immediately done without the slighest opposition.

The country of the Creek Indians, with whom the United States was at war, is situated in the western part of the state of Georgia, and the eastern part of the Mississippi territory, between the Oakmulgee and Tombigbee rivers: and extends from the Cherokee country, which borders on Tennessee, to Florida. In the course of the last summer, several families were murdered, near the mouth of the Ohio river, by a party of Indians passing from the great lakes to the Upper Creeks. The principal chiefs of the nation, on the application of the United States' agent, determined to punish the murderers by putting them to death, and a party of warriors was appointed to execute their determination. This was no sooner done, than the resentment of the friends of the murderers broke out in acts of open violence against all who had been in any way concerned in causing the murderers to be put to death, and a civil war was the consequence. It appears, however, that this circumstance only produced a premature disclosure of their object, as it has since been ascertained that most of the Upper Creeks had previously determined to take part with the northern Indians in their war with United States.

About the middle of July, the secretary at war wrote to the governor of Georgia; and at the same time transmitted a copy of his letter to the governor of Tennesee; stating, that information through various channels had reached the general government, of the hostility of a portion of the Creek nation, and of the necessity of breaking it down by some prompt and vigorous measures; and suggested the propriety of embodying a portion of the Georgia militia, who should either act separately against the enemy, or in concert with another corps of militia, drawn from Tennessee. This letter was received by governor Mitchell in the end of July, when he immediately took measures for calling out fifteen hundred of the Georgia militia, who were soon after marched to the Oakmulgee river. Their number was subsequently enlarged to a full brigade.

Meanwhile appearances became every day more threatening. The friendly Indians were forced to leave their towns and retreat towards the white settlements, and fortify themselves against the attacks of the war party. The latter proceeded in great numbers to the south, where it is asserted they were supplied by the Spanish governor of Pensacola with arms and ammunition. At last, upon the 30th of August, 1813, they commenced hostilities against the United States, by an attack upon Mim's fort, on the Tensaw, a branch of the Mobile river, in the Mississippi territory, commanded by major Beasley.

Information had been received about a week previous, that a large number ef Indians were approaching with hostile intentions, but the attack was wholly unexpected at the moment it occurred, which was about eleven in the forenoon. The whole garrison, however, was immediately under arms. The front gate being open, the enemy ran in great numbers to possess themselves of it, and in the contest for it many fell on both sides. Soon however, the action became general, the enemy fighting on all sides in the open field, and as near the stockake as they could get. The port-holes were taken and retaken several times. A block-house was contended for by captain Jack, at the head of his riflemen, for the space of an hour after the enemy were in possession of part of it; when they finally succeeded in driving his company into a house in the fort, and having stopped many of the port-holes with the ends of rails, possessed themselves of the walls. The troops made a most gallant defence from the houses, but the enemy having set fire to the roofs, and the attempt to extinguish it proving unsuccessful, the few who now remained alive attempted a retreat, having previously thrown into the flames many of the guns of the dead. Few, however, succeeded in escaping. Major Beasley fell gallantly fighting at the head of his command, near the gate, at the commencement of the action. The other officers fell nobly doing their duty; the non-commissioned officers and soldiers behaved equally well.

The loss of the Americans was great; sixty-five, including officers and men, of the Mississippi territory volunteers, and twenty-seven volunteer militia, were killed. Many respectable citizens, with numerous families, who had abandoned their farms, and fled to the fort for security, were also killed, or burnt in the houses into which they fled. A detachment which was sent from cantonement Mount Vernon, on the 21st of September to collect the bones of their countrymen, collected, and consigned to the earth, 247 persons, including men, women, and children. The detachment likewise searched the woods for bodies, where they found at least 100 dead Indians, who were covered with rails, brush, &c. These Indians had been interred with their war-dresses and implements, by which they were recognized.

On the receipt of the disastrous intelligence of the destruction of major Beasley's garrison, preparations were immediately made for collecting a large force of Tennessee militia, and providing supplies for those of Georgia which had already assembled The Tennessee militia were marched in two divisions, under the orders of major-generals Jackson and Cocke.

On the 2d of November, major-general Jackson dispatched brigadier-general Coffee from the camp at Ten-Islands, with 900 men, consisting of cavalry and mounted riflemen, on an expedition against Tallushatches towns, where a considerable force of the Creeks was concentrated. Coffee arrived within a mile and a half of the town on the morning of the 3d, where he divided his force into two divisions, and directed them to march so as completely to encircle the town, which was effected in a masterly manner. When they arrived within about half a mile of the towns, the enemy began to prepare for action, which was announced by the beating of their drums, mingled with savage yells. About an hour after sun-rise the action was brought on by two companies, who had gone within the circle of alignment, for the purpose of drawing the enemy out from their buildings. As soon as the two companies exhibited their front in view of the town, and gave a few scattering shot, the enemy formed and made a violent charge upon them, on which they gave way, and were followed by the Indians, until they reached the main body, who immediately opened a general fire, and then charged. The Indians now, in their turn, retreated firing, until they got around and in their buildings, when they made a most determined resistance, fighting to the very last moment, as long as they could stand or sit, not one shrinking or complaining; not one asking for quarter. Every warrior in the town was killed, and all the women and children were taken prisoners, except a few who were unintentionally slain, in consequence of the men flying to the houses and mixing with their families, and at the same time refusing quarter.

The number found killed of the enemy was 186, and a number of others were killed in the woods, who were not found. The number of women and children taken was eighty-four. Of the Americans, five were killed, and forty-one wounded, the greater part slightly, none mortally; two of the killed were with arrows, which appeared to form a principal part of the arms of the Indians on this occasion, every man having a bow, with a bundle of arrows, which he used after the first fire with his gun, until a leisure time for loading offered.

Coffee bestows much praise on his men, for their deliberation and firmness. "Notwithstanding our numbers," says he, "were far superior to that of the enemy, it was a circumstance to us unknown, and from the parade of the enemy we had every reason to suppose them our equals in number; but there appeared no visible traces of alarm in any; on the contrary all appeared cool and determined; and, no doubt, when they face a foe of their own, or superior number, they will show the same courage as on this occasion."

The following day general Coffee returned with his detachment to the camp.

Late on the evening of the 7th a friendly Indian arrived at the camp, who brought intelligence that the enemy had arrived in great numbers at Talledega, about thirty miles below the camp, where one hundred and sixty men of the friendly Creeks had erected a fort, the more effectually to resist the efforts of the hostile party, and where they were now stationed with their wives and children. The messenger represented that, unless speedy relief could be obtained from the army, the fort would certainly be taken. General Jackson immediately gave orders for taking up the line of march, with twelve hundred infantry and eight hundred cavalry and mounted riflemen, leaving behind the sick, the wounded, and the baggage, with a sufficient force for their protection. By twelve o'clock that night the army was in motion, and commenced crossing the river opposite the encampment, which was affected in a few hours, and on the night of the 8th the army was encamped within six miles of the enemy. At eleven that night a soldier and two Indians, who had been sent forward to reconnoitre, returned with the intelligence that the enemy were encamped within a quarter of a mile of the fort; but they had not been able to approach near enough to ascertain either their number or precise situation. At midnight the adjutant-general was ordered to prepare the line of march, and by four o'clock the army was in motion.

The infantry marched in three columns; the cavalry and mounted riflemen were in the rear, with flankers on each wing.   The advance consisted of a company of artillery with muskets, and two companies of riflemen.   A company of spies marched four hundred yards in front of the whole, to bring on the engagement.   Having arrived within a mile of the enemy at seven o'clock, two hundred and fifty of the cavalry and mounted riflemen were placed in the rear of the centre, as a *corps de reserve*, and the remainder were ordered to advance on the right and left of the infantry, and, after having encircled the enemy, by uniting the fronts of their columns, and keeping their rear connected with the infantry, to face and press inwards towards the centre, so as to leave the enemy no possibility of escape.   The infantry were ordered to advance by heads of companies, general Hall's brigade occupying the right, and general Roberts' the left.

About eight o'clock the advance, having arrived within eighty yards of the enemy, who were concealed in a thick shrubbery which covered the margin of a rivulet, received from them a heavy fire, which they immediately returned, and then charged and dislodged them from their position.   The advance now fell back, as they had been previously ordered, to the centre.   On the approach of the enemy, three of the militia companies, having given one fire, commenced a retreat, notwithstanding the utmost exertions of their officers.   To fill up the vacancy occasioned by this retreat, Jackson immediately ordered up a regiment of volunteers; but finding the advance of the enemy too rapid to admit of their arrival in time, the reserve was ordered to dismount and meet them. This order was executed with great promptitude and gallantry, and the retreating militia, seeing the spirited stand made by the reserve, immediately rallied, and recovered their position, pouring in upon the enemy a most destructive fire.   The engagement now became general; and in fifteen minutes the Indians were seen flying in every direction.   On the left they were met and repulsed by the mounted riflemen; but on the right it unfortunately happened that too great space had been left between the cavalry and infantry, by which numbers escaped.   They were pursued, however, for three miles to the mountains with great slaughter.

The force of the enemy was represented by themselves at a thousand and eighty, two hundred and ninety-nine of whom were left dead on the ground, and a great many were killed in their flight.   It is believed that very few escaped without a wound.   The American loss was fifteen killed and eighty wounded.

On the 11th of November, general Cocke, who commanded

the other division of the Tennessee militia, ordered brigadier-general White, with a detachment of mounted infantry and cavalry, to proceed from Fort Armstrong, where this division was stationed, on an expedition against the Hillibee towns of the hostile creeks on the Tallapoosie river. This expedition was completely successful. They penetrated one hundred miles into the enemy's country, and burned four of their villages, three of which they found deserted. Previous to their arrival at the fourth, they learned that a party of the hostile Creeks were assembled there. Having marched the whole of the night of the 17th, they surrounded and completely surprised the town at day-light of the morning of the 18th, and of the whole party, which consisted of three hundred and sixteen, not one escaped, sixty being killed and the remainder made prisoners. The detachment now returned to camp, where they arrived on the 23d, having lost not one drop of blood in this enterprise. The country through which they marched was exceedingly rough and hilly, and they had to pass several narrow defiles, where it was necessary to use the utmost precaution. The troops and horses, likewise, had to be subsisted, in a great degree, on such supplies as could be procured in the enemy's country, which rendered their march more tardy than it would otherwise have been.

The Georgia militia, though embodied before those of Tennessee, were not able, from the want of military supplies, to proceed to active operations till the end of November. Brigadier-general Stewart had been originally destined for the command; as the senior brigadier; but family considerations inducing him to decline its acceptance, brigadier-general Floyd was appointed in his room.

Towards the end of November, Floyd received information that numbers of the hostile Indians were assembled at Autossee, a town on the southern bank of the Tallapoosie river, about twenty miles above its junction with the Coosa. He immediately left his camp, which was situated on the west side of the Chatahouchie river, and proceeded against the enemy with nine hundred and fifty militia, and between three and four hundred of the friendly Creeks. On the evening of the 28th the detachment encamped within nine or ten miles of the place of destination, and having resumed their march about one next morning, at half past six they were formed for action in front of the town. The detachment was formed in two columns, with a rifle company on each flank, and a company of artillery in front of the right column.

It was Floyd's intention to have completely surrounded the

M

enemy, by resting the right wing of his force on Canlebee creek, at the mouth of which he was informed their town stood, and resting his left on the river bank below the town; but to his surprise, as the day dawned, he perceived a second town about 500 yards below that which he was preparing to attack. The plan, therefore, was instantly changed; three companies of infantry on the left were wheeled to the left *en echelon,** and advanced to the lower town, accompanied by a rifle company and two troops of light dragoons. The remainder of the force approached the upper town, and the battle soon became general. The Indians presented themselves at every point, and fought with desperate bravery; but the well-directed fire of the artillery and the bayonets of the infantry soon forced them to take refuge in the out-houses, thickets and copses in the rear of the town. Many, it was supposed, secured themselves in caves, previously formed for this purpose in the high bluff of the river, which was thickly covered with reeds and brush-wood. It was intended that the friendly Indians should have crossed the river above the town, and been posted on the opposite shore during the action, to fire on such of the enemy as should attempt to escape, or to keep in check any reinforcements which might be attempted to be thrown in from the neighbouring towns. Owing to the difficulty of the ford, however, and the coldness of the weather and lateness of the hour, this arrangement failed, and their leaders were directed to cross Canleebee creek, and occupy that flank, to prevent escapes from the Tallisee town. Some time after the action commenced, the friendly Indians thronged in disorder in the rear of the militia, when the hostile tribes fell on the flanks of the detachment, and fought with great intrepidity. By nine o'clock, however, the enemy was completely driven from the plains, and the houses of both towns were wrapped in flames.

It was impossible to determine the strength of the enemy, but from the information of some of the chiefs, which it is said could be relied on, there were assembled at Autossee, warriors from eight towns for its defence, it being their beloved ground, on which they proclaimed no white man could

---

* *A position in which each division follows the preceding one, like the steps of a ladder* (echelle), *from which the word is derived. A position en enchelon is convenient in removing from a direct to an oblique or diagonal line*—Duane's Military Dictionary.

approach without inevitable destruction. Neither was it possible to ascertain their loss; but from the number which were
lying scattered over the field, together with those destroyed
in the towns, and those slain on the bank of the river, whom
respectable officers affirmed they saw lying in heaps at the
water's edge, where they had been precipitated by their surviving friends, their loss, in killed alone, must have been at
least 200, among whom were the Autossee and Tallisee kings.
The number of buildings burnt is supposed to be 400; some
of them were of a superior order for the dwellings of savages,
and filled with valuable articles. The Americans had eleven
killed and fifty-four wounded, among the latter was general
Floyd.

The detachment being now sixty miles from any depot of
provisions, and their rations pretty nearly consumed, as soon
as the dead and wounded were properly disposed of, the place
was abandoned, and the troops commenced their march back
to the camp on the Chatahouchie, a measure the more necessary as they were in the heart of an enemy's country, which
in a few days could have poured from its numerous towns
hosts of warriors. They arrived at the camp in safety, having
marched 120 miles in seven days.

On the 9th of December another detachment of the Georgia militia, consisting of about 530 men, under the command
of general Adams, marched on an expedition against the Creek
towns on the Tallapoosie river. Notwithstanding the precau-
tions which they used to prevent the Indians from hearing of
their approach, they found the villages deserted, and were
unable to bring the enemy to action, though their yells were
repeatedly heard on both sides of the river. Having burnt
two of their villages, therefore, the detachment returned to
camp.

Twenty-three of the American soldiers who were made
prisoners at the battle of Queenstown, in the autumn of 1312,
were sent to England, where they were detained in rigorous
confinement as British subjects. On this being made known
to the government of the United States by the American com-
missary of prisoners at London, orders were issued to general
Dearborn to place in close confinement a like number of British soldiers, to be kept as hostages for the safety and exchange
of the American prisoners. This order was carried into execution by the imprisonment of twenty-three of the prisoners
captured at Fort George, in May 1813, of which general
Dearborn apprised the governor of Canada in a letter dated
the 31st of that month.

General Dearborn's letter was transmitted to the British government, who immediately instructed governor Prevost to state to the commander of the American forces, for the information of his government, that he was commanded "forthwith to put in close confinement forty-six American officers and non-commissioned officers, to be held as hostages for the safe keeping of the twenty-three British soldiers stated to have been put in close confinement by order of the American government.

"I have been directed at the same time to apprise you," continues Prevost, in a letter to general Wilkinson, "that if any of the said British soldiers shall suffer death by reason that any of the said soldiers of the United States now under confinement in England have been found guilty, and that the known law, not only of Great Britain, but of every independent state under similar circumstances, has been in consequence executed, that I have been further instructed to select out of the American officers and non-commissioned officers, whom I shall have put into confinement, as many as may double the number of the British soldiers who shall have been so unwarrantably put to death, and to cause such officers and non-commissioned officers to suffer death immediately. I have been further instructed by his majesty's government to notify you, for the information of the government of the United States, that the commanders of his majesty's armies and fleets on the coasts of America, have received instructions to prosecute the war with unmitigated severity against all cities, towns, and villages belonging to the United States, and against the inhabitants thereof, if, after this communication shall have been made to you, and a reasonable time given for its being transmitted to the American government, that government shall unhappily not be deterred from putting to death any of the soldiers who now are, or who may hereafter be kept as hostages for the purposes stated in the letter from major-general Dearborn."

General Wilkinson, in his answer to general Prevost's letter, states, that he should immediately transmit a copy of it to the executive of the United States. "I forbear," continues Wilkinson, "to animadvert on the acts of our superiors, whatever may be their tendency; but you must pardon me for taking exception to an expression in your letter. The government of the United States cannot be 'deterred,' by any considerations of life or death, of depredation or conflagration, from the faithful discharge of its duty to the American nation."

In a subsequent communication, general Wilkinson stated, that " the government of the United States, adhering unalterably to the principle and purpose declared in the communication of general Dearborn, on the subject of the twenty-three American soldiers, prisoners of war, sent to England to be tried as criminals; and the confinement of a like number of British soldiers, prisoners of war, selected to abide the fate of the former; in consequence of the step taken by the British government, as now communicated; ordered forty-six British officers in close confinement, and that they will not be discharged from their confinement, until it shall be known that the forty-six American officers and non-commissioned officers in question are no longer confined.

General Prevost, on the receipt of this letter, ordered all American officers, prisoners of war, without exception of rank, to be immediately placed in close confinement, as hostages for the forty-six British officers so confined, until the number of forty-six be completed, over and above those now in confinement.

A very interesting correspondence, upon a somewhat similar subject, between general Harrison and the British general Vincent, was published about this period. After the capture of the British army, in the battle on the Thames, general Proctor sent a flag with a letter to general Harrison, requesting humane treatment for the prisoners in his possession, and the restoration of private property and papers. Harrison addressed his answer on the subject to general Vincent, as the senior officer.

" With respect to the subject of General Proctor's letter," says Harrison, " those which I have the honour to enclose you from the British officers, who were taken on the fifth ultimo, to their friends, and the report of Mr. Le Briton, will satisfy you that no indulgence which humanity could claim in their favour, or the usages of war sanction, has been withheld. The disposition of the property taken on the field of action or near it, was left to the commanding officer at Detroit. The instructions given to that gentleman, and the well known generosity of his character, will ensure to the claimants the utmost justice and liberality in his decisions. In making this statement, I wish it however to be distinctly understood, that my conduct with regard to the prisoners and property taken, has been dictated solely by motives of humanity, and not by a belief that it could be claimed upon the score of reciprocity of treatment towards the American prisoners who have fallen into the hands of general Proctor. The unhappy description of persons who have es-

M 2

caped the tomahawk of the savages in the employment of the British government, who fought under the immediate orders of that officer, have suffered all the indignities and deprivations which human nature is capable of supporting. There is no single instance that I have heard of, in which the property of the officers has been respected. But I am far from believing that the conduct of general Proctor has been thought an example worthy of imitation by the greater part of the British officers; and in the character of general Vincent, I have a pledge that he will unite his exertions with mine to soften as much as possible the fate of those whom the fortune of war may reciprocally place in our power.

" But, sir, there is another subject upon which I wish an explicit declaration. Will the Indians who still adhere to the cause of his Britannic Majesty, be suffered to continue that horrible species of warfare which they have heretofore practiced against our troops, and those still more horrible depredations upon the peaceable inhabitants of our frontiers? I have sufficient evidence to show that even the latter have not always been perpetrated by amall parties of vagrant Indians, acting at a distance from the British army. Some of the most atrocious instances have occurred under the eyes of the British commander and the head of the Indian department. I shall pass by the tragedy of the river Raisin, and that equally well known which was acted on the Miami river after the defeat of colonel Dudley—and select three other instances of savage barbarity committed under the auspices of general Proctor.—In the beginning of June a small party of Indians, conducted by an Ottoway chief, who I believe is now with the British army under your command, left Malden in bark canoes, in which they coasted Lake Erie to the mouth of Portage river; the canoes were taken across the Portage to the Sandusky bay, over which the party proceeded to the mouth of Cold creek, and from thence by land to the settlements upon that river, where they captured three families, consisting of one man and twelve women and children. After taking the prisoners some distance, one of the women was discovered to be unable to keep up with them in consequence of her advanced state of pregnancy. She was immediately tomahawked, stripped naked; her womb ripped open, and the child taken out. Three or four of the children were successively butchered as they discovered their inability to keep up with the party. Upon the arrival of the Indians at Malden, two or three of the prisoners were ransomed by colonel Elliot, and the others by the citizens of Detroit, where they remained until they were taken off by their friends upon the recovery of that place by our army. I have been informed that the savage chief received from colonel E   liot *reprimand* for his cruelty.

"On the 29th or 30th of the same month, a large party of Indians were sent from Malden on a war expedition to Lower Sandusky. At a farm house near that place, they murdered the whole family, consisting of a man, his wife, son, and daughter.

"During the last attack upon Fort Meigs by general Proctor, a party headed by a Seneca, an intimate friend of Tecumseh's was sent to endeavour to detach from our interest the Shawanese of Wapockanata. In their way thither they murdered several men, and one woman who was working in her cornfield.

"I have selected, sir, the above from a long list of similar instances of barbarity, which the history of the last fifteen months could not furnish; because they were perpetrated, if not in the view of the British commander, by parties who came immediately from his camp and returned to it—who even received their daily support from the king's stores, who in fact (as the documents in my possession will show) form part of his army.

"To retaliate then upon the subjects of the king would have been justifiable by the laws of war and the usages of the most civilized nations. To do so has been amply in my power. The tide of fortune has changed in our favour, and an extensive and flourishing province opened to our arms. The future conduct of the British officers will determine the correctness of mine in withholding it. If the savages should be again let loose upon our settlements, I shall with justice be accused of having sacrificed the interests and honour of my country, and the lives of our fellow citizens, to feelings of false and mistaken humanity. You are a soldier, sir, and, as I sincerely believe, possess all the honourable sentiments which ought always to be found in men who follow the profession of arms. Use then, I pray you, your authority and influence to stop the dreadful effusion of innocent blood which proceeds from the employment of those savage monsters, whose aid (as must now be discovered) is so little to be depended upon when it is most wanted, and which can have so trifling an effect upon the issue of the war. The effect of their barbarities will not be confined to the present generation. Ages yet to come will feel the deep rooted hatred and enmity which they must•produce between the two nations.

"I deprecate most sincerely the dreadful alternative which

will be offered to me should they be continued, but I solemnly declare, that if the Indians that remain under the influence of the British government are suffered to commit any depredations upon the citizens within the district that is committed to my protection, I will remove the restrictions which have hitherto been imposed upon those who have offered their services to the United States; and direct them to carry on the war in their own way. I have never heard a single excuse for the employment of the savages by your government, unless we can credit the story of some British officer having dared to assert, that, 'as we employed the Kentuckians, you had a right to make use of the Indians.' If such injurious sentiments have really prevailed, to the prejudice of a brave, well-informed, and virtuous people, it will be removed by the representations of your officers who were lately taken on the river Thames. They will inform you, sir, that so far from offering any violence to the persons of their prisoners, these *savages* would not permit a word to escape them which was calculated to wound or insult their feelings, and this too with the sufferings of their friends and relatives at the river Raisin and Miami, fresh upon their recollection.

" P. S. I pledge myself for the truth of the above statement in relation to the murders committed by the Indians."

General Vincent, in reply, stated, that " the account given of the British officers, whom the fortune of war has lately placed at the disposal of the United States, is such, as cannot fail affording very consoling reflections to this army and their anxious friends.

" Though you must be sensible," continues he " that there are several points in your letter respecting which it is wholly beyond my power to afford you the satisfaction of an 'explicit declaration, yet be assured, sir, I shall never feel the smallest degree of hesitation in joining you in any pledge, that it will ever be my anxious wish and endeavour to alleviate as much as possible the fate of those who may fall into my power by the chances of war.

" Believe me, sir, I deprecate as strongly as yourself the perpetration of acts of cruelty committed under any pretext; and shall lament equally with yourself that any state of things should produce them. No efforts of mine will be ever wanting to diminish the evils of a state of warfare, as far as may be consistent with the duties which are due to my king and country.

" The Indians when acting in conjunction with the troops under my command, have been invariably exhorted to mercy, and have never been deaf to my anxious entreaties on this interesting subject.

" I shall not fail to transmit the original of your letter to the lower province, Tor the consideration of his excellency the commander of the forces."

The war with Great Britain, during the two first campaigns was productive of no events which materially altered the situation of the two countries. With sufficient occupation for her troops in the European peninsula, and with every nerve strained in bringing forth her pecuniary resources, for the support of her allies in Russia and Germany, Great Britain was unable to make any effectual impression on the United States, and could not even have preserved her North American provinces, but for the raw and undisciplined state of the American forces, and the want of knowledge and experience in their commanders. But, amidst all the reverses that attended the first efforts of the army of America, the native bravery of her sons was sufficiently apparent. The events even of the first two campaigns sufficiently proved, that nothing but habits of discipline and able leaders were wanting to convert this rude mass into a body of warriors, not unworthy to defend the soil of freedom, and to carry vengeance against the most powerful aggressors upon the rights of their country.

While the army was thus acquiring discipline in the fields of Upper Canada, and in the pathless desarts of Ohio, the republican navy had an apparently still more difficult task to perform. Having annihilated the navies of Europe, in the course of a twenty years war, Britain was enabled fearlessly to cover our coasts with her thousand ships of war. The navy of America was an object of ridicule with the British nation, and it was confidently predicted in her legislative assembly, that in a few short months the " half dozen fir-built frigates, with a piece of striped bunting at the mast-head" would be swept from the ocean. Nay, even the forebodings of our friends were but little more favourable. What could a few frigates and sloops of war effect against a fleet, which had succeeded in breaking down every naval power in the world, and who could exclaim almost without an hyperbole:

> " *The winds and seas are Britain's wide domain,*
> " *And not a sail but by permission spreads* "*

---

* *British Naval Register.*

But this arduous task was undertaken with undaunted firmness, and the result was as brilliant as unexpected. Frigate met with frigate, and fleet with fleet, and the flag of the conquerors of the world was repeatedly struck to the infant navy of the rude republicans. To hide the disgrace, the enemy was fain to claim kindred with those they had affected to call a degenerate and outcast race, or to resort to the more unfair and mean subterfuge of designating as " seventy-fours in disguise," the same frigates which they had had numerous opportunities of examining, both in our ports and their own, and which but a few months before they had laughed to scorn. The British vessels were also made to undergo a metamorphosis, but in an inverse ratio to that of the Americans. Their ships, brigs, schooners, and sloops were converted into gun-boats, in the futile hope of tearing the wreath from the brows of the noble Perry, whose modest demeanour and humane conduct was such as to extort the reluctant applause even of those who submitted to his prowess.

Instead, therefore, of being confined to our ports, or swept from the ocean, the little navy of America visited every sea, and every where unfurled her stripes and stars. Nor did the coasts of the mistress of the ocean escape. Vessels were even captured in her own narrow seas.

Meanwhile the Baitish navy was employed in the vain attempt of " hermetrically sealing the American ports," or in harassing the coasts of the Chesapeake by petty marauding excursions, whose prime object seems to have been the burning of farm-houses and oyster-boats, or the plundering stock and tabacco, on this extensive and defenceless frontier.

But by the occurrence of one of the most wonderful events in this most wonderful era, the war was now to assume a very different aspect. Our republican institutions were destined to undergo a fiery trial, and the hitherto problematical question to be resolved, whether a free government, which derived its chief strength from public opinion, was capable of sustaining itself single-handed during a conflict with a power possessed of apparently boundless resources, and whose armies had just returned from " conquering the conquerors of Europe," and dictating an ignominious peace in their capital. Nor were other unfavourable circumstances wanting to darken the cloud which hung over America at this eventful period. The treasury, one of the principal sinews of war was nearly beggared by the temporising policy and ruinous expedients which had been resorted to, and the policy of the enemy had succeeded in draining the country of its circulating medium to such an extent, as to induce a general stoppage of specie payments by the banks in almost every section of the country. Perhaps a more interesting period of American history never occured than this crisis presented.

The main body of the American army on the Canadian frontier, remained inactive through the winter in their cantonments at French Mills. Preparations, however, were early made for the opening of the ensuing campaign; and towards the middle of February, after having destroyed their temporary barracks, and the major part of their boats, the army marched in two columns, the one under general Brown for Sackett's Harbour, the other towards lake Champlain, under general Macomb. General Wilkinson remained one day behind for the protection of the rear, and then followed Macomb to Plattsburg. The march of both columns was unmolested by the enemy.

No further movements were made until the end of March, when general Wilkinson, learning that general Brown had marched from Sackett's Harbour against Fort Niagara determined upon attempting a diversion in his favour. He accordingly put his army in motion on the Odelltown road, and entering Canada on the 30th of March, advanced against a position occupied by the enemy on the river La Cole, where the British had fortified a large stone mill, and erected a blockhouse and other defences.

An eighteen pounder had been ordered forward to effect the destruction of the mill, but it broke down, and after being repaired the only road of approach, through a deep forest, was reported to be impracticable to a gun of such weight. An opinion prevailed with the chief engineer, and several of the best informed officers, that an iron twelve would suffice to make a breach; but after a fair and tedious experiment, at a distance of only three hundred yards, it was discovered that the battery could make no impression.

During this cannonade, which was returned by a sloop and some gun-boats from Isle aux Noix, several sorties and desperate charges were made from the mill upon the American battery; these were repulsed with great coolness by the covering corps, and the whole body engaged displayed the utmost gallantry and bravery, during the affair. The conduct of captain M'Pherson, who commanded the battery, is particularly noticed by general Wilkinson, who also states that he was admirably seconded by lieutenants Larrabee and Sheldon. M'Pherson and Larrabee were both severely wounded.

Finding all attempts to make a breach unsuccessful, general Wilkinson withdrew the battery, called in his detachments, and after removing the dead and wounded, and every thing else, fell back, unmolested, the same evening, about three miles, to Odelltown, a small town just within the Canada lines.

The force of the British at the position of La Cole, was reported, from a source on which reliance might be placed, at 2500 men. That of the Americans is unofficially stated at between three and four thousand. A small part of this force however was actually engaged. The loss of the Americans in killed and wounded on this occasion was between 80 and 90. That of the British was 10 killed, 46 wounded, and 4 missing.

This inauspicious opening of the campaign, joined to the failure of the expedition against Montreal the preceding autumn, threw a great deal of odium on general Wilkinson, and he was shortly after superceded in the command by general Izard.*

Meantime general Brown, after remaining for a short period at Sackett's Harbour, put his troops in motion towards the Niagara frontier. Expectations were entertained that he would immediately drive the enemy from his position in the American territory, but these expectations were disappointed. During the spring months, tranquility reigned uninterrupted along the whole line of the Upper Canada frontier, save by a few partial encounters, which shall be noticed in the order in which they occurred.

A small force, consisting of about 180 rangers and mounted infantry, under captain Holmes, was dispatched by lieutenant-colonel Butler, the commander at Detroit, against Delaware, a British post on the river Thames. This detachment had set out with artillery, but the state of the country presenting invincible obstacles to its transportation, it was left behind. By these means, and by sending back the sick to Detroit, Holmes' little force was diminished to about 160 men.

On the 3d of March intelligence was received, that a body of the enemy, nearly double his force, was descending the Thames, one half of whom were regulars, and the remainder militia and Indians. Holmes immediately retreated a few miles, and took an excellent position on the western bank of a creek, which ran through a deep and wide ravine. Captain

---

* General Wilkinson was tried by a court martial held at Troy, in the state of New York, on various accusations exhibited against him of misconduct during those two campaigns. He was honourably acquitted of all the charges exhibited against him.

Gill was left with a few rangers to cover the rear, and watch the motions of the enemy; but hardly had the main body encamped, before they were joined by the rangers, who had been driven in, after exchanging a few shots with the British advanced corps, in a vain attempt to reconnoitre their force.

During the night of the 3d, the British encamped upon the eastern heights, and next morning succeeded in drawing captain Holmes fnom his position by a well contrived stratagem, which, had it been skilfully followed up, could hardly have failed to eventuate in the destruction of the American detachment. Fortunately, however, this was not the case. At sun-rise the enemy exhibited a small and scattered force on the opposite heights, who retreated, after ineffectually firing at the American camp, and the reconnoitering party reported that the retreat was conducted with precipitation, the baggage left scattered on the road, and, that judging from their trail and fires, they could not exceed seventy men. Mortified at the idea of having retrogaded from this diminutive force, Holmes instantly commenced the pursuit, and resumed the idea of attacking the enemy's post. He had not, however, proceeded beyond five miles, when his advance discovered the enemy, in considerable force, arranging themselves for battle.

The stratagem of the enemy being now apparent, captain Holmes instantly took advantage of the blunder, which they had committed, in not throwing themselves in his rear, and thus placing his detachment between a fortified position and a superior force; and happily he soon regained his former position. Here, placing his horses and baggage in the centre, he formed his troops a-foot in a hollow square, to prevent the necessity of evolution, which such raw troops were incompetent to perform in action. Holmes thus calmly waited the approach of the enemy, in defiance of the murmurs of his men, who were unanimously in favour of a retreat, thinking it madness to engage with so superior a force.

The attack was commenced simultaneously on every front, the militia and Indians attacking from the north, west and south, with savage yells and bugles sounding, and the regulars charging up the heights from the ravine on the east. The latter bravely approached to within 20 paces of the American line, against the most destructive fire. But the front section being shot to pieces, those who followed much thinned and wounded, and many of the officers cut down, they were forced to abandon the charge, and take cover in the woods in diffused order, within from 15 to 30 paces of their antagonists. The charge of the British regulars thus repulsed, they had recourse to their am-

N

munition, and the firing increased on both sides with great vivacity. The American regulars, being uncovered, were ordered to kneel, that the brow of the heights might assist in screening them from the view of the enemy. But the enemy's cover also proved insufficient, a common sized tree being unable to protect even one man from the extended line of Americans; much less the squads that often stood and breathed their last together.

On the other three sides the firing was sustained with much coolness, and with considerable loss to the foe. The troops on those sides being protected by logs hastily thrown together, and the enemy not charging, both the rifle and musket were aimed at leisure, with that deadly certainty which distinguishes the American backwoodsman. Unable to sustain so unequal contest, therefore, and favoured by the shades of twilight, the British commenced a general retreat, after an hour's close and gallant conflict.

Captain Holmes declined a pursuit, as the enemy were still superior both in numbers and discipline, and as the night would have insured success to an ambuscade. Besides, as the creek would have to be passed and the heights ascended, the attempt to pursue would have given the enemy the same advantage which produced their defeat, as it could be passed on horseback at no other point; and the troops being fatigued and frost bitten, and their shoes cut to pieces by the frozen ground, it was not possible to pursue on foot. Captain Holmes accordingly returned to Detroit.

The American loss in killed and wounded, on this occasion, amounted only to a non-commissioned officer and six privates; the British official account states their loss at 14 killed, 51 wounded, 1 missing, and 1 officer wounded and taken. Two of the officers were killed, and the same number wounded. This statement does not include the loss of the Indians. The whole American force in action consisted of 150 rank and file, of whom including the rangers, 70 were militia. The British regulars alone were from 150 to 180 strong, and the militia and Indians fought upon three sides of the square.

On lake Ontario, the British still preserved the superiority which the addition to their squadron had conferred on them the preceding autumn. Measures, however, were in rapid progress at Sackett's Harbour, towards placing the hostile fleets on a more equal footing. A handsome ship, rated 44 guns, and carrying 58, was launched on the first of May. While this vessel was on the stocks, an unsuccessful attempt was made by the enemy to blow her up. The boats employed in this enterprize were discovered by the American guard boats in the bay and were forced to fly, after throwing their kegs of powder overboard.

Commodore Yeo pursued a similar policy to that which governed him the preceding summer. As long as he was manifestly superior in force to Chauncey, his fleet ruled the lake; but nothing could induce him to hazard an engagement, when the force of his rival was nearly equal to his. During that part of the summer, when this was the case, he lay snug in Kingston harbour. This is by no means said in disparagement of the British commander; for every circumstance shows that this was the wisest policy; and perhaps the only one which could have saved Upper Canada.

On the 5th of May the British naval force under Sir James Lucas Yeo, consisting of four large ships, three brigs, and a number of gun and other boats, appeared off the village of Oswego, having on board seven companies of infantry, a detachment of artillery, and a battalion of marines, under the command of lieutenant-general Drummond. This post being but occasionally, and not recently occupied by regular troops, was in a bad state of defence. It was garrisoned by about 300 regulars, under lieutenant-colonel Mitchell, who had only arrived a few days before. Lieutenant Woolsey of the navy, with a small body of seamen, was also at the village, and as soon as the fleet appeared, the neighbouring militia were called in.— About 1 o'clock the fleet approached, and 15 boats, large and crowded with troops, at a given signal moved slowly to the shore. These were preceded by gun-boats, sent to rake the woods and cover the landing, while the larger vessels opened a fire upon the fort. As soon as the debarking boats got within range of the shot from the shore batteries, a very successful fire opened upon them, which twice compelled them to retire. They at length returned to the ships, and the whole stood off from the shore for better anchorage. Several boats which had been deserted by the enemy were taken up in the evening, one of which was 60 feet long, carried thirty-six oars and three sails, and could accommodate 150 men. She had received a ball through her bow, and was nearly filled with water.

At day-break next morning the fleet appeared bearing up under easy sail, and about noon the frigates took a position directly against the fort and batteries, and opened a heavy fire, which was kept up for three hours, while the brigs, schooners, and gun-boats covered by their fire the debarkation of the troops. The Americans were now forced to retreat into the rear of the fort, where two companies met the advancing columns of the enemy, while the others engaged their flank. Lieutenant Pearce of the navy, and some seamen, joined in the attack, and fought with their characteristic bravery. After a short action, Mitchell again commenced a retreat, which was effected in good order, destroying the bridges in his rear. Indeed a retreat had become necessary for the protection of the stores at the falls 13 miles in the rear of the fort, which were supposed to form the principal object of the expedition.

Early in the morning of the 7th, the British evacuated the place, and retired to their shipping, after destroying the fort and those public stores which they could not carry away. These stores were not important, the most valuable having been deposited at the falls.

The American official account states their loss at 6 killed, 38 wounded, and 25 missing; that of the British states theirs at 19 killed and 75 wounded. Among them were several officers. Mitchell states the force landed at 1550 men, while the Americans engaged did not exceed 300, being 4 companies of the 3d artillery under captains Boyle, Romayne, M'Intyre, and Pierce, a company of light artillery under captain Melvin, and a small detachment of sailors under lieutenant Pearce of the navy.

A short time after this event, the British fleet appeared near the mouth of the Gennesee river, where about 160 volunteers were stationed, with one piece of artillery. Captain Stone, the commanding officer, dispatched expresses for assistance to different quarters. The following day the commodore's new ship came to anchor off the mouth of the river, and sent an officer on shore with a flag, demanding the surrender of the place, and promising to respect private property in case no resistance should be made, and all public property faithfully disclosed and given up. General Porter arrived while the flag was on shore, and returned for answer that the place would be defended to the last extremity. On the return of the flag, two gun-boats, with from 200 to 300 men on board, advanced to the river, which is about a mile from the town and battery, and commenced a heavy cannonade, directed partly to the town, and partly to bodies of troops who had been placed in ravines near the mouth of the river, to intercept the retreat of the gun-boats, in case they should enter.

At the expiration of an hour and a half, during which time they threw a great number of rockets, shells, and shot of different descriptions, from grape to 68lbs., a second flag was sent from the commodore's ship, requiring, in the name of the commander of the forces, an immediate surrender, and threatening that if the demand was not complied with, he would land 1200 regular troops and 400 Indians; that if he should lose a single man, he would raze the town and destroy every vestige of property; and that it was his request that the women and children might be immediately removed, as he could not be accountable for the conduct of the Indians. He was told that the answer to his demand had been already explicitly given; that they were prepared to meet him, the women and children having been disposed of; and that if another flag should be sent on the subject of a surrender, it would not be protected. The flag returned with the gun-boats to the fleet, the whole of which came to anchor about a mile from the shore, where they lay until 8 o'clock on Saturday morning, and then left the place.

On the evening of the following day, the British squadron was discovered making towards Pultneyville, another small village on the margin of lake Ontario, and information was sent to general Swift, who repaired thither in the course of the night, with 130 volunteers and militia. Next morning a flag was sent on shore, demanding a peaceable surrender of all public property, and threatening an immediate destruction of the village in case of refusal. General Swift returned for answer, that he should oppose any attempt to land, by all the means in his power. Soon after the return of the flag, however, general Swift was induced, by the pressing solicitations and entreaties of the inhabitants of the town, to permit one of its citizens to go to the enemy with a flag, and offer the surrender of the property contained in a store-house at the water's edge, consisting of about 100 barrels of flour considerably damaged, on condition that the commanding officer would stipulate not to take any other, nor molest the inhabitants. But before its return, the enemy sent their gun-boats with several hundred men on shore, who took possession of the flour in the store, and were proceeding to further depredations, when general Swift commenced a fire upon them from an adjacent wood, which wounded several, and became so harrassing as to induce them to re-embark. They then commenced a cannonade from the fleet upon the town, which was continued for some time, but with no other injury than a few shot holes through the houses.

A short time after these affairs took place, two British gunboats and five barges, some of which contained howitzers, manned by about 200 sailors and marines, under the command of captain Popham of the royal navy, were captured by a detachment of 120 riflemen and a few Oneida warriors, under

N 2

the command of major Appling, of the first United States' rifle regiment.

Major Appling had been detached to protect the cannon and naval stores at Oswego, destined for commodore Chauncey's fleet. They were embarked on board a flotilla of boats, in charge of captain Woolsey of the navy, and had arrived safely in Sandy creek. Here they were pursued by the enemy, who was gallantly met by the riflemen, and after an action of a few minutes, beaten and taken, without the loss of a man; an Indian and one rifleman only being wounded.

The riflemen were most judiciously posted along the bank, a short distance below captain Woolsey's boats, where the creek is narrow and shoal. Most of the men having withdrawn from the boats, the enemy gave three cheers at the prospect of the rich prize before him. His joy, however, was of short duration, for at this moment the riflemen poured forth their deadly fire, which in about ten minutes terminated in his total defeat, leaving an officer and 13 men killed, two officers and 28 men wounded (the officers and many of the men dangerously); the residue, consisting of 10 officers and 133 men, taken prisoners.

Major Appling speaks in the highest terms of the courage and good conduct of his officers and men. Captain Harris with his troop of dragoons, and captain Melvin with his two field-pieces, had made a rapid march, and would in a few minutes have been ready to participate in the action, had the enemy been able to make a stand.

The captured officers and men spoke in the highest terms of commendation of major Appling and his rifle corps, to whose humane and spirited conduct they are probably indebted for the preservation of their lives. The Indians were the first to reach the enemy after they submitted, and had commenced executing the savage rule of warfare, sanctioned by Anglo-Indian example at the river Raisin, Lewistown, Tuscarora, &c. of murdering their prisoners, when the major and his men happily arrived, and succeeded, by a prompt and determined course, though not without violence, in terminating the tragic scene.*

---

* An Indian chief is said to have given vent to his feelings on this occasion in language similar to the following:—" When British come to Buffalo, they kill white man, they kill Indian, they kill woman, they burn all houses—when British come here, you no let Indian kill him—you give him eat—this no good."

No further events took place on this lake during the war worth recording, excepting the capture and destruction of a gun-boat at the head of the St. Lawrence, and the burning of a vessel of war on the stocks at Presque Isle. Both these exploits were performed by lieutenant Gregory.

Nothing of importance took place on lake Erie. The only hostile event that occurred was the destruction of some mills employed in manufacturing flour for the British army, at Long Point, by colonel Campbell, with a detachment of 500 or 600 men from Erie. The mills and some houses occupied as stores were burned. About 50 dragoons stationed there as a guard made their escape, when the party returned without losing a man. This event, which was certainly not strictly justified by the laws of war, though sanctioned by the practice of the enemy, was an unauthorised act on the part of colonel Campbell. A court of enquiry was held on his conduct, whose opinion was unanimously pronounced as follows:

" That, considering the important supplies of bread-stuffs, which from the evidence it appears the enemy's forces derived from the flour-manufacturing mills at and near to Dover, colonel Campbell was warranted in destroying those mills, according to the laws and usages of war, and, for a like reason, the court think him justified in burning the distilleries under the said laws and usages. The saw-mills and carding machine, from their contiguity to the other mills, were, as the court conceives necessarily involved in one and the same burning.

" In respect to the burning of the dwelling and other houses in the village of Dover, the court are fully of opinion that colonel Campbell has erred; that he can derive no justification from the fact, that the owners of these houses were actively opposed to the American interests in the present war, or from the other facts, that some of them were at the conflagration of Buffaloe. In their partizan services it does not appear to the court, that the inhabitants of Dover have done more than their proper allegiance required of them; and the destruction of Buffaloe, by a lieutenant-general of the enemy's regular forces, was emphatically the wrong of the British government itself, rendered such by its subsequent adoption of the measure, and ought not to be ascribed to a few Canadians who were present at the time.

" Acts of retaliation, on the part of a nation proud of its rights, and conscious of the power of enforcing them, should, in the opinion of the court, be reluctantly resorted to, and only by instructions from the highest in authority. That no such instructions were given in the case under consideration, is not merely inferred from the absence of evidence to that effect, but is candidly admitted by colonel Campbell in his official report (which is in evidence), wherein he expressly states— 'This expedition was undertaken by me without orders, and upon my own responsibility.'

 " The court, in delivering the above opinion unfavourable to colonel Campbell, are fully aware of the strong incentives to a just indignation which must have been present to his mind at the time of this visit to Dover—the massacres of the Raisin and the Miami were not yet forgotten, and the more recent devastation of the entire Niagara frontier, accompanied by many acts of savage barbarity, was fresh in remembrance. That these recollections should have aroused his feelings and have swayed his judgment, does not excite wonder but regret, and there is still left for admiration, his kind and amiable treatment of the women and children of Dover, abandoned by their natural protectors."

Meanwhile general Brown was occupied in collecting and disciplining his forces, and preparing for the invasion of Canada. On the evening of the 2d of July, general orders were issued for the embarkation of the troops by day-light next morning, when the army, consisting of two brigades, and a body of New-York and Pennsylvania volunteers and Indians, under general P. B. Porter, were landed on the opposite shore, without opposition. The first brigade, under general Scott, and the artillery corps, under major Hindman, landed nearly a mile below Fort Erie, while general Ripley, with the second brigade, made the shore about the same distance above. The fort was soon completely invested, and a battery of long eighteens being planted in a position which commanded it, the garrison, consisting of 137 men, including officers, surrendered prisoners of war. Several pieces of ordnance were found in the fort, and some military stores.

Having placed a small garrison in Fort Erie to secure his rear, Brown moved forward the following day to Chippewa plains, where he encamped for the night, after some skirmishing with the enemy.

The American pickets were several times attacked on the morning of the 5th, by small parties of the British. About four in the afternoon, general Porter, with the volunteers and Indians, was ordered to advance from the rear of the American camp, and take a circuit through the woods to the left, in hopes of getting beyond the skirmishing parties of the enemy, and cutting off their retreat, and to favour this purpose the advance were ordered to fall back gradually under the enemy's fire. In about half an hour, however, Porter's advance met the light parties in the woods, and drove them until the whole column of the British was met in order of battle. From the clouds of dust and the heavy firing, general Brown concluded that the entire force of the British was in motion, and instantly gave orders for general Scott to advance with his brigade and Towson's artillery, and meet them on the plain in front of the American camp. In a few minutes Scott was in close action with a superior force of British regulars.

By this time Porter's volunteers having given way and fled, the left flank of Scott's brigade became much exposed. General Ripley was accordingly ordered to advance with a part of the reserve, and skirting the woods on the left, in order to keep out of view, endeavour to gain the rear of the enemy's right flank. The greatest exertions were made to gain this position but in vain. Such was the gallantry and impetuosity of the brigade of general Scott, that its advance upon the enemy was not to be checked. Major Jessup, commanding the battalion on the left flank, finding himself pressed both in front and in flank, and his men falling fast around him, ordered his battalion to " support arms and advance." Amidst the most destructive fire this order was promptly obeyed, and he soon gained a more secure position, and returned upon the enemy so galling a discharge, as caused them to retire.

The whole line of the British now fell back, and the American troops closely pressed upon them. As soon as the former gained the sloping ground descending towards Chippewa, they broke and ran to their works, distant about a quarter of a mile, and the batteries opening on the American line, considerably checked the pursuit. Brown now ordered the ordnance to be brought up, with the intention of forcing the works. But on their being examined, he was induced, by the lateness of the hour, and the advice of his officers, to order the forces to retire to camp.

The American official account states their loss at 60 killed, 248 wounded, and 19 missing. The British officially state theirs at 133 killed, 320 wounded, and 46 missing.

Dispirited as was the public mind at this period, the intelligence of this brilliant and unexpected opening of the campaign on the Niagara could not fail of being most joyfully received. The total overthrow of the French power had a few months before liberated the whole of the British forces in Europe. A considerable portion of lord Wellington's army, flushed with their late successes in Spain, had arrived in Canada, and were actually opposed to Brown at Chippewa, while all our maritime towns were threatened by Britain's victorious armies, whose arrival was momentarily expected on the coast.   When the intelligence of the stupendous events in Europe was first received, many consoled themselves with the idea, that the magnanimity of Great Britain would freely grant in her prosperity, what they had insisted we never could force from her in her adversity. Sincerely taking for realities the pretexts on which our neutral rights had been infringed, they thought the question of impressment, now the almost single subject of dispute, could easily be amicably arranged, when the affairs of the world were so altered as to render it nearly impossible that Great Britain could ever again be reduced to the necessity of " fighting for her existence; or, at all events, as the peace in Europe had effectually removed the cause, and as the American government declined insisting on a formal relinquishment of the practice, no difficulty would be thrown in the way of a general and complete pacification of the world.

This illusion was soon dissipated. By the next advices from Europe it was learned, that the cry for vengeance upon the Americans was almost unanimous throughout the British empire. The president was threatened with the fate of Bonaparte, and it was said that the American peace ought to be dictated in Washington, as that of Europe had been at Paris.   Even in parliament* the idea was held out that peace ought not to be thought of till America had received a signal punishment, for having dared to declare war upon them while their forces were engaged in " delivering Europe" from its oppressor.† The commencement of the negociations for peace, which had been proposed by the British court, was suspended, and strenuous efforts were made to send to America as commanding a force as possible.

Under these circumstances, a victory gained by the raw

---

* Sir Joseph Yorke, one of the lords of the admiralty, said in parliament, " we have Mr. Madison to depose before we can lay down our arms."

† At a dinner given to lord Hill, who was on the eve of sailing at the head of an expedition against New-Orleans, he stated the period when he should embark for America, and added, that " he had no doubt, with the means already there, together with those on the way, and what were promised by his prince, he should humble the Yankees, and bring the contest to a speedy and successful termination." Happy for his lordship he was soon after superseded in the command by general Packenham.

troops of America over the veterans of Wellington, superior in numbers to the victors,* upon an open plain, and upon a spot chosen by the British general, had a most beneficial tendency, by dispelling the dread which the prowess of the British troops in Spain could not have failed to have produced in the minds of their opponents. This battle was to the army, what the victory of captain Hull had been to the navy; and the confidence which it thus inspired was surely most justly founded, for every man felt that the victory had been gained by superior skill and discipline; it was not the fruit of any accidental mistake or confusion in the army of the enemy, or of one of those movements of temporary panic on one side, or excitement on the other, which sometimes give a victory to irregular courage over veteran and disciplined valour

After so signal a defeat, the British could not be induced to hazard another engagement. They abandoned their works at Chippewa, and burning their barracks, retired to fort Niagara and fort George, closely followed by Brown. Here he expected to receive some heavy guns and reinforcements from Sackett's Harbour; but on the 23d of July he received a letter by express from general Gaines, advising him that that port was blockaded by a superior British force, and that commodore Chauncey was confined to his bed with a fever. Thus disappointed in his expectations of being enabled to reduce the forts at the mouth of the Niagara, Brown determined to disencumber the army of baggage, and march directly for Burlington Heights. To mask this intention, and to draw from Schlosser a small supply of provisions, he fell back upon Chippewa.

About noon on the 25th, general Brown was advised by an express from Lewistown, that the British were following him, and were in considerable force in Queenstown and on its heights; that four of the enemy's fleet had arrived with reinforcements at Niagara during the preceding night, and that a number of boats were in view, moving up the the river. Shortly after, intelligence was brought that the enemy were landing at Lewistown, and that the baggage and stores at Schlosser, and on their way thither, were in danger of immediate

---

* The British official accounts state the American forces to have been superior in number. This apparent contradiction may be reconciled by observing, that a single brigade of the American troops achieved the victory; the volunteers having fled before the action commenced, while the brigade of general Ripley had arrived on the ground, when the British took shelter behind their works.

capture. In order to recal the British from this object, Brown determined to put the army in motion towards Queenstown, and accordingly general Scott was directed to advance with the first brigade, Towson's artillery, and all the dragoons and mounted men, with orders to report if the enemy appeared, and if necessary to call for assistance. On his arrival near the falls, Scott learned that the enemy was in force 'directly in his front, a narrow piece of woods alone intercepting his view of them. He immediatly advanced upon them, after dispatching a messenger to general Brown with this intelligence.

The report of the connon and small arms reached general Brown before the messenger, and orders were instantly issued for general Riply to march to the support of general Scott, with the second brigade and all the artillery, and Brown himself repaired with all speed to the scene of action, whence he sent orders for general Porter to advance with his volunteers. On reaching the field of battle, general Brown found that Scott had passed the wood, and engaged the enemy on the Queenstown road and on the ground to the left of it, with the 9th, 11th, and 22d regiments, and Towson's artillery, the 25th having been thrown on the right to be governed by circumstances. The contest was close and desperate, and the American troops, far inferior in numbers, suffered severely.

Meanwhile major Jessup, who commanded the 25th regiment, taking advantage of a fault committed by the British commander, by leaving a road unguarded on his left, threw himself promptly into the rear of the enemy, where he was, enabled to operate with the happiest effect. The slaughter was dreadful; the enemy's line fled down the road at the third or fourth fire. The capture of general Riall, with a large escort of officers of rank, was part of the trophies of Jessup's intrepidity and skill; and, but for the impression of an unfounded report, under which he unfortunately remained for a few minutes, lieutenant general Drummond, the commander of the British forces, would inevitably have fallen into his hands, an event which would, in all probability, have completed the disaster of the British army. Drummond was completely in Jessup's power; but being confidently informed that the first brigade was cut in pieces, and finding himself with less than 200 men, and without any prospect of support, in the midst of an overwhelming hostile force, he thought of nothing for the moment but to make good his retreat, and save his command. Of this temporary suspense of the advance of the American column, general Drummond availed himself to make his escape. Among the officers captured, was one of general Drummond's aids-de-camp, who had been dispatched from the front line to order up the reserve, with a view to fall on Scott with the concentrated force of the whole army, and overwhelm him at a single effort. Nor would it have been possible to prevent this catastrophe, had the reserve arrived in time; the force with which general Scott would then have been obliged to contend being nearly quadruple that of his own. By the fortunate capture, however, of the British aid-de-camp, before the completion of the service on which he had been ordered, the enemy's reserve was not brought into action until the arrival of general Ripley's brigade, which prevented the disaster which must otherwise have ensued.*

Though the second brigade pressed forward with the greatest ardour, the battle had raged for an hour before it could arrive on the field, by which time it was nearly dark. The enemy fell back on its approach. In order to disengage the exhausted troops of the first brigade, the fresh troops were ordered to pass Scott's line, and display in front, a movement which was immediately executed by Ripley. Meanwhile the enemy, being reconnoitered, was found to have taken a new position, and occupied a height with his artillery, supported by a line of infantry, which gave him great advantages, it being

---

* " *A trait in his conduct highly honourable to colonel Jessup is, that his humanity as a man triumphed over his technical duty as an officer. Such was, for a time, his situation in the field, that every prisoner he took, by impeding his operations against the enemy, not only injured the cause in which he was engaged, but endangered the safety of his own corps. According to the canons of war, therefore, his duty, as we believe, was, to make no prisoners, but to put to death every man who might oppose him in arms. Regardless, however, of these sanguinary statutes, and listening only to the voice of mercy, he gave quarter to all that surrendered to him, although conscious they would diminish his effective force, and that he must necessarily suffer them again to escape. This conduct was noticed by some of the British officers, and commended as highly honourable to the young American. Had Jessup been less humane as a man, and more technically rigid as an officer, he might have acted, as the aid-de-camp of general Drummond acknowledged, with more deadly effect against the enemy. But he knew the road to glory better. The fairest wreath in the hero's chaplet is that which is entwined by the hand of mercy.*"—Port Folio.*

O

the key to the whole position. To secure the victory, it was necessary to carry his artillery and seize the height. For this purpose the second brigade advanced upon the Queenstown road, and the first regiment of infantry, which had arrived that day, and was attached to neither of the brigades, was formed in a line facing the enemy's on the height, with a view of drawing his fire and attracting his attention, as the second brigade advanced on his left flank to carry his artillery.

As soon as the first regiment approached its position, colonel Miller was ordered to advance with the 21st regiment, and carry the artillery on the height by the bayonet. The first regiment gave way under the fire of the enemy; but Miller, undaunted by this occurrence, advanced steadily and gallantly to his object, and carried the heights and cannon in a masterly style. General Ripley followed on the right with the 23d regiment. It had some desperate fighting, which caused it to faulter, but it was promptly rallied, and brought up.

The enemy being now driven from their commanding ground, the whole brigade, with the volunteers and artillery, and the first regiment, which had been rallied, were formed in line, with the captured cannon, nine pieces, in the rear. Here they were soon joined by major Jessup, with the 25th, the regiment that had acted with such effect in the rear of the enemy's left. In this situation the American troops withstood three distinct desperate attacks of the enemy, who had rallied his broken corps, and received reinforcements. In each of them he was repulsed with great slaughter, so near being his approach, that the buttons of the men were distinctly seen through the darkness by the flash of the muskets, and many prisoners were taken at the point of the bayonet, principally by Porter's volunteers. During the second attack general Scott was ordered up, who had been held in reserve with three of his battalions, from the moment of Ripley's arrival on the field. During the third effort of the enemy, the direction of Scott's column would have enabled him, in a few minutes, to have formed line in the rear of the enemy's right, and thus have brought him between two fires. But a flank fire from a concealed part of the enemy falling upon the centre of Scott's command, completely frustrated this intention. His column was severed in two; one part passing to the rear, the other by the right flank of platoons towards Ripley's main line.

This was the last effort of the British to regain their position and artillery, the American troops being left in quiet possession of the field. It was now nearly midnight, and generals Brown and Scott being both severely wounded, and all the roops much exhausted, the command was given to general Ripley, and he was instructed to return to camp, bringing with him the wounded and the artillery. The pieces, however, were found in so dismantled a state, and such had been the slaughter of the horses, that to remove them at that late hour was found to be impracticable.

On the return of the troops to camp, general Brown sent for general Ripley, and after giving him his reasons for the measure, ordered him to put the troops into the best possible condition; to give to them the necessary refreshment; to take with him the picquets and camp guards, and every other description of force; to put himself on the field of battle as the day dawned, and there meet and beat the enemy if he again appeared.

General Ripley has been much blamed for the non-execution of this order, by which the captured cannon again fell into the hands of the British. General Brown, in his official report, says, " To this order he [Ripley] made no objection, and I relied upon its execution. It was not executed." On the part of general Ripley it is stated, that his orders were, in case the enemy appeared in force, " to be governed entirely by circumstances," His orders, therefore, were executed. At daybreak the army was arranged, and the march commenced, when circumstances of the most positive nature were made apparent, such as must have been in view in the discretionary part of the order, and in the full effect of which general Ripley commenced and effected the retreat which afterwards led him to Fort Erie. The troops reduced to less than 1600 men, were marched on the 26th by general Ripley towards the field of battle. Motion was commenced at day-break, but difficulties incidental to the late losses prevented the advance before some time had been spent in re-organization and arrangement. The line of march being assumed, and the Chippewa crossed, general Ripley sent forward lieutenants. Tappan of the 23d, and Riddle of the 15th, with their respective commands, to reconnoitre the enemy's position, strength, and movements. On examination, he was found in advance of his former position, on an eminence, strongly reinforced, as had been asserted by prisoners taken the preceding evening; his flanks, resting on a wood on one side, and on the river on the other, defied being turned or driven in; his artillery was planted so as to sweep the road; besides these advantages, he extended a line nearly double in length to that which could be displayed by our troops. To attack with two-thirds the force of the preceding evening an enemy thus increased, was an act of madness that the first thought rejected. The army was kept in the field and in motion long enough to be assured of the strength and position of the enemy; that information being confirmed, there remained but one course to prevent that enemy from impeding a retreat, which, had he been vigilant, he would previously have prevented. The army, therefore, immediately retrograded, and the retreat received the sanction of general Brown, previous to his crossing the Niagara.*

The American official account states their loss in this battle at 171 killed, 572 wounded, and 117 missing; the return of British prisoners presents an aggregate of 179, including major-general Riall, and a number of other officers.—The British state their loss to be 84 killed, 559 wounded, 193 missing; their loss in prisoners they stated only at 41. Major-general Brown and brigadier-general Scott were among the wounded of the Americans, and lieutenant-general Drummond and major-general Riall among those of the British.

In consequence of the wounds of generals Brown and Scott, the command devolved on general Ripley, who pursued his retreat across the Chippewa, destroying the bridges in his rear, and throwing every possible impediment in the way of the enemy; in order to obstruct his advance. On the 27th of July, the army reached Fort Erie. Here it was determined to make a stand, and accordingly the lines of defence and fortification were immediately marked out, and by the unremitted exertions of the army, were completed on the 3d of August, the very day of the arrival of the enemy before them.

Early in the morning of the 3d, an attempt was made to surprise Buffalo, with the intention, it is supposed, of re-capturing general Riall, and other British prisoners there, and destroying the public stores. About 2 in the morning, nine boat-loads of troops were landed on the American side, half a mile below Conjocta creek, on the upper bank of which, suspecting their intention, major Morgan had taken a position with a battalion of the first rifle regiment, consisting of 240 men. Here, during the preceding night, he had thrown up a battery of a few logs, and torn away the bridge. About four o'clock the British commenced the attack, sending a party before to repair the bridge, under cover of their fire. So heavy and deadly, however, was the fire opened by the riflemen, that they were compelled to retire. They then formed in the skirt of the wood, and kept up the fight at long shot, continually re-

* *Port Folio, Memoir of Major General Ripley.*

inforcing from the Canada shore, until they had 23 boat-loads, when they attempted to outflank, by sending a large body up the creek to ford it. But a detachment of about 60 men being sent to dispute the passage, they were repulsed with considerable loss. The object now appearing unattainable, the enemy commenced their retreat, having previously thrown some troops on Squaw Island, which enfiladed the creek, thus preventing their retreat from being harassed. Their superior numbers enabled them to take their wounded and most of their killed off the field; though some of the latter were afterwards found. A number of muskets and accoutrements were also collected, and some clothing that appeared to have been torn for the purpose of binding their wounds. Six British prisoners were taken, who stated their force to have consisted of from 12 to 1500 men. Although the action continued for two hours and a half, the loss of the Americans was but trifling—two killed and eight wounded. The loss of the British was never ascertained, but it must have been quite disproportioned to that of the Americans.

On the arrival of the British before Fort Erie, they perceived that the opportunity was lost of carrying the American works by a coup-de-main. Driving in the pickets, therefore, they made a regular investment of the place. The following day general Gaines arrived from Sackett's Harbour, and being senior in rank assumed the command. On the 6th, the rifle corps was sent to endeavour to draw out the enemy, in order to try his strength. Their orders, were to pass through the intervening woods, to amuse the British light troops until their strong columns should get in motion, when they should retire slowly to the plain, where a strong line was posted in readiness to receive the enemy. The riflemen accordingly met and drove the light troops into their lines, but although they kept the wood near two hours, they were not able to draw any part of the enemy's force after them. The British left eleven dead and three prisoners in the hands of the riflemen; but their loss was supposed to be much more considerable. The loss of the riflemen were five killed and three or four wounded.

The main camp of the British was planted about two miles distant. In front of it they threw up a line of partial circumvallation, extending around the American fortifications. This consisted of two lines of entrenchment, supported by block-houses; in front of these, at favourable points, batteries were erected, one of which enfiladed the American works.

The American position was on the margin of lake Erie, at the entrance of the Niagara river, on nearly a horizontal plain, twelve or fifteen feet above-the surface of the water, possessing few natural advantages. It had been strenghtened in front by temporary parapet breast-works, entrenchment, and abbatis, with two batteries and six field-pieces   The small unfinished fort, Erie, with a 24, 18, and 12 pounder, formed the north-east, and the Douglass battery, with an 18 and 6 pounder near the edge of the lake, the south-east angle on the right. The left was defended by a redoubt battery with six field-pieces, just thrown up on a small ridge. The rear was left open to the lake, bordered by a rocky shore of easy ascent. The battery on the left was defended by captain Towson; Fort Erie by captain Williams, with major Trimble's command of the 19th infantry; the batteries on the front by captains Biddle and Fanning; the whole of the artillery commanded by major Hindman. Parts of the 11th, 9th, and 22d infantry, were posted on the right under the command of lieutenant-colonel Aspinwall. General Ripley's brigade, consisting of the 21st and 23d, defended the left. General Porter's brigade of New York and Pennsylvania volunteers, with the riflemen, occupied the centre.

During the 13th and 14th, the enemy kept up a brisk cannonade, which was sharply returned from the American batteries, without any considerable loss. One of their shells lodged in a small magazine, in Fort Erie, which was almost empty. It blew up with an explosion more awful in appearance than injurious in its effects, as it did not disable a man or derange a gun. A momentary cessation of the thunders of the artillery took place on both sides. This was followed by a loud and joyous shout by the British Army, which was instantly returned on the part of the Americans, who, amidst the smoke of the explosion, renewed the contest by an animated roar of the heavy cannon.

From the supposed loss of ammunition, and the consequent depression such an event was likely to produce, general Gaines felt persuaded that this explosion would lead the enemy to assault, and made his arrangements accordingly. These suspicions were fully verified, by an attack that was made in the night between the 14th and 15th of August.

The night was dark, and the early part of it raining, but nevertheles one third of the troops were kept at their posts. At half past two o'clock, the right column of the enemy approached, and though enveloped in darkness, was distinctly heard on the American left, and promptly marked by the musquetry under major Wood and captain Towson. Being mounted at the moment, Gaines repaired to the point of attack, where the sheet of fire rolling from Towson's battery, and the musquetry of the left wing, enabled him to see the enemy's column of about 1500 men approaching on that point; his advance was not checked until it had approached within ten feet of the infantry. A line of loose brush, representing an abattis, only intervened; a column of the enemy attempted to pass round the abattis, through the water, where it was nearly breast-deep. Apprehending that this point would be carried, Gaines ordered a detachment of riflemen and infantry to its support; but at this moment the enemy were repulsed. They instantly renewed the charge, and were again driven back.

On the right, the fire of cannon and musquetry announced the approach of the centre and left columns of the enemy, under colonel Drummond and Scott. The latter was received and repulsed by the 9th, under the command of captain Foster, and captains Boughton and Harding's companies of New York and Pennsylvania volunteers, aided by a six-pounder, judiciously posted by major M'Kee, chief engineer.

But the centre, led by colonel Drummond, was not long kept in check; it approached at once every assailable point of the fort, and with scaling-ladders ascended the parapet, where, however, it was repulsed with dreadful carnage. The assault was twice repeated, and as often checked; but the enemy having moved round in the ditch, covered by darkness, encreased by the heavy cloud of smoke which had rolled from the cannon and musquetry, repeated the charge, re-ascended the ladders, and with their pikes, bayonets, and spears fell upon the American artillerists, and succeeded in capturing the bastion. Lieutenant M'Donough, being severely wounded, demanded quarter. It was refused by colonel Drummond. The lieutenant then seized a handspike, and nobly defended himself until he was shot down with a pistol by the monster who had refused him quarter, who often reiterated the order—" give the damned yankees no quarter." This officer, whose bravery, if it had been seasoned with virtue, would have entitled him to the admiration of every soldier—this hardened murderer soon met his fate. He was shot through the breast, while repeating the order " to give no quarter."

Several gallant attempts were made to recover the right bastion, but all proved unsuccessful. At this moment every operation was arrested by the explosion of some cartridges deposited in the end of the stone building adjoining the contested bastion. The explosion was tremendous and decisive; the bastion was restored by the flight of the British. At this moment captain Biddle was ordered to cause a field-piece to be posted so as to enfilade the exterior plain and salient glacis. Though not recovered from a severe contusion in the shoulder, received from one of the enemy's shells, Biddle promptly took his position, and served his field-piece with vivacity and effect. Captain Fanning's battery likewise played upon them at this time with great effect. The enemy were in a few moments entirely defeated, taken, or put to flight, leaving on the field 221 killed, 174 wounded, and 186 prisoners, including 14 officers killed and 7 wounded and prisoners. A large portion were severely wounded; the slightly wounded, it is presumed, were carried off.

The loss of the Americans during the assault was seventeen killed, fifty-six wounded, and eleven missing. The British acknowledge only 57 killed, 309 wounded, and 539 missing. During the preceding bombardment, the loss of the Americans was 7 killed, 19 severely and 17 slightly wounded. The loss of the British is not mentioned in their official account. This bombardment commenced at sun-rise on the morning of the 13th, and continued without intermission till 8 o'clock, P. M.; recommenced on the 14th, at day-light, with increased warmth; and did not end until an hour before the commencement of the assault on the morning of the 15th.

During the night preceding the commencement of the bombardment of Fort Erie, an unfortunate affair for the American arms took place on the lake, just behind the fort, in the surprise and capture of two schooners, by a number of boats full of British soldiers. On the boats being hailed, they answered " provision boats," a manœuvre which deceived the American officers, as boats from the fort had been in the habit of passing and repassing through the night. The force being overwhelming, and the surprise complete, but little effectual resistance was made, and the enterprise was completely successful. The Americans had one killed and nine wounded. The loss of the assailants was more considerable.

A short time after the assault on Fort Erie, general Gaines received a serious wound from the bursting of a shell, by which means the command once more devolved on general Ripley, till the 2d of September, when the state of his health allowed general Brown again to place himself at the head of his army.

The troops in Fort Erie began now to be generally considered as in a critical situation, and much solicitude to be expressed for the fate of the army that had thrown so much glory on the American name, menaced as it was in front by an enemy of superior force, whose numbers were constantly receiving additions, and whose batteries were every day becoming more formidable, while a river of difficult passage lay on their rear. Reinforcements were ordered on from Champlain, but they were yet far distant. But the genius of Brown was fully equal to the contingency, and the difficulties with which he was environed served only to add to the number of his laurels.

Though frequent skirmishes occurred about this period, in which individual gallantry was amply displayed, yet no event of material consequence took place till the 17th of September, when having suffered much from the fire of the enemy's batteries, and aware that a new one was about to be opened, general Brown resolved on a sortie in order to effect their destruction. The British infantry at this time consisted of three brigades, of 12 or 1500 men each, one of which was stationed at the works in front of Fort Erie, the other two occupied their camp behind. Brown's intention therefore was, to storm the batteries, destroy the cannon, and roughly handle the brigade upon duty, before those in reserve could be brought into action.

On the morning of the 17th, the infantry and riflemen, regulars and militia, were ordered to be paraded and put in readiness to march precisely at 12 o'clock. General Porter with the volunteers, colonel Gibson with the riflemen, and major Brooks with the 23d and 1st infantry, and a few dragoons acting as infantry, were ordered to move from the extreme left upon the enemy's right, by a passage opened through the woods for the occasion. General Miller was directed to station his command in the ravine between Fort Erie and the enemy's batteries, by passing them by detachment through the skirts of the wood—and the 21st infantry under general Ripley was posted as a corps of reserve between the new bastions of Fort Erie—all under cover, and out of the view of the enemy.

The left column, under the command of general Porter, which was destined to turn the enemy's right, having arrived near the British entrenchments, were ordered to advance and commence the action. Passing down the ravine, Brown judged from the report of the musquetry that the action had commenced. Hastening, therefore, to general Miller, he directed him to seize the moment, and pierce the enemy's entrenchments between the batteries No. 2 and 3. These orders were promptly and ably executed. Within 30 minutes after the first gun was fired, batteries No. 2 and 3, the enemy's line of entrenchments, and his two block-houses, were in possession of the Americans.

Soon after, battery No. 1 was abandoned by the British. The

guns in each were then spiked or otherwise destroyed, and the magazine of No. 3 was blown up.

A few minutes before the explosion, the reserve had been ordered up under general Ripley, and as soon as he arrived on the ground, he was ordered to strengthen the front line, which was then engaged with the enemy, in order to protect the detachments employed in demolishing the captured works. While forming arrangements for acting on the enemy's camp during the moment of panic, Ripley received a severe wound. By this time, however, the object of the sortie being accomplished beyond the most sanguine expectations, general Miller had ordered the troops on the right to fall back; and, observing this movement, Brown sent his staff along the line to call in the other corps. Within a few minutes they retired from the ravine, and thence to the camp.

Thus, says general Brown, in his dispatch, 1000 regulars and an equal portion of militia, in one hour of close action, blasted the hopes of the enemy, destroyed the fruits of fifty days' labour, and diminished his effective force 1000 men at least.

In their official account of this sortie, the British published no returns of their loss, but from their vigorous resistance it must no doubt have been very great. Their loss in prisoners was 385. On the part of the Americans the killed amounted to 83, the wounded to 216, and the missing to a like number.

A few days after this battle the British raised the siege, and retreated behind the Chippewa. Meanwhile the reinforcements from Plattsburg arrived at Sackett's Harbour, and after a few days rest proceeded to the Niagara. They crossed that river on the ninth of October, when general Izard, being the senior officer, superceded general Brown in the command. On the 14th the army moved from Fort Erie, with the design of bringing the enemy to action. An attempt was made to dispute the passage of a creek at Chippewa plains, but the American artillery soon compelled the enemy to retire to their fortified camp, when attempts were repeatedly made to draw them out the following day, but without effect. A partial engagement took place on the 19th, which closed the campaign on this peninsula.

General Bissell marched from Black Creek on the morning of the 18th, with a body of about 900 men, for the purpose of seizing some provisions intended for the British troops. After driving before them a picket, of which they made the commanding officer prisoner, they encamped for the night, in the course of which the advanced picket was attacked by two companies of the Glengary light infantry, who were repulsed with loss. Next morning Bissell was attacked by a corps of about 1200 men, commanded by the marquis of Tweedale. The light corps and riflemen sustained the whole fire for about fifteen minutes, with the greatest gallantry, until the other troops were formed, and brought to their support.

The 5th regiment, under colonel Pinckney, was ordered to skirt the woods and turn the right flank of the enemy; the 14th, under major Bernard, to form in front, and advance to the support of the light troops; the 15th and 16th regiments were ordered to act as circumstances might require. The well-directed fire of the light corps, and the charge of the 14th, soon compelled the enemy to give ground; and on discovering that his right flank was turned by the 5th, he retreated in the utmost confusion, leaving some killed, wounded, and prisoners behind. Bissell pursued them to a ravine, some distance from the scene where the action commenced. Not knowing the ground, he did not think proper to push them further, but soon after, the country being reconnoitered, it was discovered that they had retreated to their strong holds. A large quantity of grain was found and destroyed; and, after burying the few soldiers who fell, and the enemy's dead who were left on the ground, the detachment returned to camp. The killed, wounded, and missing in this affair amounted to 67, of whom 12 were killed.

Before leaving the affairs on this frontier, it will be proper to mention the expedition of mounted men under general M'Arthur, which proceeded from Detroit towards Burlington Heights, for the purpose of destroying the resources of general Drummond's army, and paralising any efforts which might be made against Detroit during the winter.

The detachment, consisting of about 720 Ohio and Kentucky volunteers, and a few Indians, left Detroit about the end of October. To mask the object of the expedition, a movement round lake St. Clair was rendered absolutely necessary. This circuit caused the troops to be exposed to many difficulties and hardships in wading frequently along the shores of the lake; in the passage of several deep and rapid rivers, sometimes without boats, and on all occasions encountering swamps; yet, notwithstanding these obstacles, such was the secrecy and rapidity of the expedition, that the detachment was enabled to enter the town of Oxford, 140 miles in the enemy's country, before the inhabitants were apprised that a force was approaching.

On the succeeding day, the detachment proceeded to Bur-

ford, where the militia had been embodied in expectation of
this expedition; but it was found that they had retreated, a few
hours before, to Malcolm's mills, where they were joined by
the militia from Long Point.

It was M'Arthur's intention to cross Grand River, as soon
as possible, without regarding the militia collected at Malcolm's
mills, and attack Burlington.   But to his great mortification,
the river was found high and rapid from the late excessive
rains.   Here also the news reached him that the American
troops had re-crossed the Niagara, leaving only a strong garrison in Fort Erie.   These and other considerations presented
serious objections to any attempt to pass the river; it was
therefore determined to attack and defeat, or disperse the militia at Malcolm's mills, move down the Long Point road through
the Grand River settlement, destroy the valuable mills in that
quarter, and then return to the American territory, either by a
movement across Grand River at the mouth, to Fort Erie, or
along Talbot-street to the Thames.

To that effect, a detachment was directed to remain and engage the attention of the enemy, whilst the principal force
should be withdrawn and marched to Malcolm's mills.   The
enemy, consisting of four or five hundred militia and a few Indians, was found fortified on commanding ground beyond a
creek, deep and difficult of passage, except at a bridge immediately in front of their works, which had been destroyed.   Arrangements were made for a joint attack on the fort and rear.
The Ohio troops, with the advance guard and Indians, were accordingly thrown across the creek under cover of a thick wood,
to approach the enemy in rear, whilst the Kentucky troops
were to attack in front, as soon as the attention of the enemy
was engaged by the attack in the rear.   The enemy would
have been completely surprised and captured, had not an unfortunate yell by the Indians announced the approach of the
detachment destined to attack their rear; they were, however,
defeated and dispersed, with the loss, in the skirmishes on that
day, of one captain and seventeen privates killed, nine privates
wounded, and three captains, five subalterns, and one hundred
and three privates made prisoners; whilst the loss of the Americans was only one killed and six wounded.   Early next morning the enemy were pursued on the road to Dover, many made
prisoners, and five valuable mills destroyed.

Apprehensive that the troops could not be supplied on the
route to Fort Erie, and that difficulties would occur in the passage of Grand River, together with the uncertainty which existed as to the position of general Izard's army, M'Arthur was

induced to return to Detroit by the way of Talbot-street and the Thames, which was happily effected on the 17th of November.

Thus this active body of men penetrated two hundred miles into the enemy's territory, destroyed two hundred stand of arms, together with five of their most valuable mills; paroled or dispersed the greater portion of the efficient militia of that part of Upper Canada west of Grand River; and then returned in safety to Detroit, with the loss of only one man.

Meanwhile, the approach of winter rendering it necessary for the army to retire to comfortable quarters, general Izard crossed the major part of his troops into the American territory, leaving a garrison in Erie, which also was soon after withdrawn.

Thus ended a third campaign in Upper Canada without a single important conquest being secured. The operations of the army under Brown, however, are not to be considered as worthless and inefficient. They have, in the most complete manner, effaced the stain thrown on the army by the imbecile efforts of its infancy, and have cast a lustre on the American name, by a series of the most brilliant victories, over troops heretofore considered matchless. Nor ought we to lose sight of the effect produced by these events on the country at large, actively engaged as was almost every citizen, in repelling, or in preparing to repel, the invaders of their homes. This effect was without doubt extensively beneficial; and perhaps it may not be improper to ascribe to Brown and his gallant companions in arms a part of that renown which the arms of the United States have acquired by the defeat, in almost every instance, of the powerful forces with which it has been assailed.

The British squadron in the Chesapeake, under admiral Cockburn, still continued their system of plunder and devastation along the coasts of the bay, and the numerous rivers of which it forms the estuary. The principal, if not the only naval protection to this exposed coast, consisted of the flotilla under commodore Barney, but this presented but a very imperfect protection to this extensive line of frontier.

On the 1st of June, the flotilla, making sail from the mouth of the Patuxent, with the wind from the northward, discovered two of the enemy's schooners down the bay. The schooners made signals and fired guns; when a large ship was seen getting under way, which dispatched a number of barges to the assistance of the schooners. Unfortunately at this time the wind shifted, which brought the ship to windward, and Barney

P

was thus forced to put back into the Patuxent, whither he was followed by a seventy-four, three schooners, and seven barges with a fresh wind. But the gun-boats being in the rear, particularly one which was laden with provisions, Barney soon found it necessary to hazard an engagement to prevent their capture. Accordingly, bringing his sloop and one of the gun-boats to an anchor, he sent men on board of the provision boat, to assist in bringing her in, and made signals for his barges to return and join him. At this moment his sloop and gun-boat opened a fire on a schooner of the enemy, which was leading in, with a number of barges. She immediately bore up, and got her boats ahead to tow her off, seeing which, the American barges rowed down upon her and the other schooners, and gave them a number of shot at long distance. But the chase was soon given up, and the flotilla returned to port. During the firing, a British barge threw a number of rockets, which did no execution.

On the 8th, the enemy being reinforced with a razee and a sloop of war brig, the flotilla moved up the Patuxent to the mouth of St. Leonard's creek, and on being followed by the British squadron, they moved up the creek about two miles, and moored in line, abreast, across the channel, where they prepared for action. The creek not being accessible to ships; the barges of the enemy, fifteen in number, were dispatched against the flotilla. As they approached, they advanced a rocket barge, at which several shot were fired by the flotilla, but they fell short, as rockets can be thrown a greater distance than shot. Barney, therefore, got his barges, thirteen in number, under weigh, and leaving the sloop and gun-boats at anchor, they rowed down upon the enemy, who precipitately fled from their position. The pursuit was continued till the flotilla came near the enemy's shipping, when, after firing a few shot, the American barges returned to their moorings. In the afternoon, the British barges again came up, again threw rockets, and were again pursued out of the creek.

During these encounters, the British are said to have suffered considerably. The large schooner was nearly destroyed, having several shot through her at the water's edge; her deck torn up, gun dismounted, and mainmast nearly cut off about half way up, and otherwise much cut. They ran her ashore to prevent her sinking. The commodore's boat was cut in two; a shot went through the rocket boat; one of the small schooners, carrying two thirty-two pounders, had a shot which raked her from aft forward. The boats generally suffered, but their loss was not ascertained.

On the 15th, the enemy having received further reinforcements, sent a detachment of boats up the river, which took possession of Benedict and Marlborough, the latter only 18 miles from Washington. After plundering a quantity of stock, and burning the tobacco warehouses, which, according to the British statement, contained 2500 hogsheads of tobacco, they returned to their ships.

Shortly after this affair, in order to extricate the flotilla from its confined situation, a battery was hastily thrown up on a point of land at the junction of St. Leonard's creek and the Patuxent, and a combined attack being made by the flotilla and a small body of infantry and artillery, the British squadron was forced to drop down the Patuxent, which enabled commodore Barney to pass his flotilla up that river.

At this time no apprehension was entertained of any serious attack being made on any important point by the enemy's forces in the Chesapeake. But towards the end of June, certain intelligence was received of the complete success of the allies in the subjugation of France, and government were led to believe, as well from communications received from our ministers abroad, as from the tone of the British prints, that a powerful force was about to be sent to the United States. A variety of considerations pointed to Washington City and Baltimore as prominent objects of attack.

Immediate measures of defence had therefore become necessary; and accordingly a new military district was created, embracing the state of Maryland, the District of Columbia, and that part of Virginia lying between the Rappahannock and Potomack, the command of which was given to general Winder. A requisition was made on certain states for a corps of 93,500 militia, and the executive of each state was requested to detach and hold in readiness for immediate service their respective quotas. Of that requisition, 2000 effectives from the quota of Virginia; 5000 from that of Pennsylvania; 6000, the whole quota of Maryland; and 2000, the estimated number of the militia of the District of Columbia, were put at the disposition of general Winder, making an aggregate of 15,000, exclusive of about 1000 regulars. But this force, which had it been well organized, and ready to meet the foe at any threatened point, would have been amply sufficient for defence, totally failed in the hour of need. From the tardiness incident to the present imperfect militia system of the United States, the Virginia and Pennsylvania troops could not be organized in time to meet the enemy, although the battle which sealed the fate of Washington did not take place till a month after they were called out. And even of the Maryland militia, nearly one half joined the army but half an hour before the action. A considerable part of this delay was occasioned by general Winder's not recieving the authority to call out the state troops for some time after it was issued, owing to his being constantly in motion at this period, in order to acquire a complete knowledge of the topography of the district.

During the month of July, the enemy's fleet ascended both the Potomack and Patuxent, and committed great depredations, particularly on the former river. Admiral Cochrane arrived in the Chesapeake in the beginning of August, and on the 17th, the fleet, then in great force, was joined by admiral Malcolm, with the expedition from Bermuda, destined against Baltimore and Washington.

The circumstance of Barney's flotilla having taken shelter at the head of the Patuxent proved extremely favourable to an attack on Washington, as it masked the intention of the enemy. This attack, therefore, being determined on, Cochrane moved his squadron up the river. Previously to his entering the Patuxent, however, he detached captain Gordon, with a number of ships and bombs to the Potomack, to bombard fort Warburton, with a view of destroying that fort, and opening a free communication above, as well as to cover the retreat of the army, should its return by the Bladensburg road be found too hazardous. Sir Peter Parker, with the Menelaus and some small vessels, was sent up the Chesapeake to make a diversion in that quarter. The remainder of the naval force, and the troops, moved up the Patuxent to Benedict, where the army was landed upon the 19th and 20th.

So soon as the necessary provisions and stores could be assembled and arranged, major-general Ross, with his army, moved towards Nottingham, while the British flotilla, consisting of the armed launches, pinnaces, barges, and other boats of the fleet, under admiral Cockburn, passed up the river, keeping on the right flank of the army, for the double purpose of supplying it with provisions, and, if necessary, of passing it over to the left bank of the river, which secured a safe retreat to the ships, should it be judged necessary. The army reached Nottingham on the 21st, and the following day arrived at Marlborough. The flotilla, keeping pace with the army, arrived within sight of Barney's flotilla on the 22d. It was instantly set on fire by a small party of sailors who had been left for that purpose, the commodore having previously joined general Winder with the greater part of his force. The flotilla soon blew up, excepting one vessel, which fell into the hands of the enemy.

While a large regular army, well disciplined and accoutred, accompanied with a strong naval force, was thus within 16 miles of the American capital, the principal part of the force destined to defend it had not arrived, and a considerable portion still remained at their homes. The actual force under general Winder only amounted to about 3000 men, of whom 1400 were regulars, including the marines and sea-fencibles under commodore Barney; the remainder were volunteers and militia, principally from the District of Columbia. The force of the enemy at this time was variously estimated. The best opinion made them from 5000 to 7000. They were without cavalry, and had only two small field-pieces and one howitzer, drawn by men. Four hundred of the American troops were cavalry, and they had 17 pieces of artillery.

On the afternoon of the 23d the British army again set out, and after some skirmishing with the American advance, in which the latter were compelled to retreat, bivouacked for the night five miles in advance of Marlborough. Towards sunset, general Winder ordered his troops to retreat to Washington, that he might effect a union of his whole forces. To this he was also induced by the fear of a night attack, from the superiority of the enemy, and want of discipline in his troops, and knowing that in such an attack his superiority in artillery could not be used.

Meanwhile general Stansbury arrived at Bladensburg on the 22d with about 1300 Baltimore militia, and on the evening of the 23d he was joined by colonel Sterret with another militia regiment from Baltimore, about 500 strong, a rifle battalion of about 150 men, and two companies of volunteer artillery, also about 150 strong; making Stansbury's whole force about 2100. Most of these troops were extremely fatigued by their march from Baltimore.

General Stansbury encamped during the night of the 23d on a hill near Bladensburg, with the intention of attacking the enemy at reveille next morning, in compliance with previous orders from general Winder. Near midnight, a firing from the advanced pickets on the road by which the enemy was expected, caused the troops to be prepared for action, and they were kept under arms till after two the following morning; and hardly had they again retired to their tents, when information was received from general Winder that he had retreated to the city by the Eastern branch bridge. As this movement of Winder exposed both the rear and right flank of Stansbury's troops, and his officers, whom he immediately consulted, were unanimous in opinion that his situation on the hill could not be defended with the force then under his command, worn down with hunger and fatigue as they were, it was considered indispensably necessary that the troops should immediately retire across the bridge at Bladensburg, and take a position which they could defend on the road between that place and the city. Orders were therefore instantly given to strike tents and prepare to march. In about thirty minutes, without noise or confusion, the whole were in motion, and about half past three in the morning passed the bridge at Bladensburg, which leads to the city of Washington. Securing the rear from surprise, the troops halted in the road till the approach of day, with a view of finding some place where water could be had, that the men might partake of some refreshment.

Early in the morning of the 24th, the troops were again put in motion towards the city, with a view of taking a stand on some more favourable ground for defence, when orders were received from general Winder to give the enemy battle at Bladensburg, should he move that way, and that he would join, if necessary. Stansbury immediately ordered his troops to retrace their steps to Bladensburg, and took a position to the west of that place, in an orchard on the left of the Washington road. Here his artillery, consisting of six six-pounders, posted themselves behind a small breastwork of earth, which had been lately thrown up, and the riflemen and infantry were posted in the rear and to the left, so as to protect the position. This battery commanded the pass into Bladensburg, and the bridge leading to Washington.

Meanwile general Winder's troops, including commodore Barney's command, made a rapid march from Washington, and arrived upon the ground just as the enemy made their appearance behind Bladensburg. Colonel Beal, with about 800 militia from Annapolis, had crossed the bridge about half an hour before, and posted himself on the right of the Washington road. The force which had arrived from the city was formed in a second line on the right and left of the road in the rear of Stansbury's and Beall's command, the heavy artillery under commodore Barney being posted on or near the road.

About half after 12, while the second line was forming, the enemy approached, and the battle commenced. The Baltimore artillery opened their fire, and dispersed the enemy's light troops now advancing along the street of the village, who took a temporary cover behind the houses and trees, in loose order, and presented objects only occasionally for the fire of the cannon. The enemy then commenced throwing his rockets, and his light troops began to concentrate near the bridge, and to press across it and the river, which was fordable above. The Baltimore riflemen now united with the fire of the battery; and for some time with considerable effect. The enemy's column was not only dispersed while in the street, but while approaching the bridge they were thrown into some confusion, and the British officers were seen exerting themselves to press the soldiers on. Having now gained the bridge, the enemy passed it rapidly, and immediately flanked, formed the line, and advanced steadily on, which compelled the artillery and riflemen to give way. But they were soon rallied, and united with the other Baltimore troops at a small distance in the rear of their first position. One of the pieces of artillery was abandoned and spiked.

A company of volunteer artillery from the city, under the command of captain Burch, and a small detachment near it, now opened a cross fire on the enemy, who were partially sheltered by the trees of an orchard, and kept up a galling fire on part of the American line. Colonel Sterret, with one of the Baltimore regiments, was ordered to advance, and made a prompt movement until ordered to halt; for at this moment the other two Baltimore regiments were thrown into confusion by the rockets of the enemy, and began to give way. In a few minutes they took to flight, in defiance of all the exertions of generals Winder and Stansbury and other officers. Burch's artillery and Sterret's regiment remained firm, until, being out-flanked, they were ordered to retreat, with a view of reforming at a small distance in the rear. But instead of retiring in order, the militia regiment retreated in disorder and confusion. Thus was the first line, which consisted almost exclusively of Baltimore militia, totally routed and put to flight.

On the right, colonels Beall and Hood, commanding the Annapolis militia, had thrown forward a small detachment, under colonel Kramer. After maintaining their ground for some time with considerable injury to the enemy, this advance was driven back on the main body. Their retreat exposed the enemy's column in the road to the city artillery, under major Peter, which continued an animated discharge on them till they came in contact with commodore Barney's command. Here the enemy met the greatest resistance, and sustained the greatest loss, while advancing upon the retreating line. When the British came in full view, and in a heavy column in the main road, Barney ordered an eighteen pounder to be opened upon them, which completely cleared the road, and repulsed them. In several attempts to rally and advance, the enemy

were again repulsed, which induced them to flank to the right
of the American line in an open field. Here three twelve-
pounders opened upon them, and the flotilla men acted as infantry with considerable effect. The enemy continued flanking to the right, and pressed upon the Annapolis militia, which
gave way after three or four rounds of ineffectual fire, while
colonel Beall and other officers attempted to rally the men upon their high position. Commodore Barney's command now
had the whole force of the enemy to contend with. The British never again, however, attempted to appear in force in front,
but continuing to outflank, pushed forward a few scattering
sharp-shooters, by whom Barney was wounded, and several of
his officers killed or wounded. Being now completely out-
flanked on both sides, the ammunition-waggons having gone off
in disorder, and that which the marines and flotilla men had,
being exhausted, Barney ordered a retreat; in consequence of
his wound, he himself was made prisoner. His pieces fell into
the hands of the enemy.

The Georgetown and city militia, and the few regulars which
were on the field, still remained firm; but being now also out-
flanked, they were ordered by general Winder to retreat, which
was effected with as much order as the nature of the ground
would permit. After retiring five or six hundred paces, they
were halted and formed, but were again ordered to retreat, and
to collect and form on the height near the capitol. Here they
were joined by a regiment of Virginia militia, who had arrived
in the city the preceding evening, but had been detained there
by some difficulties which had arisen in furnishing them with
arms and ammunition.

General Winder had endeavoured to direct the retreat of
the Baltimore troops towards the city, but from the confusion
in which they fled, was not able to effect it, and they directed
their course northwardly towards Montgomery court-house.—
This wrong direction to their course was pincipally caused
by their ignorance of there being a second line of troops behind them, general Winder's forces having arrived just as the
action commenced.

The British estimated their loss in this battle at 64 killed,
and 185 wounded. The loss of the Americans was estimated
by the superintending surgeon at 10 or 12 killed, and about 30
wounded some of whom afterwards died. The most probable
estimate of the British force made it about 4500; of the American 6000; but it must be recollected that the enemy's troops
were all regulars, who had seen service, and were led by able
officers of great experience, while the American troops were

all militia, with the exception of a few hundred seamen and regulars; that one half of them were not collected together till the day before the engagement, and about 800 did not arrive till a few minutes before its commencement; that from the uncertainty whether Baltimore, the city of Washington, or Fort Washington, would be selected as the point of attack, it was necessary that the troops should frequently change their positions, owing to which, and to alarms causlessly excited on the night of the 23d, they were all much fatigued, and many of them nearly exhausted, at the time when the hostile army was crossing the bridge; and finally, that the officers commanding the troops were generally unknown to general Winder, and but a very small number of them had enjoyed the benefit of military instruction or experience. When these circumstances are taken into consideration, we think we shall not hazard much in asserting, now that the violent feelings of the moment have subsided, that the American militia rather gained than lost honour on the field of Bladensburg. The Baltimore troops fought gallantly, until forced to retreat by their flanks being turned.—While retreating, by order of their commander, they were thrown into confusion by a new mode of warfare, of which the effects were to them totally unknown.* The bravery of Barney's command needs no comment, and the orderly retreat of the Annapolis and District of Columbia militia, in the face of a regular army of superior numbers, (now that the Baltimore troops had dispersed) is above all praise.

A remarkable circumstance attendant on this battle was the presence of the American president and heads of departments. They retreated with the second line of troops to Washington, where a consultation was held with the commanding general as to the propriety of making a stand on the heights near the capitol, or in the capitol itself. General Winder stated, that the diminution of his force was such as to render it impossible to place his troops in a position which would prevent the enemy from taking him on the flanks as well as in front; and that no reasonable hope could be entertained, that any of the troops could be relied on to make a resistance as desperate as necessary, in an isolated building, which could not be supported by a sufficiency of troops without: indeed it would have taken nearly the whole of the troops, he said, to have sufficiently filled

* *Some of the finest troops of France were thrown into confusion by the rocket brigade at the battle of Leipsic.*

the two wings,* which would have left the enemy masters of every other part of the city, and given him the opportunity, without risk, in 24 hours to have starved them into a surrender. The objection equally applied to the occupation of any particular part of the city. It was accordingly determined to retire through Georgetown, and take post on the heights in the rear of that place, with a view of collecting together the whole of the forces.

It is impossible, says the commander of the militia of the district, in his dispatch, to do justice to the anguish evinced by the troops of Washington and Georgetown, on the receipt of this order. The idea of leaving their families, their houses, and their homes, at the mercy of an enraged enemy, was insupportable. To preserve that order which was maintained during the retreat, was now no longer practicable. As they retired through Washington and Georgetown, numbers were obtaining and taking leave to visit their homes, and again rejoining; and with ranks thus broken and scattered, they halted at night on the heights near Tenly Town, and on the ensuing day assembled at Montgomery court-house.

Meanwhile general Ross, after halting his army a short time for refreshment, pushed on towards Washington, where he arrived unmolested about eight in the evening. Having stationed his main body on the heights about a mile and a half east of the capitol, he led his advance, consisting of about 700 men, into the deserted city.

Washington, though denominated a city, and though the seat of the federal government, possesses but an inconsiderable population, which is sparely scattered over an extensive scite: The capitol stands near the centre of the city; the president's palace and navy yard are each distant about a mile from that building, in opposite directions. Around each of these situations, stands what would elsewhere be denominated a village, and a few scattering rows of buildings have been erected on the avenue leading from the capitol to the president's house, and thence to Georgetown, each about a mile in length. The number of houses in the city does not exceed nine hundred; its inhabitants amount to about eight thousand. The capitol and the president's house are built of a beautiful white free-

---

* *The two wings constituted the whole of the capitol, the central part of the building never having been erected. The wings were connected by a slight wooden gallery.*

stone, and have been deservedly esteemed the finest specimens of architecture in the United States, if not upon the continent. The capitol was in an unfinished state, the two wings only having been erected; the upper part of the north wing contained the senate chamber with the committee rooms and office containing their archieves, and the congressional library, a valuable collection of books; in the lower part was the hall of the Supreme Court of the United States. The southern wing was exclusively devoted to the hall of the house of representatives and their necessary offices, the whole of the upper part being occupied by the hall and its galleries.

Washington, thus abandoned to the British arms, presented now a most deplorable scene. Though surrendered without the slightest opposition, and though totally without fortifications, the British naval and military commanders (admiral Cockburn and general Ross) immediately issued orders for, and personally superintended the conflagration of the public buildings, with all the testimonials of taste and literature which they contained. The capitol and the president's house, together with the costly and extensive buildings erected for the accommodation of the principal officers of government in the transaction of public business, were, on the memorable night of the 24th of August, consigned to the flames. The large hotel on the capitol hill, the great bridge across the Potomac, and the private rope-walks, shared the same fate.

A consultation had been held by the president and the heads of departments on the subject of the navy yard, on the morning preceding the battle of Bladensburg. The secretary of the navy described the situation of the public vessels, and the nature of the public property, at that establishment; the vast importance of the supplies, and of the shipping, to the enemy, particularly as there appeared to be no doubt of his squadron forming a junction with his army, should it succeed in the conquest of the capitol (general Winder having distinctly stated on the same morning, that Fort Washington could not be defended); and as, in this event nothing could be more clear than that he would first plunder, and then destroy the building and improvements; or, if unable to carry off the plunder and the shipping, he would destroy the whole. And if the junction should be formed, it would be a strong inducement to the enemy to remain, in order to launch the new frigate, which the force at his command would accomplish in four or five days. He would then carry off the whole of the public stores and shipping, and destroy the establishment; and, in the mean time, greatly extend the field of his plunder and devastation.

Thus, in either case, whether the junction was formed, or whether the army alone entered the city, the loss or destruction of the whole of the public property at the navy yard was certain.   It was, therefore, determined, as the result of this consultation, that the public shipping, and naval and military stores, and provisions at the navy yard, should be destroyed, in the event of the enemy's obtaining possession of the city.   Agreeably to this determination, the trains, which had been previously laid, were fired on the approach of the enemy, and the public buildings, stores, and vessels were soon wrapped in flames, and were all destroyed, excepting the new schooner Lynx, which escaped in an extraordinary manner.   The issuing store of the yard, and its contents, which had escaped the original conflagration, were soon after totally destroyed by the enemy.

The only loss which the enemy sustained in the city was at Greenleaf's point.   A detachment was sent down to destroy it, and in the midst of their devastations, a firebrand having been thrown into a dry well in which a quantity of powder had been previously hidden, it exploded with great violence, by which a number of lives were lost.

Nearly the whole of the male population having joined the army, a great number of houses were broken open and plundered by the blacks and a few disorderly inhabitants.   The conduct of the British in general was orderly.*

The utmost efforts of general Winder were now devoted to collect his troops, and to prepare them to move down toward the city, and hang upon and strike at the enemy whenever an opportunity occured.   The next morning, however, intelligence was received that the enemy had moved from Washington the preceding night, and was in full march for Baltimore. Winder accordingly advanced as rapidly as was practicable to that city; but on his arrival at Snell's bridge, on the Patuxent, Winder learned that the enemy was proceeding to Marlborough, and not toward Baltimore.

Having completed the destruction of the public buildings in the course of the 25th, the British left the city at nine

---

* The famous (or rather infamous) Cockburn must be excepted from this remark.   He so far laid aside the dignity of a British admiral as meanly to revenge himself on the property of a printer, who, he said, had been giving him some hard rubs. A file of soldiers were employed to ransack his office and destroy his types and presses.   What a magnanimous spectacle ! what a chivalrous spirit was here displayed!

that night, and by a rapid march reached Marlborough in the course of the next day. On the evening of the 29th they reached Benedict, and re-embarked the following day.

Meanwhile captain Gordon proceeded up the Potomac with his squadron, consisting of two frigates, two bomb-vessels, two rocket-ships, and a schooner. Owing to the shoals, and contrary winds, they were not able to reach Fort Washington, about fifteen miles below the city, until the evening of the 27th, two days after the army under Ross had commenced their retreat. The bomb-ships immediately began to bombard the fort; but on the bursting of the first shell, the garrison was observed to retreat, and in a short time, to the great surprise of the British commander, the fort was blown up.

When the British army first left the Patuxent, their destination could not be foretold by general Winder. Baltimore, Fort Washington, and the Federal city seemed equally threatened. Fort Washington, which commands the Potomac, was considered almost impregnable to any attack by water, though too weak to be defended against any large force by land. Captain Dyson, the commander, therefore, was instructed, in case the British army should approach his rear, to blow up the fort, and proceed with his command across the Potomac. But nothing was farther from the intention of general Winder than that this important post should be deserted, on being attacked by a naval force.*

Nothing was now left to oppose the progress of the British squadron, and they proceeded slowly up the river to Alexandria, with their barges employed in sounding in advance.

On the day preceding the battle of Bladensburg, a committee of vigilance, which had been appointed by the inhabitants to watch over the safety of Alexandria, in this time of peril, despairing, they allege, of receiving any assistance from the general government, and having information of the rapid approach of the enemy towards the capital by land, and that their squadron was approaching Alexandria by water, deemed it

---

* *Captain Dyson alledged, in justification, that he had learnt that the enemy had been reinforced at Benedict, 2000 strong, and that they were on their march to co-operate with the fleet, in addition to the force which left the city. But surely he should not have deserted his post on a vague rumour, which this must have been. He was shortly after tried by a court-martial, and dismissed the service.*

Q

their duty to recommend to the common council the passage of a resolution, that in case the British vessels should pass the fort, or their forces approach the town by land, and there should be no sufficient force to oppose them, with any reasonable prospect of success, they should appoint a committee to carry a flag to the officer commanding the enemy's force about to attack the town, and to procure the best terms in their power for the safety of persons, houses, and property. This resolution was unanimously adopted by the common council, and on the arrival of the British at Washington, a flag was sent to the British commander there, to know what treatment might be expected from him, in case his troops should approach Alexandria, and should succeed in obtaining possession of the town. The deputation were assured by admiral Cockburn, that private property of all descriptions should be respected; that it was probable that fresh provisions and some flour might be wanted, but that whatever they did take should be paid for.

After the blowing up of Fort Washington a similar deputation was dispatched to the naval commander. But Gordon had other intentions than those avowed by Cockburn. He would give no reply until he had placed his shipping in such a position before the town, as would ensure assent to the hard terms he had decided to enforce. These were, the surrender of all naval and ordnance stores, public and private, and all the shipping and merchandise of the town. Gordon having arranged his vessels along the town, the defenceless inhabitants were forced to submit; and the plunderers took possession of three ships, three brigs, several bay and river craft, 16,000 barrels of flour, 1000 hogsheads of tobacco, 150 bales of cotton, and wine, sugar, and other articles to the value of about 5000 dollars.

But though Gordon, with his buccaneering crew, had thus taken possession of Alexandria, without a single gun being fired against him, he was not destined to carry off his booty entirely unmolested. General Hungerford arrived near Alexandria with the Virginia militia, and commodores Rodgers, Porter, and Perry, with a detachment of sailors from Baltimore. It was not deemed proper to disturb the enemy at Alexandria, as that would probably cause the destruction of the place. Commodore Porter, therefore, proceeded down the river, and threw up an entrenchment on a bluff, not far from the ruins of the fort, on the opposite side of the river; and commodore Perry threw up another a little below. The arrival of a small despatch vessel, which had to fight its way past Porter's battery, convinced Gordon he had no time to lose, and he therefore precipitately left Alexandria, without waiting to destroy the stores which he had not the means of carrying off.

To endeavour to clear the passage, Gordon first sent down a bomb-ship and two barges, one carrying a long thirty-two pounder, the other a mortar. These vessels commenced their operations on Porter's battery, the bomb-ship throwing shells in front, out of the reach of shot, the barges flanking on the right.

When the small vessel passed upwards, the preceding day, Porter had only two small four-pounders, but the same evening two eighteen pounders reached his position. His force consisted principally of sailors; some navy and militia officers and private citizens acted as volunteers. General Hungerford's militia, who were ordered to co-operate, were stationed in the woods on each side of the battery, in such positions as would effectually protect its rear, in the event of the enemy's landing. These positions, it was supposed, would have enabled them to clear the enemy's decks with their musquetry, and in a great measure serve to divert his fire from the battery, while the thick woods on the high bank would conceal them from view.

The firing lasted all day without intermission; several shells fell near, and burst over the battery, but this had no other effect than to accustom the militia to the danger. In the afternoon, Porter took an eighteen pounder to a more advanced point, about a mile distant, and commenced a fire on the bomb-ship, which did so much execution as to draw on him the fire of all the vessels, including a schooner and an eighteen gun brig which had dropped down that day.

The following day (August 3) Gordon left Alexandria with his prizes, which he anchored above the battery, out of the reach of the cannon. The bombarding vessels were reinforced by another bomb-ship, and a sloop of war fitted up as a rocket ship. The latter anchoring within reach of the battery, Porter was enabled to play on her with great effect, and compelled her to change her position. All this day and the succeeding night, the enemy kept up a brisk fire of shot, shells, and rockets.

Within a few hours of the departure of the enemy, commodore Rodgers arrived at Alexandria from above, with three small fire-vessels, under the protection of four barges or cutters manned with about 60 seamen armed with muskets. He immediately proceeded to attack two frigates and a bomb-ship, which lay about two miles below. The failure of the wind, just as they were within reach of the enemy, prevented any beneficial effect being produced. On their approach, the whole of the enemy's boats were put in motion. Some were employed in towing off the fire-vessels, and the remainder in pursuit of Rodgers' cutters. They did not, however, venture to come within musket shot, though much superior both in force and numbers, but continued at a distance firing their great guns for about half an hour, and then retired to their ships.

The following day another fire-vessel was prepared; but it being calm, Rodgers ordered his lieutenant and the four cutters to proceed with a lighter, carrying an eighteen pounder, to attack a bomb-ship, which, in the anxiety of the enemy to get below the works which Porter and Perry had thrown up, had been left exposed to attack. At sunset, however, just as he was about to give orders to attack the bomb, Rodgers discovered one of the enemy's frigates behind a point, which obliged him to relinquish this determination, and give orders to proceed across to the Virginia shore, to haul up the boats, and place the lighter in a situation to be defended against the barges of the enemy.

About nine o'clock at night, Rodgers again shifted his situation to the opposite shore, owing to a man being seized under suspicious circumstances on the beach, near a small boat, about a mile above the enemy's headmost ship. The cutters were now hauled up, the lighter placed in an advantageous position, and the seamen on the top of a cliff overlooking the river. Scarcely had this arrangement been completed, when an attack was made by all the enemy's barges. It was met with great intrepidity, the enemy were thrown into confusion, and driven back with loss. The only injury which Rodgers sustained, was one man wounded on board the lighter.

The work at Porter's battery continued to go on; five light field-pieces, from four to six pounders, arrived and were planted, and hopes were entertained of soon receiving some long thirty-two pounders from Washington; a furnace was built for hot shot, and time only appeared necessary to make the battery formidable. The whole of the 4th and 5th, an incessant fire was kept up by the enemy night and day. He had once attempted landing at night, it is supposed with an intention of spiking the guns of the battery, but was repulsed by the picket guard. The plan of annoying him by advancing guns was now adopted with better effect than before. The rocket-ship lying close in shore, was much cut up by a twelve-pounder and two sixes carried to a point; scarcely a shot missed its hull, and for one hour the fire of all the enemy's force was drawn to this point.

The want of ammunition now caused a suspension of firing at the battery at a most unfortunate moment, just as commodore Rodgers was approaching with his last fire-ship. The enemy being thus enabled to direct the whole of their attention towards him, Rodgers was forced to fire the vessel prematurely, and order his boats to retire, to prevent their being taken possession of by the numerous barges of the enemy.

Some thirty-two pounders now arrived at the battery, and carpenters were employed to make carriages. Two mortars, a large quantity of ammunition, and an abundance of shot and shells were also received; two barges were equipping, and every thing promised that the battery would speedily be put in a proper state for annoying the enemy. In the evening two frigates anchored above, making the whole force of the enemy opposed to the battery three frigates, three bomb-ships, a sloop of war, a brig, a schooner, and two barges, carrying altogether 173 guns. The guns mounted in the battery were three 18 pounders, two 12 pounders, six 9 pounders, and two fours. The two mortars were without carriages, as were all the thirty-two's, for notwithstanding every effort was made, both at Washington and on the spot, they could not be completed in time.

On the morning of the 6th, the enemy showing a disposition to move, intelligence to that effect was sent to general Hungerford, and preparations made to meet them at the battery with hot shot. About 12 o'clock the two frigates got under way, with a fair wind and tide, and stood down; the rocket-sloop, bomb-vessels, brig, schooner, and prizes followed in succession, the gun-boats endeavouring to flank the battery on the right. Porter immediately dispatched an officer to general Hungerford, to request him to take the position agreed upon in the woods on the heights; but from the distance of his camp, and the quick approach of the enemy, he was unable to march before the firing commenced, and, after that period, it was rendered impossible, from the vast quantities of shot, shells, and rockets which were showered over the hills and fell among his troops.

As the enemy approached, a well-directed fire was kept up from the battery with hot and cold shot. The officers and men stood the broadsides of the ships with unparalleled firmness. But from the militia not making their appearance, the whole of the enemy's fire was directed at the battery. Porter, therefore, finding that in a few minutes all the enemy's force would be brought to bear on him, and entertaining no hopes of preventing his passing, as some of his men had already been killed and wounded, he determined not to make a useless sacrifice. When the enemy was on the point of anchoring abreast the battery, therefore, after sustaining his fire an hour and a quarter, the commodore directed the officers and men to retire behind a hill on the left, and be in readiness to charge the enemy if he should land to spike the guns. The two frigates anchored abreast, the bombs, sloops, and smaller vessels passed outside them, all pouring into the battery and neighbouring woods a tremendous fire of every description of missive. In the woods on the left, a company of riflemen from Jefferson county, Virginia, under captain George W. Humphreys, greatly distinguished themselves by a well-directed fire on the enemy's decks, as did a company of militia under the command of captain Gena, who was posted on the right. The first lost one man killed, and one sergeant and four privates wounded; the latter, two privates killed. After the bombs, gun-vessels, and prizes had all passed, the frigates proceeded down and anchored abreast of commodore Perry's battery, where a constant firing was kept up until after sun-set.

But the guns of Perry's battery were of too small calibre to make much impression on the enemy. A single eighteen pounder, which arrived only thirty minutes before the firing began, ill supplied with ammunition, was the only gun that could be of much service. The ammunition of this gun, and that of several of the six-pounders, being expended, and the fire of the enemy being very heavy, it was thought advisable to retire a short distance in the rear. This was done in good order, after sustaining their fire for more than an hour.

The advantageous situation of this battery prevented the enemy from doing much injury. Only one man was wounded. The number of killed and wounded at commodore Porter's battery did not exceed thirty. The loss of the enemy was seven killed, and thirty-five wounded.

Sir Peter Parker, who was sent up the Chesapeake to make a diversion in favour of this expedition, was the least fortunate of the commanders. He met his death in a conflict with a small body of militia on the eastern shore of Maryland, under the command of colonel Reid.

A force of about 150 men was landed at night from his vessel, at the head of which he placed himself, with the intention of surprising the militia in their camp. The movement of the British barges, however, had been discovered, and every preparation was made to give them a warm reception. The camp and baggage were removed, and the troops posted on a rising ground, flanked on both sides with woods, with the artillery in the centre. The head of the enemy's column soon appeared, and received the fire of the American advance at 70 paces distance. Being pressed by superior numbers, the advance were ordered to retire, and form on the right of the line. The fire now became general, and was sustained by the militia with the most determined valour. The enemy pressed in front; but being foiled, he threw himself on the left flank; where his efforts were equally unavailing.

The fire of the enemy had nearly ceased, when Reid, the commander of the militia, was informed that the cartridges were entirely expended in some parts of the line, and that none of the men had more than a few rounds, although each had brought twenty into the field. The artillery cartridges were entirely expended. Under these circumstances, the troops were ordered to fall back to a convenient spot where a part of the line was fortified, for the purpose of distributing the remaining cartridges.

But the enemy having sustained a severe loss found it more prudent to retreat than to pursue. They retired to the beach, carrying with them all the wounded they could find, among whom was sir Peter Parker, who expired a few minutes after being carried from the field. The loss of the British on this occasion was 14 killed and 27 wounded. The Americans had only three wounded. Nothing but the want of ammunition could have saved the whole party of the British from capture.

With the multitude, success in war is generally supposed to indicate wisdom in our rulers, while defeat is uniformly attributed either to their folly and weakness, or to treasonable purposes. The clamour which arose out of the disaster of our arms, which led to the capture of Washington, was particularly directed against general Winder, who commanded the American forces, and general Armstrong, the secretary of war, but chiefly against the latter. So violent was the ferment of the public mind in the District of Columbia, that the president was forced to yield to the clamour, and request the secretary to resign. His place was filled *pro tem.* by colonel Monroe, the secretary of state.

The conduct of the British while in possession of Washington and Alexandria, is without a parallel in the history of civilized nations. In the wars of modern Europe, no examples of the kind, even among nations the most hostile to each other, can be traced. In the course of the last ten or twelve years, most of the capitals of the principal powers of Europe have been entered by Bonaparte, at the head of his victorious troops, yet no one instance of such wanton and unjustifiable destruction has been seen. And yet this is the chief whose conduct the British have affected to consider as outraging all the laws of civilized war.

But it has been attempted to justify this wanton destruction, under the plea of retaliation. Admiral Cochrane, in a letter to the secretary of state, dated the day previous to the debarkation of Ross's army, though not delivered till after the destruction at Washington, stated, that having been called upon by the governor-general of the Canadas to aid him in carrying into effect measures of retaliation against the inhabitants of the United States, for the wanton destruction committed by their army in Upper Canada, it had become imperiously his duty, conformably with the nature of the governor-general's application, to issue to the naval force under his command an order to destroy and lay waste such towns and districts upon the coast as might be found assailable.

This general accusation was rebutted by Mr. Monroe, in his answer to this letter. The secretary declared it to have been the resolution of government, from the very commencement of the war, to wage it in a manner most consonant to the principles of humanity, and to those friendly relations which it was desirable to preserve between the two nations, after the restoration of peace. This resolution had never been deviated from, although it was perceived, with the deepest regret, that a spirit so just and humane was neither cherished nor acted upon by the British government. Without dwelling on the deplorable cruelties committed by the savages in the British ranks, and in British pay, on American prisoners at the river Raisin, which to this day have never been disavowed or atoned, I refer, continued the secretary, as more immediately connected with the subject of your letter, to the wanton desolation that was committed at Havre-de-Grace, and at Georgetown, early in the spring of 1813. These villages were burnt and ravaged by the naval forces of Great Britain, to the ruin of their unarmed inhabitants, who saw with astonishment that they derived no protection to their property from the laws of war. During the same season, scenes of invasion and pillage, carried on under the same authority, were witnessed all along the waters of the Chesapeake, to an extent inflicting the most serious private distress, and under circumstances that justified the suspicion, that revenge and cupidity, rather than the manly motives that should dictate the hostility of a high-minded foe, led to their perpetration.

Although these acts of desolation invited, if they did not impose on the government, the necessity of retaliation, yet in no instance has it been authorised.*   The burning of the village of Newark, in Upper Canada, was posterior to the early outrages above enumerated.   The village of Newark adjoined Fort George, and its destruction was justified by the officer who ordered it, on the ground that it became necessary in the military operations there.   The act, however, was disavowed by the government.   The burning which took place at Long Point was unauthorised by the government, and the conduct of the officer subjected to the investigation of a military tribunal.   For the burning at St. David's, committed by stragglers, the officer who commanded in that quarter was dismissed without trial, for not preventing it.

I am commanded by the president distinctly to state, continued the secretary, that it as little comports with any orders which have been issued to the military and naval commanders of the United States, as it does with the established and known humanity of the American nation, to pursue a system which it appears you have adopted.   This government owes it to itself, to the principles which it has ever held sacred, to disavow, as justly chargeable to it, any such wanton, cruel, and unjustifiable warfare.   Whatever unauthorised irregularity may have been committed by any of its troops, it would have been ready, acting on these principles of sacred and eternal obligation, to disavow, and as far as might be practicable, to repair.

But the government, it appears, was mistaken in attributing this general charge against the American troops in Upper Canada, to the destruction of the villages alluded to in the secretary's letter.   The governor of Canada, in an address to the provincial parliament, on the 24th of January, 1815, asserted, " that, as a just retribution, the proud capitol at Washington, had experienced a similar fate to that inflicted by an American force on the seat of government in Upper Canada;"

---

* *We have always been of opinion, that our government was highly reprehensible, if not in the failure to adopt retaliatory measures, at least to make a solemn appeal to the British government and to the world, on the subject of these devastations. The outrages were not committed in the heat of the moment, or by an inferior officer, but by parties which were generally led by an admiral, and apparently in a systematic manner. We cannot bring ourselves to believe, that if a decided stand had been taken, this abominable system of outrage would have continued to desolate the shores of the Chesapeake to the end of the war.*

and the chancellor of the exchequer, in a debate in the British parliament, on an address to the prince regent, in November, 1814, was still more explicit. The Americans at York, he asserted, "not only burnt the house of the governor, but also every house belonging to the meanest individual, even to a shell, and left the populace in the most wretched condition."

Thus, in the great as in the little world, one wrong inevitably treads on the heels of another. The same cowardly spirit which dictated the orders for devastating the American coast, was apparent on this occasion, when, cowering under the reproaches of their compatriots for the stain they had cast on the British arms, the ministry were forced to shelter themselves under the most base and malignant untruths. But the reign of falsehood is always short. These official assertions produced an investigation of the subject by congress, which must cover with shame the authors of this slander.

From this investigation it appears, that nothing was destroyed by the American commander, excepting the barracks and public storehouses. That several of the most valuable public buildings were destroyed by the explosion of a magazine, which the British set fire to as the Americans entered the place, and which proved fatal to general Pike, and to a vast number of his brave followers. That, notwithstanding this great provocation for burning the town, nothing of the kind took place; a strong guard was set, with positive orders to prevent any plunder or depredation on the inhabitants; and when leaving the place, the commander of the American troops received a letter from judge Scott, chief justice of the superior court, in which he expressed his thanks for the humane treatment the inhabitants had experienced from his troops, and for the commander's particular attention to the safety of their persons and property. The destruction of public edifices for civil uses was not only unauthorised, but positively forbidden by the American commanders. It has recently however appeared, that a public building, of little value, called the parliament-house (not the government house), had been burnt, in which an American scalp was found, (as appears by the official letter of commodore Chauncey, to the secretary of the navy), as a part of the decoration of the speaker's chair, whether it was an accidental consequence of the confusion in which the explosion of the magazine involved the town, or the unauthorised act of some exasperated individual, has not been ascertained. The silence of the military and civil officers of the provincial government of Canada, seem to indicate that the transaction was not deemed, when it occurred, a cause, either for retaliation or reproach.

The burning of Newark and of the Indian towns on the river Thames, commonly called the Moravian towns, are also adverted to in the report arising out of this investigation. The burning of Newark, it is stated, was vindicated by the American general, as necessary to his military operations; but as soon as the American government heard of it, instructions, dated the 6th of January, 1814, were given by the department of war, to major-general Wilkinson, " to disavow the conduct of the officer who committed it, and to transmit to governor Prevost a copy of the order, under colour of which that officer had acted." This disavowal was accordingly communicated, and on the 10th February, 1814, governor Prevost answered, " that it had been with great satisfaction he had received the assurance, that the perpetration of the burning of the town of Newark, was both unauthorised by the American government, and abhorrent to every American feeling; that if any outrages had ensued the wanton and unjustifiable destruction of Newark, passing the bounds of just retaliation, they were to be attributed to the influence of irritated passions, on the part of the unfortunate sufferers by that event, which, in a state of active warfare, it had not been possible altogether to restrain, and that it was as little congenial to the disposition of his majesty's government, as it was to that of the government of the United States, deliberately to adopt any plan of policy, which had for its object the devastation of private property."

But the disavowal of the American government was not the only expiation of the unauthorised offence committed by its officer; for the British government undertook itself to redress the wrong. A few days after the burning of Newark, the British and Indian troops crossed the Niagara for this purpose; they surprized and seized Fort Niagara; they burnt the villages of Lewistown, Manchester, Tuscarora, Buffaloe, and Black Rock, desolating the whole of the Niagara frontier, and dispersing the inhabitants in the extremity of the winter. Sir George Prevost himself appears to have been satisfied with the vengeance that had been inflicted; and, in his proclamation of the 12th of January, 1814, he expressly declared, that for the burning of Newark, " the opportunity of punishment had occurred; that a full measure of retaliation had taken place, and that it was not his intention to pursue further a system of warfare, so revolting to his own feelings, and so little congenial to the British character, unless the future measures of the enemy should compel him again to resort to it." With his answer to major-general Wilkinson, which has been already noticed, he transmitted a copy of the proclamation, " as

expressive of the determinatian as to his futnre line of conduct," and added, "that he was happy to learn, that there
was no probability, that any measures, on the part of the
American government, would oblige him to depart from it."

The places usually called tne Moravian towns, were mere
collections of Indian huts and cabins, on the river Le Trench
or Thames, not probably worth, in the whole, one thousand
dollars. The Indians who inhabited them, among whom were
some notoriously hostile to the United States, had made incursions the most cruel into their territory. When, therefore,
the American army under general Harrison invaded Canada
in 1813, the huts and cabins of the hostile Indians were destroyed. But this species of warfare has been invariably pursued by every nation engaged in war with the Indians of the
American continent. However it may be regretted on the
score of humanity, it appears to be the necessary means of
averting the still greater calamities of savage hostility; and it
is believed, that the occurrence would never have been made
the subject of a charge against the American troops, if the
fact had not been misrepresented or misunderstood. Many
people at home, and most people abroad, have been led to suppose, that the Moravian towns were the peaceable settlements
of a religious sect of Christians, and not the abode of a hostile
tribe of savages.

But while excuses are thus framed with a view of palliating
the devastation committed by the British army, not one attempt is made to palliate or excuse the navy for its plunder of
the wealthy town of Alexandria, or for the system of pitiful
pilfering which was carried on for two summers in the Chesapeake. Is the plunder and devastation of the property of private individuals, then less heinous than the destruction of public edifices? or is the world so accustomed to the system of
wholesale privateering, unauthorised by the laws of naval warfare, as to pass over without comment, when committed by
naval officers, not only the sack of a large town, but the desolation of whole districts?

The general orders of Brown, on crossing the Niagara, form
a pleasing contrast to the devastating threat of Cochrane.
"Upon entering Canada," says he, "the laws of war*

---

* "*War is at best a savage thing, and wades through a sea
of violence and injustice; yet even war itself has its laws, which
men of honour will not depart from.*"—Plutarch, life of Camil-
lus.

will govern; men found in arms, or otherwise engaged in the service of the enemy, will be treated as enemies; those behaving peaceably, and following their private occupations, will be treated as friends. Private property will in all cases be held sacred; public property, wherever found, will be seized and disposed of by the commanding general. 'Any plunderer shall be punished with death, who shall be found violating this order."

An intelligent French writer, in noticing the capture of Berlin by the Russians in 1760, remarks, that two important military principles may be deduced from that event. 1st. That the possession of a capital does not decide the fate of a state, or even of a campaign. 2d. That in the modern art of war, *men* are of more importance than fortified places, and that a general should never acknowledge himself vanquished, though all his strong holds be subdued, if he retain his soldiers and his constancy. If these observations be correct in their application to European capitals, how much more forcibly do they apply to that of the federal government, a mere open village, of about 8000 inhabitants, and in a country thinly populated! Indeed the capture of Washington cannot be viewed in any other light than as a predatory incursion, under the pretence of retaliation, but really with the view of striking terror and inducing submission, and at the same time producing an effect in Europe, where the occupation of the capital of their enemy, it was doubtless conceived, would be viewed as a most brilliant exploit. General Ross had neither the intention nor the means of holding Washington. Without artillery or stores, he was unable to remain longer than 24 hours, when a retreat was commenced under favour of the night, and even then this retreat would have been extremely hazardous, but for the disorganized state of his opponents, and their blameable deficiency in the article of intelligence. It is true, that had they remained a few days longer, a communication with their shipping would have been opened by the Potomac, but this arose from a circumstance that could not have been foreseen, and Ross certanly acted wisely in not calculating on the destruction of Fort Washington by its commander.

But the capture of Washington produced in Europe a very different effect from what was expected. The Gothic barbarity displayed in the wanton destruction of the public buildings roused the indignation of the whole continent, and even produced such a sensation in the British parliament, as to cause its instigators to resort to falsehood to shield them from the public odium. The agitation of the question also drew

R

from the ministry a statement, that instructions had been sent
to the coast of America to desist from further inflictions of
vengeance.

The threats of devastation and their piratical operations in
the district of Columbia, produced an electric effect throughout the union. A spirit of patriotism was kindled by the
flames of the capitol, before which all party considerations
and honest differences of opinion vanished. The war, at its,
commencement, was considered an inexpedient measure, by a
large and respectable portion of the community. The mode
of conducting it also, by the invasion of Canada, was con-
demned as inefficacious; as resembling more a war for foreign
conquest, than a resolute assertion of our naval rights, which
ought, it was said, to be conquered on the ocean. All aid,
either in men or money, was consequently as much as possible withheld by those who embraced these sentiments. Party
considerations had no doubt their effect in producing this result. It was not to be expected, that the opposition would
fail to make use of the same popular topics which had been
so successfully wielded against them when in power, and
which had finally driven them from their seats.

But at this interesting crisis a new spirit pervaded the nation,
which aroused it almost instantaneously to arms. Party ran-
cour, for a moment, seemed utterly extinct; " this is not the
time for speaking, but for acting," became the universal cry.
All classes seemed inspired with military ardour; the young
and the old, the rich and the poor, rushed into the ranks, came
forward with their contributions, and assisted in the labour of
raising works of defence. Nor were even the females idle at
this trying moment. Their labours were united in accoutring
the volunteers, and in providing for their necessities.

These movements were little if at all regulated by the governments either of the states or of the union. It appeared
as if the people, perceiving that the powers with which they
had entrusted their rulers were either incompetent to the crisis,
or had not been sufficiently acted on, had determined sponta-
neously to arise in their might, and take the defence of their
respective neighbourhoods upon themselves. Committees of
vigilance or defence were every where appointed by the people in the town meetings, who collected money, arms, and
ammunition, regulated the military movements of the citizens,
and superintended their voluntary labour at the fortifications.
Nor was the public enthusiasm unavailing. From this moment, almost every encounter with the enemy shed new lustre on the American arms, till the war finally closed in a blaze
of glory at New-Orleans.

The unanimity which prevailed at this period cannot perhaps be exemplified more strikingly than by the proclamations of governor Chittenden.—Shortly after his election to the chief magistracy of Vermont, in the fall of 1813, Chittenden issued a proclamation, ordering a brigade of Vermont militia, then at Plattsburg, in the service of the United States, to return to their homes, on the pretence that it was highly improper that the militia should be placed under the command of, and at the disposal of an officer of the United States, and out of the juris-diction or controul of the executive of Vermont, and marched to the defence of a sister state, fully competent to all the purposes of self-defence. The militia refused compliance with this requisition, and the officers publicly addressed the governor, stating at large their reasons for this refusal. " We are not of that class," say they, " who believe that our duties as citizens or soldiers are circumscribed within the narrow limits of the town or state in which we reside; but that we are under a paramount obligation to our common country, to the great confederacy of states." " We conceive it our duty," they continue, " to declare uequivocally to your excellency, that we shall not obey your excellency's order for returning; but shall continue in the service of our country, until we are legally and honourably discharged. An invitation or order to desert the standard of our country will never be obeyed by us, although it proceeds from the governor and captain-general of Vermont." Adding, " We cannot perceive what other object your excellency could have in view than to embarrass the operations of the army, to excite mutiny and sedition among the soldiers, and to induce them to desert, that they might forfeit the wages to which they are entitled for their patriotic services.'

At this important crisis a very different stand was taken by the same governor. In his proclamation, dated September 19, 1814, he declares, that the war has assumed an entirely different character, since its first commencement, and has become almost exclusively defensive, and is prosecuted by the enemy with a spirit, unexampled during pending negociations for peace, which leaves no prospect of safety but in a manly and united determination to meet invasion at every point, and expel the invader. That, as the conflict has become a common and not a party concern, the time has now arrived when all degrading party distinctions and animosities, however we may have differed respecting the policy of declaring, or the mode of prosecuting the war ought to be laid aside; that every heart may be stimulated, and every arm nerved, for the protection of our common country, our liberty, our altars, and our firesides; in the defence of which we may, with an humble confidence, look to heaven for assistance and protection. He therefore earnestly exhorts all the good people of Vermont, by that love of country, which so signally distinguished their fathers, in their glorious and successful struggle for independence, to unite both heart and hand, in defence of their common interest, and every thing dear to freemen.

The British army having re-embarked on board the fleet in the Patuxent, admiral Cochrane moved down that river, and proceeded up the Chesapeake, and on the evening of the 10th of September appeared at the mouth of the Patapsco, about 14 miles from the city of Baltimore. Anticipating the debarkation of the troops, general Smith, who commaned at Baltimore, had ordered general Stricker to march, with a portion of his militia, towards North Point, near the mouth of the river, where it was expected the British would make a landing. His force consisted of 550 of the 5th regiment, under lieutenant-colonel Sterrett; 620 of the 6th, under lieutenant-colonel Donald; 500 of the 27th under-lieutenant-colonel Long; 450 of the 39th, under lieutenant-colonel Fowler; 700 of the 51st, under lieutenant-colonel Amey; 150 riflemen, under captain Dyer; 140 cavalry, under lieutenant-colonel Biays; and the Union Artillery of 75 men, with six four-pounders, under captain Montgomery; making an aggregate of 3,185 effective men. Major Randal, with a light corps of riflemen and musquetry, taken from general Stansbury's brigade and the Pennsylvania volunteers, was detached to the mouth of Bear Creek, with orders to co-operate with general Stricker, and to check any landing which the enemy might attempt in that quarter.

The troops moved towards North Point, by the main road, on the 11th, and at 3 o'clock, P. M. reached the meeting-house, near the head of Bear Creek, seven miles from the city. Here the brigade halted, with the exception of the cavalry, who were pushed forward to Gorsuch's farm three miles in advance, and the riflemen, who took post near the blacksmith's shop, two miles in advance of the encampment. At 7 o'clock, on the morning of the 12th, information was received from the advanced videtts, that the enemy were debarking troops from and under cover of their gun-vessels, which lay off the bluff of North Point, within the mouth of Patapsco river. The baggage was immediately ordered back under a strong guard, and general Stricker took a good position at the junction of the two roads leading from Baltimore to North Point, having his right flanked by Bear Creek, and his left by a mash. He here waited the approach of the enemy, having sent on an advanced corps,

BATTLE AT NORTH POINT AND DEATH OF GEN^L. ROSS.

under the command of major Heath, of the 5th regiment. This advance was met by that of the enemy, and after some skirmishing it returned to the line, the main body of the enemy being at a short distance in the rear of their advance. During this skirmishing, major-general Ross received a musket-ball through his arm into his breast, which proved fatal to him on his way to the water side for re-embarkation. The command of the enemy's forces then devolved on colonel Brook. Between 2 and 3 o'clock, the enemy's whole force came up and commenced the battle by some discharges of rockets, which were succeeded by the cannon from both sides, and soon after, the action became general along the line. General Stricker gallantly maintained his ground against a great superiority of numbers during the space of an hour and twenty minutes, when the regiment on his left (the 51st) giving way he was under the necessity of retiring to the ground in his rear, where he had stationed one regiment as a reserve. He here formed his brigade; but the enemy not thinking it advisable to pursue, he in compliance with previous arrangements, fell back and took post on the left, a half mile in advance of the entrenchments, which had been thrown up on the hills surrounding Baltimore. About the time general Stricker had taken the ground just mentioned, he was joined by general Winder, who had been stationed , 1 the west side of the city, but was now ordered to march with general Douglas' brigade of Virginia militia, and the United States' dragoons, under captain Bird, and take post on the left of general Stricker. During these movements, the brigades of generals Stansbury and Foreman, the seamen and marines, under commodore Rodgers, the Pennsylvania volunteers, under colonels Cobean and Findley, the Baltimore artillery, under colonel Harris, and the marine artillery, under captain Stiles, manned the trenches and batteries, and in this situation spent the night, all prepared to receive the enemy.

Next morning, the British appeared in front of the entrenchments, at the distance of two miles, on the Philadelphia road, from whence he had a full view of the position of the Americans. He manœuvred during the morning towards his right, as if with the intention of making a circuitous march, and coming down on the Hartford or York roads. Generals Winder and Stricker were ordered to adapt their movements to those of the enemy, so as to baffle this supposed intention. They executed this order with great skill and judgment, by taking an advantageous position, stretching across the country, when the enemy was likely to approach the quarter he seemed to threaten. This movement induced the British to concentrate their forces in front, pushing his advance to within a mile of the entrenchments; driving in the videttes, and shewing an intention of attacking the position that evening. Smith, therefore, immediately drew generals Winder and Stricker nearer to the right of the enemy, with the intention of falling on his right or rear should he attack the entrenchments, or, if he declined it, of attacking him in the.morning.

As soon as the British troops had debarked at North Point, the fleet proceeded up the Patapsco, to bombard Fort M'Henry, which commands the entrance to the harbour of Baltimore. On the 13th, about sunrise, the British commenced the attack from their bomb-vessels, at the distance of about two miles, when, finding that the shells reached the fort, they anchored, and kept up an incessant and well-directed bombardment.

Fort M'Henry was commanded by lieutenant-colonel Armistead. The garrison consisted of one company of United States' artillery, under captain Evans, and two companies o sea-fencibles, under captains Bunbury and Addison. Of these three companies, 35 men were unfortunately on the sick list and unfit for duty. In contemplation of the attack, Armistead had been furnished with two companies of volunteer artillery from the city of Baltimore, under captain Berry and lieutenant-commandant Pennington, a company of volunteer artillerists, under judge Nicholson, who had proffered their services, a detachment from commodore Barney's flotilla, under lieutenant Redman, and about six hundred infantry, under the command of lieutenant-colonel Stewart and major Lane, consisting of detachments from the 12th, 14th, 36th, and 38th regiments of United States troops—the total amounting to about a thousand effective men. Two batteries to the right of Fort M'Henry, upon the Patapsco, were manned, the one by lieutenant Newcombe, with a detachment of sailors, the other by lieutenant Webster, of the flotilla. The former was called Fort Covington, the latter the City Battery.

As soon as the British commenced the bombardment, the batteries at the fort were opened in return; but the firing soon ceased on the part of the Americans, as it was found that all the shot and shells fell considerably short sf the British vessels. This was a most distressing circumstance to the troops in the fort, as it compelled them to remain inactive, though exposed to a constant and tremendous shower of shells. But though thus inactive, and without that security, which, in more regular fortifications, is provided for such occasions, not a man shrunk from his post.

About 2 o'clock, P. M. one of the twenty-four-pounders on the south-west bastion, under the immediate command of captain Nicholson, was dismounted by a shell, the explosion from which killed his second lieutenant, and wounded several of his men; the bustle necessarily produced in removing the wounded, and remounting the gun, probably induced the British to suspect that the garrison was in confusion, as three bomb-ships were immediately advanced. But the fire, which now opened from the fort, soon compelled them to seek shelter, by again withdrawing out of the reach of the guns, when the garrison gave three cheers, and again ceased firing.

The British continued throwing shells, with one or two slight intermissions, for twenty-five hours, viz. from sunrise of the 13th till 7 o'clock, A. M of the 14th of September. During the night, whilst the bombardment was the most severe, two or three rocket vessels and barges succeeded in passing Fort M'Henry, and getting up the Patapsco, but they were soon compelled to retire by the forts in that quarter. These forts also destroyed one of the barges, with all on board. It is supposed that the vessels that passed the fort contained picked men, with scaling ladders, for the purpose of storming.

In the course of the night, admiral Cochrane held a communication with the commander of the land forces, and the enterprise being considered impracticable, it was mutually agreed to withdraw. Accordingly, while the bombardment still continued, in order to distract the attention of the Americans, the retreat was commenced. Owing to the extreme darkness; and a continued rain, it was not discovered till daylight, when general Winder commenced a pursuit, with the Virginia brigade and the United States' dragoons; at the same time major Randal was dispatched with his light corps in pursuit of the enemy's right, whilst the whole of the militia cavalry was put in motion for the same object. All the troops were, however, so worn out with continued watching, and with being under arms during three days and nights, exposed the greater part of the time to very inclement weather, that it was found impracticable to do any thing more than pick up a few stragglers.

The naval forces, as was before observed, continued the bombardment till seven o'clock. About nine they retired to North Point, where the embarkation of the troops commenced that evening, and was completed next day at one o'clock. It would have been impossible, even had the American troops been in a condition to act offensively, to have cut off any part of the enemy's rear guard during the embarkation, as the point where it was effected was defended from approach by a line of defences extending from Back river to Humphreys' creek, on the Patapsco, which had been thrown up previous to the arrival of the British.

The loss of the Americans, at the battle near North Point, was 24 killed, 139 wounded, and 50 prisoners. The loss of the British in this action was 39 killed, and 251 wounded. The loss in the fort was only 4 killed and 24 wounded; no list of killed and wounded on board the squadron has been published. From the best calculations that could be made, from fifteen to eighteen hundred shells were thrown by the enemy. A few of these fell short. A large proportion burst over the fort, throwing their fragments around, and threatening destruction. Many passed over, and about four hundred fell within the works. Two of the public buildings were materially injured, the others but slightly.

The effect produced by the joyful intelligence of the failure of the attempt upon Baltimore, may be more easily conceived than expressed, when it is considered that almost every large town being equally threatened with devastation, the case of Baltimore came home to every individual bosom. But one moment before, the public dismay seemed to have reached its acme; and the most gloomy anticipations seemed about to be realized.

While admiral Cochrane was threatening the country along the Chesapeake, by order of sir George Prevost, the latter was leading an army and navy into the United States, but holding very different language. Though he could direct the British forces in the south to lay waste and desolate, he was too fearful of the re-action of such barbarous orders to dare to utter them at the head of his own troops. Here his language was of the softest and most conciliatory nature. On entering the state of New-York, he " makes known to its peaceable and unoffending inhabitants, that they have no cause for alarm from this invasion of their country, for the safety of themselves and families, or for the security of their property. He explicitly assures them, that as long as they continue to demean themselves peaceably, they shall be protected in the quiet possession of their homes, and permitted freely to pursue their usual occupations. It is against the government of the United States, by whom this unjust and unprovoked war has been declared, and against those who support it, either openly or secretly, that the arms of his majesty are directed. The quiet and unoffending inhabitants, not found in arms, or otherwise not aiding in hostilities, shall meet with kind usage and generous treatment; and all just complaints against any of his majesty's subjects, offering violence to them, to their families, or to their possessions, shall be immediately redressed." With these fair words, sir George Prevost led his army against Plattsburg, about the beginning of September, while the fleet proceeded on his left up the lake, in order to make a contemporaneous attack on the Americans by land and water.

Previous to this invasion, no military movements took place in this quarter, excepting an attack which was made on an American battery at the mouth of Otter Creek, on the 14th of May, by the British naval forces on the lake. In this affair the British were repulsed with loss.

But during the months of July and August, the army from the Garonne, which had so greatly distinguished itself under general Wellington, arrived in the St. Lawrence; and part of the troops being sent up to the Niagara, the remainder, consisting of about 14,000 men, were organized by sir George Prevost, agreeably to the orders of the prince regent, for the purpose of undertaking an expedition into the state of New-York. There is good reason to suppose, that if this expedition had been successful, a powerful attempt would have followed from another quarter on the city of New-York, in order, by seizing the line of the Hudson, completely to cut off the New England states.

The British troops were concentrated on the frontiers of Lower Canada, and took possession of Champlain on the 3d of September. The best part of the American troops in this quarter had previously been formed into a division, which had marched towards the Niagara, under general Izard. General Macomb, as senior officer, had been left in command. But excepting four companies of the 6th regiment, he had not an organized battalion. The garrison was composed of convalescents and recruits of the new regiments, not exceeding 1500 effective men for duty; all in the greatest confusion, as well as the ordnance and stores, and the works in no state of defence.

Finding, from the proclamations of the enemy, and his impressment of the waggons and teams in his vicinity, that an attack on Plattsburg was determined on, every exertion was made to place the works in a state of defence; and, to create an emulation and zeal among the officers and men, they were divided into detachments, and placed near the several forts; Macomb declaring in orders, that each detachment was the garrison of its own work, and bound to defend it to the last extremity.

As soon as the force of the enemy was ascertained, general Macomb called on general Mooers, of the New-York militia, and arranged with him plans for bringing forth the militia en masse. The inhabitants of Plattsburg fled with their families and effects, except a few men and some boys, who formed themselves into a party, received rifles, and were exceedingly useful.

By the 4th of the month general Mooers collected about seven hundred militia, and advanced seven miles on the Beckman Town road, to watch the motions of the enemy, and to skirmish with him as he advanced; also to obstruct the roads with fallen trees, and to break up the bridges. On the lake road, at Dead Creek bridge, two hundred men had been posted under captain Sproul of the 13th regiment, with orders to abbatis the woods, to place obstructions in the road, and to fortify himself; to this party were added two field-pieces. In advance of this position, was lieutenant-colonel Appling, with 110 riflemen, watching the movements of the enemy, and procuring intelligence.

It was ascertained, that before day-light on the 6th, the enemy would advance in two columns, on the two roads before mentioned, dividing at Sampson's, a little below Chazy village. The column on the Beckman Town road proceeded with great rapidity; the militia skirmished with his advanced parties, and, except a few brave men, fell back precipitately, in the greatest disorder, although the British troops did not deign to fire on them, except by their flankers and advanced patroles. The night previous major Wool had been ordered to advance with a detachment of 250 men to support the militia, and set them an example of firmness. Captain Leonard, of the light artillery, was also directed to proceed with two pieces to be on the ground before day; but he did not make his appearance until 8 o'clock, when the enemy had approached within two miles of the village. Major Wool, with his party, disputed the road with great obstinacy, but the militia could not be prevailed on to stand, notwithstanding the exertions of their general and staff officers; although the fields were divided with strong stone walls, and they were told that the enemy could not possibly cut them off. The state dragoons of New-York wear red coats, and they being on the heights to watch the enemy, gave constant alarm to the militia, who mistook them for the enemy, and feared his getting in their rear.

Finding the enemy's columns had penetrated within a mile of Plattsburg, general Macomb dispatched his aid-de-camp to bring off the detachment at Dead Creek, and to order lieutenant-colonel Appling to fall on the enemy's right flank. The colonel fortunately arrived just in time to save his retreat, and to fall in with the head of a column debouching from the woods. Here he poured in a destructive fire from his riflemen, and continued to annoy the column until he formed a junction with Major Wool. The field-pieces did considerable execution among the enemy's columns. So undaunted, however, was the enemy, that he never deployed in his whole march, always pressing on in column. This column, however, was much impeded by obstructions thrown in the way, and by the removal of the bridge at Dead creek, as it passed the creek and beach, the galleys kept up on it a lively and galling fire.

The village of Plattsburg is situated on the north-west side of the small river Saranac, near where it falls into lake Champlain. The American works were situated on the opposite side of the river.

Every road was now full of troops crowding on all sides in upon Plattsburg. The field-pieces were therefore ordered to retire across the bridge, and form a battery for its protection, and to cover the retreat of the infantry, which was accordingly done, and the parties of Appling and Wool, as well as that of Sproul, retired alternately, keeping up a brisk fire until they got under cover of the works. The enemy's light troops then took possession of the houses near the bridge, and kept up a constant firing from the windows and balconies, but a few hot shot from the American works, which put the houses in flames, soon obliged these sharp-shooters to retire. The whole day, until it was too late to see, the enemy's light troops endeavoured to drive the guards from the bridge, but they paid dearly for their perseverance. An attempt was also made to cross the upper bridge, where the militia resolutely drove them back.— The troops being now all on the south side of the Saranac, the planks were taken off the bridges, and piled up in the form of breastworks to cover the parties intended to dispute the passage, which afterwards enabled them to hold the bridges against very superior numbers.

From the 7th to the 11th, the enemy was employed in getting on his battering train, and erecting his batteries and approaches, and constantly skirmishing at the bridges and fords. By this time the militia of New-York and the volunteers of Vermont were pouring in from all quarters. They were all placed along the Saranac, to prevent the enemy's crossing the river, excepting a strong body sent in his rear to harrass him day and night, and keep him in continual alarm. The militia behaved with great spirit after the first day, and the volunteers of Vermont were exceedingly serviceable. The regular troops, notwithstanding the constant skirmishing, and repeated endeavours of the enemy to cross the river, kept at their work day and night strengthening the defences, and evinced a determination to hold out to the last extremity.

Meanwhile the British were strenuously engaged in preparing the fleet, which was destined to co-operate with the land forces. It appeared in view at Plattsburgh early in the morning of the 11th. This fleet consisted of the frigate Confiance, carrying 39 guns, 27 of which were twenty-four-pounders; the brig Linnet, carryng 16 guns; the sloops Chub and Finch, each carrying 11 guns; and thirteen galleys, five of which carried two, and the remainder one gun each. The American force consisted of the Saratoga, carryng 26 guns, eight of which were long twenty-four-pounders; the Eagle, 20 guns; the Ticonderoga 17; the Preble 7; and ten galleys, six of which carried two, the remainder one gun each. The British were superior, both in size and number of guns.

At 8 in the morning, the American look-out-boat announced to commodore Macdonough, the commander of the squadron, the approach of the enemy. He at this time lay at anchor in Plattsburg bay, calmly awaiting the approach of the British squadron, the fleet being moored in line, abreast of the works with a division of five gun-boats on each flank. At 9, the British fleet anchored in line abreast the American squadron, at about 300 yards distance, the Confiance opposed to the Saratoga, the Linnet to the Eagle; the British galleys and one of the sloops to the Ticonderoga, Preble, and the left division of the American galleys; the other sloops to the right division of the American galleys.

In this situation the whole force on both sides became engaged, the Saratoga suffering much from the heavy fire of the Confiance. But the fire of the Saratoga was also very destructive to her. The Ticonderoga likewise gallantly sustained her full share of the action. At half past 10 o'clock the Eagle, not being able to bring her guns to bear, cut her cable and anchored in a more elligible position, between, the Saratoga and the Ticonderoga, where she very much annoyed the enemy, but unfortunately left the Saratoga exposed to a galling fire from the enemy's brig. The guns on the starboard side of the Saratoga being nearly all dismounted, or not manageable, a stern-anchor was let go, the bower-cable cut and the ship winded with a fresh broadside on the enemy's ship, which soon after surrendered. A broadside was then sprung to bear on the brig, which surrendered in about fifteen minutes after.

The sloops that was opposed to the Eagle had struck some time before and drifted down the line; the sloop which was with their galleys having struck also. Three of the enemy's galleys were sunk, the others pulled off. The American flotilla were about obeying with alacrity the signal to follow them, when all the vessels were reported to the commodore as in a sinking state; it then became necessary to annul the signal to the galleys, and order their men to the pumps. The enemy's galleys thus got off in a shattered condition, for there was not a mast in either squadron that could stand to make sail on; the lower rigging, being nearly all shot away, hung down as though it had been just placed over the mast heads.

The Saratoga had fifty-five round shot in her hull; the Confiance one hundred and five. The Saratoga was twice set on fire by hot shot from the Confiance. The enemy's shot must have principally passed just over the heads of the sailors, as there were not twenty whole hammocks in the nettings at the close of the action, which lasted without intermission two hours and twenty minutes.*

This naval engagement was in full view of both armies at Plattsburg. The killed on board the American squadron amounted to 52, the wounded to 58. The killed on board the captured vessels amounted to 84, including captain Downie, the commander of the squadron; the wounded amounted to 110; the loss on board the British galleys has never been ascertained. The number of men in the American squadron was 820; the British were supposed to exceed 1000.

The batteries on shore were opened on the American works at the same instant that the engagement commenced on the lake, and continued throwing bomb-shells, sharpnells, balls, and Congreve rockets, until sun-set, when the bombardment ceased, every battery of the British being silenced. Three efforts were made to pass the river at the commencement of the cannonade and bombardment, with a view of assaulting the works, and an immense number of scaling ladders had been prepared for that purpose. One of these attempts was made at the village bridge, another at the upper bridge, and a third at a ford about three miles from the works. The two first were repulsed by the regulars; at the ford by the volunteers and militia. Here the enemy suffered severely in killed, wounded, and prisoners; a considerable body having crossed the stream, all of whom were either killed, taken, or driven back. A whole company of the 76th regiment was here destroyed, the three lieutenants and twenty-seven men prisoners,

---

* A cock, the " bird of war," was in the Saratoga, and repeatedly crowed from the shrouds during the action. A similar circumstance occurred in Fort M'Henry during the bombardment.

the captain and the rest killed. The woods at this place were very favourable to the operations of the militia.

The further prosecution of the expedition having become impracticable by the capture of the fleet, an event totally unlooked-for, at dusk the enemy withdrew his artillery from the batteries, and raised the siege; and at nine, under the cover of the night, sent off in a great hurry all the baggage he could find transport for, and also his artillery. At two, the next morning, the whole army precipitately retreated, leaving behind their sick and wounded; the commander left a note with the surgeon, requesting for them the humane attention of general Macomb.

Vast quantities of provisions were left behind and destroyed; also an immense quantity of bomb-shells, cannon-balls, grape-shot, ammunition, flints, &c. entrenching tools of all sorts, and tents and marquees. A great deal was afterwards found concealed in the ponds and creeks, and buried in the ground, and a vast quantity was carried off by the inhabitants.

Such was the precipitancy of the retreat of the British, that they arrived at Chazy, a distance of eight miles, before their flight was discovered. The light troops, volunteers, and militia pursued immediately; and some of the mounted men made prisoners of a few of the rear guard. A continual fall of rain, and a violent storm, prevented further pursuit. Upwards of 300 deserters came in.

The British officers of the army and navy who were killed, were buried with the honours of war. The humane treatment of the Americans to the wounded, and their generous and polite attention to the prisoners, were gratefully mentioned by captain Pring (who succeeded to the command of the British fleet on the fall of captain Downie) in his official dispatch to the admiralty. *

Thus were two formidable invasions, in which both the sea

---

* *The humane attention to their prisoners, for which the Americans have been so remarkable, has led to most singular conclusions in England. Lord Liverpool said in parliament, that "in many places a strong disposition had been shown by the American people to put themselves under our protection, and that their treatment of our officers led to any conclusion rather than to the belief that they entertain any animosity against this country, or that they were not fully persuaded that the war was a war of unprovoked aggression on the part of their own government."*

and land forces of Great Britain co-operated, totally frustrated, nearly at the same moment, while another British squadron was added to the trophies of the American navy.

During the first years of the war, the British affected to conciliate the New-England states, by exempting their harbours from blockade, by refraining from the predatory incursions with which they teazed the southern coasts, and in one case, even proclaiming that a system of perfect neutrality was to be observed towards them by the sea and land forces of Great Britain. A different system was adopted this summer. The ports of New-England were included in the sweeping system of blockading the whole of the American coast, repeated incursions were made for the destruction of private property, and finally a large portion of the District of Maine was invaded and captured by a powerful force by land and water.

One of the most remarkable attacks, which occurred in the course of the campaign, was that made by Sir Thomas Hardy, upon Stonington, a small village in Connecticut, about 20 miles east from New-London. On the 9th of August, commodore Hardy appeared off the village with one 74, one frigate, one bomb-ship, and two gun-brigs, and immediately summoned the place to surrender. In the course of the day, a number of flags passed to and from the place, the conditions required were, that the family of Mr. Stewart, late consul at New London, should be immediately sent off to the squadron; that the two guns in the battery should be removed; and that no torpedoes should be fitted from, or suffered to be in, the harbour. The terms being sent over to New London to general Cushing, the commanding officer of this district, he replied, that the request for the removal of Mr. Stewart's family would be forwarded to Washington; with the others he would not comply.

In the evening, the British commenced the attack with rockets from one of the brigs: a great number of rockets were thrown, with little or no effect. The brig then hauled up within a short distance of the battery, and kept up a heavy and well-directed fire from guns of a very large calibre, which was returned by the two eighteen-pounders in the little battery, till their ammunition was expended. During this time the brig had grounded. A supply of ammunition having arrived from New London, the fire from the battery was re-commenced, and with such effect, that the brig slipped her cables, and towed off, out of reach of the eighteen-pounders, she having previously swung clear of the ground.

On the 10th, a number of flags passed; the commodore still

insisting on his former terms. On the following morning, the last flag passed, with Hardy's ultimatum, at 11 o'clock, viz.: that Mrs. Stewart should be put on board by two o'clock, P. M. or he would destroy the place. He, however, did not commence till 3 o'clock, at which time the bomb-ship commenced from two mortars, one a 15 inch and the other 13. The bombardment continued from this time till half past 8 in the evening, without intermission; the place was several times on fire, and as, often put out by the soldiers and inhabitants.

At day-light on the 12th, the attack was re-commenced from the bomb-ship, seventy-four, and frigate, and continued, with little intermission, till half past 9, A. M. when the tide began to ebb, and the ships thought proper to haul off. In the afternoon, they set sail, and left the sound by dark.

As commodore Hardy has never favoured the world with his official account of this valiant and famous affair, we are entirely at a loss to conjecture what could have been his motive. One *horse*, and one *goose*, constituted the whole list of killed on shore; a lieutenant and three privates, of the militia, were slightly wounded by the bursting of a shell, and two men in the battery by a piece going off at half charge. The town was but little damaged, considering the tremendous cannonade and bombardment it sustained: one half of the houses were untouched, and not one entirely demolished, although every ship threw its shot completely over the point. Nearly 300 shells and fire-carcasses were thrown into the village, making, it was estimated, 50 tons of metal. Three or four tons of shot, carcasses, and bombs were collected by the inhabitants.—After the bombardment, it was learnt from good authority, that the British had a number killed, and several badly wounded, by the fire from the two eighteen-pounders on shore.

A few weeks after the declaration of war, sir J. C. Sherbroke, governor of Nova Scotia, &c. issued his proclamation, ordering and directing all his majesty's subjects, under his government, to abstain from molesting the inhabitants living on the shores of the United States, contiguous to Nova Scotia and New Brunswick; and on no account to molest the goods and unarmed coasting vessels, belonging to defenceless inhabitants on the frontiers, so long as they shall abstain on their part from any act of hostility and molestation towards the inhabitants of Nova Scotia and New Brunswick; on the ground that predatory warfare, carried on against defenceless inhabitants, could answer no good purpose.

Another proclamation of the same date was issued by governor Sherbroke and admiral Sawyer, purporting, that having

understood that the inhabitants of Eastport had manifested a
disposition to avoid hostilities with the subjects of Great Britain, it is made known to them and all concerned, that from a
wish to discourage, as far as possible, every species of depredatory warfare, which can only have a tendency to distress private individuals; they have respectively issued orders to the
naval and land forces, to respect the persons and property of the
inhabitants of Eastport, so long as they shall carry on their
usual and accustomed trade and intercourse with any part of
these provinces, and reciprocally abstain from acts of hostility.
Adding, that this system of perfect neutrality towards Eastport
should not be departed from without due and timely notice
being previously given to the inhabitants.

Though some expressions in these proclamations appear as
if they were intended as a mere cover for smuggling transactions, yet the humanity and good sense displayed in the acknowledgment " that no good could result from depredatory
warfare, which can only have a tendency to distress private individuals," is worthy of high commendation, and it is sincerely
to be regretted that the same principle had not been universally acted on. It would have been worthy of two great and
magnanimous nations to have waged war, " in a manner most
consonant to the principles of humanity, and to those friendly
relations, which it was desirable to preserve between the two
nations, after the restoration of peace."

Whether " due and timely notice was previously given" to
the inhabitants of Eastport of the departure from this system
of perfect neutrality, we have no means of ascertaining. But
about two years after the date of this proclamation, (*July* 11,
1814) the island on which it stands was captured by a British
squadron, and formally taken possession of in the name of his
Britannic majesty.

Eastport is situated on Moose Island, in Passamaquoddy bay.
Although this island has been held by the Americans since the
revolutionary war, the right of its sovereignty has never been
settled, it being considered both by the Americans and British
as within their boundary line. As soon as it was taken possession of by the British, the inhabitants were ordered to appear
and declare their intention, whether they would take the oath
of allegiance to his Britannic majesty; and were further noti-
fied, that all persons not disposed to take this oath, would be
required to depart from the island in the course of seven days,
unless special permission was granted to them to remain for a
longer period. But a communication was also sent to the government of Massachusetts, stating, that the object of the Bri-

tish government was to obtain possession of the islands of Passamaquoddy bay, in consequence of their being considered within their boundary line; that they had no intention of carrying on offensive operations against the people residing on the continent, unless their conduct should oblige them to resort to the measure; and in the event of their remaining quiet, they should not be disturbed either in their property or persons.

This resolution, however, of avoiding hostile operations against the inhabitants of the continent was adhered to for a much shorter period than the "system of perfect neutrality," promised to be observed towards the inhabitants of Eastport For the British ministry, elevated by the success of their arms in Europe, had come to the resolution to demand large and important cessions of territory from the United States. One of those cessions included that part of the District of Maine which lies eastward of Penobscot river, which they considered desirable on account of its securing to them a direct communication between Halifax and Quebec. Instructions were accordingly sent out to lieutenant general Sherbroke, governor of Nova Scotia, &c. to effect the conquest of that part of Maine, of which it was intended to demand the cession. Towards the end of August an expedition sailed from Halifax to accomplish the object in view. The troops were commanded by governor Sherbroke, the naval forces by rear admiral Griffith.

It was governor Sherbroke's original intention first to have taken possession of Machias, and then proceed to Castine, on the Penobscot; but on the 30th of August the fleet fell in with the Rifleman sloop of war, from which information was obtained that the United States' frigate Adams had arrived in the Penobscot; and that, from the apprehension of being attacked by British cruizers, if she remained at the entrance of the river, she had run up as high as Hampden, where her guns had been landed, and mounted on shore for her protection.

This information determined governor Sherbroke to proceed first to the Penobscot, in order to arrive there before the Americans had time to strengthen themselves. The fleet arrived off Castine on the 1st of September. The small garrison in the fort not being able to resist the overwhelming force of the British, discharged their guns, blew up the fort, and retired. The enemy then took possession without opposition.

The following day a considerable force was despatched up the river to Hampden, in order to capture or destroy the Adams. Captain Morris, the commander, had received intelligence the day before of the arrival of the expedition off Castine, which was immediately forwarded to brigadier general

Blake, of the militia, with a request that he would direct such force as could be collected to repair immediately to Hampden. As the ship was prepared for heaving down, and in no situation to receive her armament, the attention of the seamen was immediately directed to the occupation of such positions on shore as would best enable them to protect her. By great and unremitted exertions, and the prompt assistance of all the inhabitants in the immediate vicinity, during the 1st and 2d, nine pieces were transported to a commanding eminence near the ship, one to the place selected by general Blake for his line of battle, fourteen upon a wharf commanding the river below, and one on a point covering the communication between the hill and wharf batteries—temporary platforms of loose plank were laid, and such other arrangements made as would enable them to dispute the passage of a naval force. Want of time prevented Morris from improving all the advantages of his position, and he was compelled to leave his rear and flanks to the defence of the militia, in case of attack by land troops.

Favoured by a fresh breeze, the British had advanced to within three miles of the Adams at sun-set on the 2d, with the Sylph mounting 22, and Peruvian 18 guns, and one transport, one tender, and ten barges, manned with seamen from the Bulwark and Dragon, under the command of commodore Barrie. Troops were landed, under the command of colonel John, opposite their shipping, without any opposition, their numbers unknown, but supposed to be about 350. To oppose these troops, about 370 militia were then collected, assisted by lieutenant Lewis, of the United States artillery, who, by a forced march, had arrived from Castine, with his detachment of 28 men.

Many of the militia were without arms, and most of them without any ammunition, and, as the seamen were barely sufficient to man the batteries, the ship's muskets were distributed among the militia; the sick were sent across the creek, with orders for such as were able, to secure themselves in the woods, in case of defeat. These arrangements were not concluded until late on the evening of the 2d.

During the night, the militia were reinforced by three companies. The British were also landed, and at five next morning, marched towards Hampden, in front of which the militia were advantageously posted. But they were not able to withstand the attack of the British regulars; they soon gave way and fled in confusion. Captain Morris and his sailors had now no alternative but precipitate retreat or captivity; their rear and flanks being entirely exposed, while they were destitute of any other defence on that side than their pikes and cutlasses. Lieutenant Wadsworth was therefore ordered to spike the guns, and retire across the bridge, which was done in perfect order, the marines under lieutenant Watson covering the rear. The remainder of Morris's force was at the same time ordered to spike the guns at the lower battery, fire the ship, and then join their companions across the creek.

Before these last orders were fully executed, the enemy appeared on the hill from which the militia had retired, and the seamen were consequently exposed to their fire for a short time while completing them. When they commenced their retreat, it was found to be impossible to gain the bridge; but they succeeded in fording the creek, and rejoining their companions, without receiving the slightest injury from the fire of the enemy.

The loss of the militia was estimated by the British at 30 or 40 killed, wounded, and *missing*, while their loss was only one killed, 8 wounded, and 1 missing. Captain Morris's loss was only a seamen and a marine made prisoner. He estimates the loss of the naval force opposed to him at 8 or 10 killed, and from 40 to 50 wounded, principally by the eighteen-pounder under charge of lieutenant Lewis, of the United States artillery.

Machias being now the only post remaining between the Penobscot and Passamaquoddy bay, a brigade was sent against it from Castine. It was taken without resistance, and colonel Pilkington, the British commander, was making arrangements to proceed into the interior of the country, when he received a letter from brigadier-general Brewer, commanding the district, engaging that the militia within the county of Washington should not bear arms, or in any way serve against his Britannic majesty during the war. A similar offer having been made by the civil officers and principal citizens of the county, a cessation of arms was agreed upon. Thus was this large district of country from the Penobscot eastward, taken possession of almost without resistance.

Having now reviewed the most important transactions of the campaign on our maritime frontier, we will next direct our attention to the upper lakes in the north-west. After the capture of the British fleet on lake Erie, in 1813, an expedition against the important post of Michillimackinac had been contemplated; but the lateness of the season prevented its being carried into effect. Preparations were therefore made the following summer, and an expedition sailed from Detroit against the fort on the 3d of July, 1814; the troops under the command of colonel Croghan, the naval forces under captain Sinclair. The difficulties encountered on the flats of lake St. Clair, where there was only eight feet water, and the rapid current of the river, prevented the squadron from reaching lake Huron till the 12th. Thence the squadron shaped its course for Matchadash bay, and used every possible effort to gain it, but without effect. Not being able to find a pilot for that unfrequented part of the lake, and finding it filled with islands and sunken rocks, which must inevitably have proved the destruction of the fleet had they persisted, it being impossible to avoid them on account of the impenetrable fog with which the lake is almost continually covered; and finding the army already growing short of provisions, it was agreed between colonel Croghan and the commodore to push for the island of St. Joseph's near the head of the lake, where the British had a small establishment, and here they arrived on the 20th. The fort being found deserted was destroyed.

Whilst the squadron remained wind-bound at St. Joseph's, a detachment of infantry and artillery, under major Holmes, was dispatched in the launches, under the command of lieutenant Turner, to St. Mary's, to break up the establishment at that place, and capture a schooner which lay there waiting for a cargo of flour for the North-West company's establishments on lake Superior, which had fallen into the hands of the American squadron by the capture of the schooner Minx, on its way from Michillimackinac to St. Mary's. The establishment, against which this expedition was directed, is a factory of the Montreal company, situated at the foot of the falls of St. Mary, the stream by which lake Superior discharges its waters into lake Huron. These falls are surmounted by a canal, by which goods are passed in boats from the vessels which navigate one lake to those which traverse the other.

The launches, under lieutenant Turner, were rowed night and day; but the distance being 60 miles, against a strong current, information of their approach reached the enemy about two hours before their arrival, carried by Indians in their light canoes. No resistance was made at the fort, but the British and Indians made their escape, carrying with them all the light valuable articles, such as peltry, clothes, &c. Turner, with his sailors and a few of the infantry, instantly proceeded to the head of the rapids, where the enemy, finding he could not get off with the vessel Turner was in quest of, set fire to her in several places and scuttled her. Turner, however, succeeded in boarding her, and by considerable exertions extinguished the flames, and secured her from sinking. But every effort failed to get her through the falls in safety. She bilged on her passage, and being immediately run on shore, was burnt. A part of the public property was brought away, and the remainder destroyed. All private property was respected.

On the return of the launches to St. Joseph's, the squadron proceeded to Michillimackinac, where they arrived on the 26th. This place is, by nature, a second Gibraltar, being a high rock, inaccessible on every side, except the west: from the landing to the heights is nearly two miles, through a very thick wood. Finding that the British had strongly fortified the height overlooking the old fort, Croghan at once despaired of being able, with his small force, to carry the place by storm. He therefore determined to land and establish himself on some favourable position, whence he would be enabled to annoy the enemy by gradual and slow approaches, under cover of his artillery, of which he was superior to the enemy in point of metal. He was also induced to adopt this step by the supposition, that it would either induce the enemy to attack him in his strong holds, or force the Indians and Canadians, the enemy's most efficient, and only disposable force, off the island, as they would be very unwilling to remain after a permanent footing should be taken.

Unfavourable weather prevented the landing of the troops till the 4th of August, when the whole force was disembarked on the west end of the island, under cover of the guns of the shipping. The line being quickly formed, advanced towards a field, which had been recommended as a suitable place for a camp, by persons who had lived several years on the island. Hardly had the troops arrived at the edge of the field, before intelligence was conveyed to colonel Croghan that the enemy was a short distance a-head, and in a few seconds a fire of shot and shells opened on the Americans, from a battery of four pieces.

The enemy's position was well selected; his line reached along the edge of the woods, at the farther extremity of the field, and was covered by a temporary breastwork. On reconnoitering the enemy, Croghan determined to change his position, which was now two lines, the militia forming the front. He accordingly ordered the battalion of regulars under major Holmes, to advance to the right of the militia, thus to outflank the enemy, and by a vigorous effort gain his rear. But before this movement could be executed, a fire was opened by some Indians posted in a thick wood near the American right, which proved fatal to major Holmes, and severely wounded captain Desha, the next officer in rank. This unlucky fire, by depriving the battalion of the services of its most valuable officers, threw that part of tho line into confusion, from which the best exertions of the officers were not able to recover it.

Finding it impossible to gain the enemy's left, owing to the impenetrable thickness of the woods, a charge was ordered to be made by the regulars immediately against the front. This charge, though made in some confusion, served to drive the enemy back in the woods, whence an annoying fire was kept up by the Indians. Lieutenant Morgan was now ordered up with a light piece to assist the left, which, at this time, was particularly galled; its fire soon forced the enemy to retire to a greater distance.

The position contemplated for the camp being now occupied, was found to be by no means tenable, from being interspersed with thickets, and every way intersected by ravines. Croghan determined, therefore, no longer to expose his force to the fire of an enemy deriving every advantage which could be obtained from numbers and a knowledge of the position, and therefore ordered a retreat towards the shipping, which was immediately effected.

The loss of the Americans in this affair was 13 killed, 51 wounded, and 2 missing. The loss of the British has not been ascertained.

Michillimackinac being thus found impregnable by assault, measures were adopted for starving it into submission, by cutting off its supplies. The whole of the troops, except three companies, were therefore dispatched in two of the vessels, to join general Brown on the Niagara, and the rest of the squadron directed their course to the east side of the lake, in order to break up any of the establishments of the enemy in that quarter. The only practicable lines of communication with the lower country, while the Americans were masters of lake Erie, was with Montreal by Outawas, or Grand river, which is connected by means of a portage or carrying-place, with lake Nipissing, which latter empties itself into lake Huron by means of French river; or with York, by means of lake Simcoe and Nautauwasaga river. The first of these communications was learnt to be impracticable during the present season, on account of the marshy state of the portages. The squadron, therefore, proceeded to the mouth of the Nautauwasaga, where it arrived on the 13th of August, and the troops were immediately disembarked on the peninsula formed by the river and lake, for the purpose of fixing a camp.

On reconnoitering this position, a schooner, the only one possessed by the British in this quarter, was discovered in the river, a few hundred yards above, under cover of a block-house erected on a commanding situation on the opposite shore. On the following morning, a fire was opened by the shipping on the block-house for a few minutes, but with little effect, owing to a thin wood intervening to obscure the view. Two howitzers, however, being landed, they commenced throwing shells; and in a few minutes one of the shells burst in the block-house, which shortly after blew up his magazine, allowing the enemy barely time to make his escape. The explosion set fire to a train which had been laid for the destruction of the vessel, and in an instant she was in flames. The necessary preparations had been made by commodore Sinclair for getting on board of her; but frequent and heavy explosions below deck made it too great a risk to attempt saving her. She was, therefore, with her cargo, entirely consumed.

Colonel Croghan not thinking it advisable to fortify and garrison Nautauwasauga, the communication from York being so short and convenient, that any force left there might easily be cut off in the winter, the Scorpion and Tigress were left to blockade it closely, until the season should become too boisterous for boat transportation, and the remainder of the squadron returned to Detroit. But this blockade, which, had it been properly enforced, would probably soon have made a bloodless conquest of Michillimackinac, was soon put an end to by the capture of both the schooners. The Tigress was carried by boarding from the enemy's boats on the night of the 3d of September, and the Scorpion was surprised and taken by the Tigress, on the 6th, at the dawn of day. And thus, by the negligence of the officers, was the capture of Michillimackinac completely frustrated for this season.

The forces employed in the war with the Creek Indians, a part of whose operations has already been detailed in the former part of this volume, were the Tennessee militia, under major-general Jackson, whose head-quarters were at Fort Strother, upon the Coosee river; the Georgia militia, under brigadier-general Floyd, whose operations were directed from the Chatahouchie; and a body of volunteers, in the southern part of the country of the Creeks, under the command of brigadier-general Claiborne. The settlements of the hostile Creeks were principally on and between the Tallapoosee and Coosee rivers. Here stood the towns of Tallushatches, Talledega, and Hillibee, which gave their names to the battles so called, which have already been noticed. The town of Autossee stood on the left bank of the Tallapoosee.

Notwithstanding the decisive victories that have been obtained by the American troops, and the heavy losses of the Indians, and the destruction of their principal towns, this brave people were still unsubdued. General Claiborne, therefore, marched a detachment from Fort Claiborne, on the 13th of December, 1813, with a view to the further destruction of their towns. Fort Claiborne is situated on the Alabama river, at no great distance above where, by its junction with the Tombigbee, it forms the Mobile river. The object in view was a town, called by the Creeks, Eccanachaca, or Holy Ground.—This place, Claiborne was informed, was occupied by a large body of the enemy, under the command of Weatherford, a half-bred chief, who commanded the Indians that commenced the war by the destruction of the garrison at Fort Mims.

When about 30 miles from the town, a stockade was erected for the security of the sick and the heavy baggage, and on the morning of the 22d the troops resumed their line of march. Their course lay chiefly through woods, without a track to guide them. On the morning of the 23d, the disposition for the attack was made. The troops advanced in three columns, a small body acting as a corps de reserve. About noon the right column came in view of the town, and was immediately vigorously attacked by the enemy, who had been apprised of their approach,·and had chosen their field of action. Before the centre or the left could come generally into action, the·enemy were repulsed, and flying in all directions, many of them casting away their arms.

Thirty of the Creeks were killed in this rencontre, and, judging from appearances, many were wounded. The loss on the part of the Americans was one killed and six wounded.

A pursuit was immediately ordered; but from the nature o the country nothing was effected. The town was nearly surrounded by swamps and deep ravines, which rendered the approach of the troops difficult, while it facilitated the escape of the Indians. In the town was found a large quantity of provisions, and immense property of various kinds, which the enemy, flying precipitately, were obliged to leave behind. All were destroyed, together with the village, consisting of about 200 houses. The Indians had barely time to remove their women and children across the Alabama, which runs near where the town stood. The town had been built since the commencement of hostilities, and was established as a place of security for the inhabitants of several villages.

In the house of Weatherford, the commander, was found a letter from the Spanish governor of Pensacola to the leader of

T

the Creeks, stating, that he had presented their request of arms and munitions to the captain-general in Havanna, but had as yet received no answer. He was in hopes, however, he stated, of receiving them; and as soon as that took place, they should be informed.

The following day was occupied by the troops in destroying a town consisting of 60 houses, eight miles higher up the river, and in taking and destroying the boats of the enemy. At this place three Indians of some distinction were killed.

The term of service of the volunteers having now generally expired, they marched to Fort Stoddart, in order to be paid off.

Soon after the battle of Talledega, general Jackson's army had been almost entirely broken up, by the expiration of the time of the militia, but on the 14th of January, he was joined at Fort Strother by about 800 new-raised volunteers from Tennessee, making his whole force, exclusive of Indians, 930.— The term of service of the volunteers being short, and the men full of ardour to meet the enemy, he determined immediately to employ them in active service; and to this he was particularly induced by the information, that the Indians were concentrating with the view of attacking Fort Armstrong, a position about 50 miles above Fort Strother, on the same river, and also by his desire to make a diversion in favour of general Floyd, who was about making a movement to the Tallapoosee river, near its junction with the Coosee.

The volunteers therefore were marched across the river the day after their arrival, and on the next day, Jackson followed with the remainder of his force, consisting of the artillery company with one six-pounder, one company of infantry of 48 men, two companies of spies, of about 30 men each, and a company of volunteer officers, headed by general Coffee, who had been abandoned by his men, under some misapprehension as to their term of service, and who still remained in the field waiting the orders of the government.

On the 17th, the troops took up the line of march, and on the night of the 18th encamped at Talledega Fort, where they were joined by between 200 and 300 friendly Indians; 65 of whom were Cherokees, the remainder Creeks. On the 20th, they encamped at Enotachopco, a small Hillibee village, about 12 miles from Emuckfau. Here Jackson began to perceive very plainly how little knowledge the spies had of the country, of the situation of the enemy, or of the distance the army was from them. The insubordination of the new troops, and the want of skill in most of their officers, also became more and more apparent. But their ardour to meet the enemy was not diminished; and Jackson had a sure reliance upon the guards, and the company of old volunteer officers, and upon the spies, in all about 125.

On the morning of the 21st, the troops marched from Enotachopco, as direct as possible for the head of the Tallapoosee, and about 2 o'clock, P. M. the spies having discovered two of the enemy, endeavoured to overtake them, but failed. In the evening a large trail was perceived, which led to a new road, much beaten and lately travelled. Knowing that he must have arrived within the neighbourhood of a strong force, and it being late in the day, Jackson determined to encamp, and reconnoitre the country in the night. He accordingly chose the best scite the country would admit, encamped in a hollow square, sent out spies and pickets, doubled the centinels, and made the necessary arrangements before dark for a night attack. About 10 o'clock at night one of the pickets fired at three of the enemy, and killed one, but he was not found until the next day. At 11, the spies returned with the information, that there was a large encampment of Indians at the distance of about three miles, who, from their whooping and dancing, seemed to be apprized of the approach of the troops. One of these spies, an Indian in whom Jackson had great confidence, assured him that they were carrying off their women and children, and that their warriors would either make their escape or attack him before day. Being prepared at all points, nothing remained to be done but to await their approach, if they meditated an attack, or to be ready, if they did not, to pursue and attack them at day-light.

While the troops were in this state of readiness, the enemy, about 6 o'clock in the morning, commenced a vigorous attack on the left flank, which was as vigorously met; the action continued to rage on that flank, and on the left of the rear, for about half an hour. So soon as it became light enough to pursue, the left wing, having sustained the heat of the action, and being somewhat weakened, was reinforced by a company of infantry, and was ordered and led on to the charge by general Coffee, who was well supported by all the officers and privates who composed that line. The enemy was completely routed at every point, and the friendly Indians joining in the pursuit, they were chased about two miles with considerable slaughter.

The chase being over, general Coffee was detached with 400 men and all the Indian force to burn the encampment; but with orders, if it was fortified, not to attack it, until the artillery could be sent forward to reduce it. On viewing the encampment and its strength, the general thought it most prudent to return, and guard the artillery thither. The wisdom of this step was soon discovered—in half an hour after his return to camp, a considerable force of the enemy made its appearance on Jackson's right flank, and commenced a brisk fire on a party of men, who had been on picket-guard the night before, and were then in search of the Indians they had fired upon. General Coffee immediately requested 200 men to turn their left flank, which were accordingly ordered; but, through some mistake, not more than 54 followed him, among whom were the old volunteer officers. With these, however, he immediately commenced an attack on the left flank of the enemy, and Jackson ordered 200 of the friendly Indians to fall in upon their right flank, and co-operate with general Coffee. This order was promptly obeyed, and what was expected was realized. The enemy had intended the attack on the right as a feint, and expecting to direct all Jackson's attention thither, meant to attack him again, and with their main force, on the left flank, which they had hoped to find weakened and in disorder. But they were disappointed; for Jackson had ordered the left flank to remain firm to its place, and the moment the alarm-gun was heard in that quarter, he repaired thither, and ordered captain Ferrill, part of the reserve, to support it. The whole line met the approach of the enemy with astonishing intrepidity, and having given a few fires, they forthwith charged with great vigour. The effect was immediate and inevitable. The enemy fled with precipitation, and were pursued to a considerable distance, by the left flank and the friendly Indians, with a galling and destructive fire.

In the mean time general Coffee was contending with a superior force of the enemy. The Indians who had been ordered to his support, and who had set out for this purpose, hearing the firing on the left, had returned to that quarter, and when the enemy were routed there, entered into the chase. That being now over, 100 of them were sent to the relief of Coffee, and as soon as they reached him, the charge was made and the enemy routed: they were pursued about three miles, and 45 of them slain, who were found. General Coffee was wounded in the body, and his aid-de-camp, A. Donaldson, killed, together with three others.

The camp was now fortified, in order that the troops might be the better prepared to repel any attack which might be made the following night, and next morning the troops set out on their return to Fort Strother, general Jackson not deeming it prudent to proceed farther, on account of the scarcity of supplies, the number of his wounded, and the probability of the Indians receiving reinforcements from below. The retreat commenced at 10 o'clock on the 23d, and the troops were fortunate enough to reach Enotachopco before night, having passed a dangerous defile without interruption. The camp was again fortified. Having another defile to pass in the morning, across a deep creek, and between two hills, which Jackson had viewed with attention, as he passed on, and where he expected he might be attacked, he determined to pass it at another point, and gave directions to the guide and fatigue-men accordingly. The general's expectation of an attack in the morning was increased by the signs of the night, and with it his caution. Before the wounded were removed from the interior of the camp, the front and rear-guards were formed, as well as the right and left columns, and the centre moved off in regular order, leading down a ridge to Enotachopco creek, at a point where it was clear of reeds, except immediately on its margin. A general order had been previously issued, pointing out the manner in which the men should be formed in the event of an attack on the front, or rear, or on the flanks, and the officers had been particularly cautioned to halt and form accordingly, the instant the word should be given.

The front guard had crossed with part of the flank columns, the wounded were over, and the artillery in the act of entering the creek when an alarm-gun was heard in the rear. Having chosen the ground, Jackson expected there to have entirely cut off the enemy, by wheeling the right and left columns on their pivot, re-crossing the creek above and below, and falling in upon their flanks and rear. But, to his astonishment and mortification, when the word was given to halt and form, and a few guns had been fired, the right and left columns of the rear-guard precipitately gave way. This shameful retreat was disastrous in the extreme: it drew along with it the greater part of the centre column, leaving not more than 25 men, who being formed by colonel Carroll, maintained their ground as long as it was possible to maintain it. There was then left to repulse the enemy, the few who remained of the rear-guard, the artillery company, and captain Russell's company of spies. Their conduct, however, exceeded the highest expectations. Lieutenant Armstrong, who commanded the artillery company in the absence of captain Deadrick, who was confined by sickness, ordered them to form, and advanced to the top of the hill, whilst he and a few others dragged up the six-pounder. Never was more bravery displayed than on this occasion. Amidst the most galling fire from the enemy, more than ten times their number, they ascended the hill and maintained their position, until their piece was hauled up, when, having levelled it, they poured upon the enemy a fire of grape, re-loaded and fired again, charged and repulsed them.*

A number of the troops now crossed the creek, and entered into the chase. Captain Gordon of the spies, who had rushed from the front, endeavoured to turn the left flank of the enemy, in which he partially succeeded, and colonel Carroll, colonel Higgins, and captains Elliot and Pipkins, pursued the enemy for more than two miles, who fled in consternation, throwing away their packs, and leaving 26 of their warriors dead on the field. This last defeat was decisive, the troops being no more disturbed in their retreat.

The loss sustained in these several engagements was 20 killed and 75 wounded, 4 of whom afterwards died. The loss of the enemy could not be accurately ascertained: 189 of their warriors were found dead; but this must fall considerably short of the number really killed. Their wounded can only be guessed at.

Meanwhile general Floyd was advancing towards the Indian territory from Chatahouchie river. On the 27th of January his camp was attacked by a large body of Indians, at the hour usually chosen for their operations, viz. about an hour before day. They stole upon the centinels, fired upon them, and then with great impetuosity rushed upon the line. In 20

---

* *General Jackson, in his official report, states some instances of perhaps the most deliberate bravery that have ever been recorded. The individuals mentioned were lieutenant Armstrong, Constantine Perkins, and Craven Jackson, all of the artillery, the two latter acting as gunners. In the hurry of the moment, in separating the gun from the limbers, the rammer and picker of the cannon were left tied to the limber: no sooner was this discovered, than Jackson, amidst the galling fire of the enemy, pulled out the ramrod of his musket and used it as a picker; primed with a cartridge, and fired the cannon. Perkins having pulled off his bayonet, used his musket as a rammer, and drove down the cartridge; and Jackson, using his former plan, again discharged her. Lieutenant Armstrong fell, just after the first fire of the cannon, exclaiming, as he lay, " my brave fellows, some of you may fall, but you must save the cannon."*

minutes the action became general, and the front of both flanks were closely pressed, but the gallant conduct of the officers, and the firmness of the men, repelled them at every point. As soon as it became light enough to distinguish objects, Floyd strengthened his right wing to prepare them for a charge, and the cavalry was ordered to form in their rear, to act as circumstances should dictate. The order for the charge was promptly obeyed, and the enemy fled in every direction before the bayonet. The order was then given for the charge of the cavalry, who pursued and sabred fifteen of the enemy.

Thirty-seven Indians were left dead on the field. From the effusion of blood, and number of the war-clubs and head-dresses found in various directions, their loss must have been considerable. Floyd's loss was 17 killed, and 132 wounded.

The Creeks being rather inspirited than cast down by their last encounters with the whites, more vigorous efforts became necessary. General Jackson, therefore, having received rein-forcements of militia from Tennessee, and being joined by a considerable body of Cherokee and friendly Creek Indians, set out on another expedition to the Tallapoosee river. He put his army in motion from the Coosee river on the morning of the 24th of March, and having a passage of fifty-two and a half miles over the ridges which divide the waters of the two rivers, reached the bend of the Tallapoosee, three miles beyond where the engagement of the 22d of January took place, and at the southern extremity of New Youca, on the morning of the 27th.

This bend resembles in its curvature that of a horse-shoe, and is thence called by that name among the whites. Nature furnishes few situations as eligible for defence; and barbarians never rendered one more secure by art, than was this by the Creeks. Across the neck of land which leads into it from the north, they had erected a breastwork, of the greatest compact-ness and strength, from five to eight feet high, and prepared with double rows of port-holes very artfully arranged. The figure of this wall manifested no less skill in the projectors of it, than its construction; an army could not approach it with-out being exposed to a double and cross fire from the enemy, who lay in perfect security behind it. The area of this penin-sula, thus bounded by breastworks, included about 80 or 100 acres.

In this bend the warriors from Oakfuskee, Oakchaya, New Youca, Hillabees, the Fish Ponds, and Eufauta towns, appriz-ed of Jackson's approach, had collected their strength. Their exact number was not ascertained; but it was believed to have

been about 1000: and relying with the utmost confidence upon their strength, their situation, and the assurances of their
prophets, they calculated on repusing Jackson with great
ease.

Early on the morning of the 27th, having encamped the preceding night at the distance of six miles from the bend, Jackson detached general Coffee. with the mounted men and nearly the whole of the Indian force, to pass the river at a ford
about three miles below their encampment; and to surround
the bend in such a manner that none of them should escape by
attempting to cross the river.   With the remainder of the
forces Jackson proceeded along the point of land, which led
to the front of their breastwork; and at half past 10 o'clock,
planted his artillery on a small eminence, distant from the nearest point of the breastwork about 80 yards, and from its farth-
est about 250; from which a brisk fire was immediately opened
upon its centre.   Whenever the enemy showed themselves
behind their works, or ventured to approach them, a galling
fire was opened upon them with musquetry and rifles.

Meanwhile general Coffee, having crossed below, turned up
the river, bearing away from its cliffs.   When within half a
mile of the village, which stood at the extremity of the peninsula, the savage yell was raised by the enemy.   Expecting an
immediate attack, Coffee drew up his forces in line of battle,
in open hilly woodland, and moved forward in that position.
The friendly Indians had been previously ordered to advance
secretely and take possession of the bank of the river, and prevent the enemy from crossing on the approach of Jackson's
main body in front.   Accordingly, the fire of Jackson's cannon
commencing when Coffee's troops were within about a quarter of a mile from the river, his Indians immediately rushed
forward with great impetuosity to its banks.   The militia were
halted, and kept in order of battle, an attack on the rear being
expected from the Oakfuskee villages, which lay on the river
about eight miles below.

The fire of the cannon and small arms becoming now general and heavy in front, animated the Indians on the bank; and
seeing about 100 of the warriors, and all the squaws and children of the enemy running about among the huts of the village on the opposite shore, they could no longer remain silent spectators.   While some kept up a fire across the river
(here about 120 yards wide), to prevent the enemy's approach
to the bank, others plunged into the river and swam across for
canoes, that lay on the other side in considerable numbers.—
Having succeeded in bringing them over, numbers embarked,

and landing in the peninsula, advanced into the village, and soon drove the enemy from the huts up to the fortification, where they pursued and continued to annoy them during the whole action.

This movement of the friendly Indians leaving the river bank unguarded, made it necessary that a part of Coffee's line should take their place. A company of rangers were accordingly posted on the bank of the upper part, and a lieutenant with 40 men took possession of an island in the lower part of the bend.

Finding that the friendly Indians, notwithstanding the determined bravery they displayed, were wholly insufficient to dislodge the enemy, and that general Coffee had secured the opposite banks of the river, Jackson determined upon taking possession of the works by storm. Never were men better disposed for such an undertaking, than those by whom it was to be effected. They had entreated to be led to the charge with the most pressing importunity; and received the order which was now given, with the strongest demonstration of joy. The effect was such as this temper of mind foretold. The regular troops, led by colonel Williams and major Montgomery, were presently in possession of the nearer side of the breastwork; and the militia accompanied them in the charge with a vivacity and firmness which could not have been exceeded, and have seldom been equalled by troops of any description.

Having maintained for a few minutes a very obstinate contest, muzzle to muzzle, through the port-holes, in which many of the enemy's balls were welded to the American bayonets, they succeeded in gaining possession of the opposite side of the works. The event could then no longer be doubtful; the enemy, although many of them fought to the last with that kind of bravery which desperation inspires, were routed and cut to pieces. The whole margin of the river which surrounded the peninsula, was strewed with the slain: 557 were found, besides a great number who were thrown in the river by their surviving friends, and killed in attempting to pass it, by general Coffee's men, stationed on the opposite banks. Not more than 20 could have escaped. Among the dead was found their famous prophet Manahoee, shot in the mouth by a grape-shot, and two other prophets. Two or three women and children were killed by accident. The number of prisoners taken exceeded 300, all women and children excepting three or four.

The battle may be said to have continued with severity for about five hours; but the firing and the slaughter continued until it was suspended by the darkness of the night. The next morning it was resumed, and 16 of the enemy slain, who had concealed themselves under the banks.

Jackson's loss was 26 white men killed, and 107 wounded, 18 Cherokees killed, and 36 wounded; 5 friendly Creeks killed, and 11 wounded.

This most decisive battle completely broke the spirit as well as power of the hostile Creeks, who were never after able to make head against the troops of the United States. Jackson shortly after completely scoured the Coosee and Tallapoosee rivers, and the entervening country. A part of the enemy on the latter river, just before his arrival, made their escape across it, and fled in consternation towards Pensacola. Most of the inhabitants on the Coosee and the neighbouring country came in, and surrendered unconditionally. Many of the negroes taken at Fort Mims were delivered up, and one white woman, with her two children.

A detachment of militia from North and South Carolina, under the command of colonel Pearson, scoured the country below, upon the Alibama, took a number of prisoners, and received the submission of a great number of Creek warriors and prophets. On the return of Pearson's expedition, he had with him upwards of 600 of the late hostile Creeks, and nearly all the remaining negroes that had been captured at Fort Mims.

On the 1st of August, the principal chiefs of the hostile Creeks met general Jackson at the fort called by his name, for the purpose of concluding articles of agreement and capitulation, which were agreed upon the 9th of the same month. By this treaty a large and valuable portion of their territory was ceded to the United States, as an equivalent for the expenses incurred in prosecuting the war, and the right of the United States to establish military posts and trading-houses, and to open roads within their territory, was acknowledged, as also the right to the free navigation of all their waters. The Creeks also engaged to make an immediate surrender of all the persons and property taken from the citizens of the United States, the friendly part of the Creek nation, the Cherokee, Chickasaw, and Choctaw nations, to the respective owners; and to surrender all the prophets and instigators of the war, whether foreigners or natives, who had not submitted to the arms of the United States, and become parties to these articles, if ever they should be found within the territory of the Creeks. It was also stipulated, that the Creeks should abandon all communication, and cease to hold any intercourse with any British or Spanish post, garrison, or town; and that they should not admit among them any agent or trader, who should not derive authority to hold commercial or other intercourse with them, by license from the president or authorised agent of the United States. The United States engaged to guarantee the remainder of their territory, and to restore all their prisoners; and, in consideration of the nation being reduced to extreme want, and not having at present the means of subsistance, the United States engaged, from motives of humanity, to continue to furnish them gratuitously with the necessaries of life, until the crops of corn could be considered competent to yield the nation a supply; and to establish trading-houses, to enable the nation by industry and economy to procure clothing.

Thus ended the Creek war, after a prodigious slaughter of those brave, misguided men, and the unconditional submission of the remainder, excepting a few who took refuge in Florida. Nearly the whole of the Creek towns were destoyed.

But hardly was the Indian war at an end, before new troubles sprang up in this quarter, and general Jackson was forced to encounter a much more formidable enemy. After concluding the treaty with the Creeks, Jackson moved his head quarters to Mobile, where, on the 27th of August, he received information by express, from Pensacola, that three British vessels had arrived there on the 25th, which, on the following day, had disembarked an immense quantity of arms, ammunition, munitions of war, and provisions; and marched into the Spanish fort between two and three hundred troops. He was likewise informed that thirteen sail of the line, with a large number of transports, bringing 10,000 troops, were daily expected.

On the receipt of this information, Jackson immediately dispatched an express to the governor of Tennessee, at Nashville, requesting that the whole of the quota of the militia of that state should be organized, equipped, and brought into the field, without delay, and his adjutant-general, then in Tennessee, was instructed to make the necessary arrangements for immediately provisioning and bringing the troops to head-quarters.

The three vessels which had arrived at Pensacola, joined by another, soon after sailed from that port for Mobile, and on the 15th of September appeared off Fort Bowyer. The town of Mobile, where general Jackson had his head-quarters, is situated on the west side of the Mobile river, at its entrance into the bay of the same name. Mobile bay is about 30 miles long, and of considerable breadth; but its entrance is only five miles broad, and is completely commanded by Fort Bowyer, which is situated at the extreme point on the east side of the bay.—The fort was occupied by a small garrison, commanded by major Lawrence, of the 2d infantry.

The British squadron, consisting of two ships and two brigs, appeared in sight about noon of the 15th, standing directly for the fort. At 4, in the afternoon, the battery was opened upon them; the firing was immediatly returned from all the vessels. A force of 110 marines, commanded by colonel Nicholls, 200 Creek Indians, headed by captain Woodbine, of the British navy, and about 20 artillerists, had been previously landed in the rear of the fort, and opened a fire upon it from a twelve-pounder and a howitzer, but they did no execution, and were soon silenced by a few shot. The action continued without intermission on either side for nearly three hours, when three of the vessles were compelled to retire. The commodore's ship, which mounted 22 thirty-two-pound carronades, having anchored nearest the fort, had her cable cut by the shot, and was so much disabled that she drifted on shore, within 600 yards of the battery; when the other vessels being out of reach, such a tremendous fire was opened upon her, that she was set on fire and abandoned by such of her crew as survived. Out of a crew of 170 men, the commander and 20 men only escaped. On board of the other ship, 85 were killed and wounded; one of the brigs also was very considerably damaged; but her loss was not ascertained. The effective force in the fort was about 120 men; their loss was only four killed and five wounded.—During the hottest part of the action the flag-staff being shot away, the flag was immediately regained under a heavy fire of grape and cannister, hoisted on a sponge staff, and planted on the parapet. The land-forces retreated by land to Pensacola, after having re-embarked their pieces.

A short time previous to this attack, a proclamation was issued by Edward Nicholls, commanding his Britannic majesty's forces in the Floridas, and dated head-quarters, Pensacola, addressed to the inhabitants of Louisiana, Kentucky, and Tennessee. In this address the natives of Louisiana are called upon to assist the British forces in liberating their paternal soil from a fruitless, imbecile government; to abolish the American usurpation, and put the lawful owners of the soil in possession. The inhabitants of Kentucky and Tennessee are told that they have too long borne with grievous impositions; that the brunt of the war has fallen on their brave sons; and they are intreated to be imposed on no more, but either to range themselves under the standard of their forefathers, or observe a strict neutrality. If they complied with either of these offers, the address assured them, that whatever provisions they sent down should be paid for in dollars, and the safety of the persons bringing it, as well as the free navigation of the Mississippi, guaranteed.

The proclamation then calls to the view of the "men of Kentucky the conduct of those factions which hurried them into this cruel, unjust, and unnatural war, at a time when Great Britain was straining every nerve in defence of her own and the liberties of the world; when she was expending millions of her treasure in endeavouring to pull down one of the most formidable and dangerous tyrants that ever disgraced the form of man. When groaning Europe was in her last gasp, when Britons alone showed an undaunted front, basely did these assassins endeavour to stab her from the rear; she has turned on them renovated from the bloody but successful struggle. Europe is happy and free, and she now hastens justly to avenge the unprovoked insult. Shew them," continued Nicholls, "that you are not collectively unjust—leave that contemptible few to shift for themselves; let those slaves of the tyrant send an embassy to Elba, and implore his aid; but let every honest, upright American spurn them with merited contempt. After the experience of 21 years, can you any longer support those brawlers of liberty, who call it freedom, when themselves are no more free than their impostors? Be no longer their dupes, accept my offers, and all that is promised you in the proclamation, I guarantee to you, on the sacred word of a British officer."

A greater degree of ignorance of the nature of the people addressed, was perhaps never displayed, than was manifested in this proclamation. Nicholls himself was enabled to take a pretty favourable view of its reception a few days after it was issued, as he headed the land forces employed agaist Fort Bowyer.

Previous to the attack upon Mobile, Nicholls had held out the most seducing offers to induce a band of lawless men, who had formed an establishment on the island of Barrataria, to enter into the British service in the operations planned against Lower Louisiana. But although these men were acting in the most lawless manner, and though they were actually proscribed by the American government, they would not consent to act the part of traitors. Instead of accepting the British offers, they procrastinated their answer, and immediately dispatched the intelligence to New Orleans.

U

The Barratarians principally consisted of the officers and crews of French privateers, who, on the capture of Guadaloupe, the last of the French West-India islands, had repaired to Carthagena, and accepted commissions from the new government which had been established there. For the convenience of disposing of their prizes, these men resorted to Barrataria, and formed establishments in the island of Grand Terre, and other places along the coast of Louisiana to the west of the Mississippi, whence, it is said, they preyed indiscriminately upon the commerce of all nations, not excepting even that of the United States, in whose dominions they had thus unwarrantably settled themselves. The chief intercourse of the Barratarians was with New Orleans, almost all their prize goods being smuggled into that port.

In the year 1813, this lawless colony excited the attention of the government of Louisiana, and a company was ordered out to break up the establishment. But this small force proved quite ineffectual: the whole party were surprised and captured before they reached the settlements of this resolute set of men. The naval force however, being considerably strengthened in the summer of 1814, a new expedition was fitted out. On the 11th of September, commodore Patterson left New Orleans with a detachment of 70 of the 44th regiment of infantry, commanded by colonel Ross, and being joined by the schooner Caroline at Placquemine, and the gun-boats at the Balize, on the morning of the 16th made the island of Barrataria, and discovered a number of vessels in the harbour, some of which shewed Carthagenian colours. As soon as the squadron was perceived, the Barratarians formed their vessels, ten in number, into a line of battle near the entrance of the harbour; and Patterson also formed his vessels into a line of battle, consisting of six gun-boats, a tender, and a launch; the schooner Caroline drawing too much water to cross the bar. On the approach of the squadron, however, the Barratarians abandoned their vessels, and took to flight in all directions in their small boats, having previously fired two of their best schooners. The launch, with two gun-barges and the small boats, were immediately sent in pursuit, and all the vessels in the harbour were taken possession of, and the establishment on shore completely destroyed.

The unprecedented conduct of the governor of Pensacola, in harbouring and aiding the British and their Indian allies, and in allowing them to fit out expeditions against the United States from that port, had been forcibly remonstrated against by general Jackson, but hitherto without effect. Having been

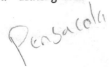

reinforced by about 2000 Tennessee militia, which had marched to Mobile through the Indian country, Jackson, therefore, advanced towards Pensacola to demand redress. He reached the neighbourhood of that post on the afternoon of the 6th of November, and immediately sent a flag to communicate the object of his visit to the governor; but it was forced to return, being fired on from the batteries. Jackson then reconnoitered the fort, and finding it defended by both English and Spanish troops, determined to storm the town, and accordingly made the necessary arrangements for carrying his determination into effect the next day.

The troops were put in motion for the attack early on the 7th. Being encamped to the west of the town, Jackson calculated that the attack would be expected from that quarter. To cherish this idea, part of the mounted men were sent to show themselves on the west, while the remainder of the troops passed in the rear of the fort, undiscovered, to the east of the town. When at the distance of a mile, the town appeared in full view. The troops, principally militia, with a few regulars, and some Choctaw Indians, advanced with the most undaunted courage, although a strong fort appeared ready to assail them on the right, seven British armed vessels on the left, and strong block-houses and batteries of cannon in front. On entering the town, a battery of two cannon was opened on the centre column, composed of the regulars, with ball and grape, and a shower of musquetry from the houses and gardens. The battery was immediately stormed, and the musquetry was soon silenced by the steady and well-directed fire of the regulars.

The governor now made his appearance with a flag, and begged for mercy, offering to surrender the town and fort unconditionally. Mercy was granted, and protection given to the citizens and their property, although the officer commanding the fort refused to give it up, and held it till near mid night, when he evacuted it with his troops. The British moved down to the Barrancas, a strong fort commanding the harbour, and, finding that Jackson had gained possession the town, next morning spiked and dismounted the cannon, and blew up the fort, just as the American troops were preparing to march and storm the place.

The British then withdrew to their shipping, and general Jackson, having accomplished his object, evacuated the town, and returned to the American dominions.

The dangers impending over New Orleans, from the threatened expedition of the British, now rendered the presence of general Jackson highly necessary at that city. He arrived there with his troops on the 2d of December, and immediate measures of defence were adopted, by embodying the militia, repairing the forts on the river, &c.

A few days after Jackson's arrival, the British fleet made their appearance in the Bay of St. Louis, and on the 12th, the fleet appeared in such strength off Ship island, as to induce lieutenant Jones, who commanded the American flotilla of gun-boats, to retire higher up the lake, to take a position to defend the passes to New-Orleans. On the 13th, the American schooner Seahorse, which had been sent by the commodore that morning to the Bay of St. Louis, to assist in the removal of some public stores, was attacked by three of the enemy's barges. These were driven off, but being reinforced by four others, the schooner was blown up by her crew, and the store-house set on fire. On the following day, the American flotilla, while becalmed, was attacked by 42 heavy launches and gun-barges, manned with 1000 men and officers, and after a vigorous resistance, for upwards of an hour, against this overwhelming force, the whole flotilla was captured by the enemy.

The news of the arrival of the British squadron in these waters reached New Orleans on the 12th of December, and in a day or two after, martial law was proclaimed in the city, and the militia called out *en masse*. Large appropriations were made by the legislature of Louisiana for the erection of batteries, and granting bounties to seamen to enlist in the service; an embargo was laid for three days in order to stop the departure of those individuals; and a requisition was made by general Jackson of negroes to work on the fortifications, and all those found in the streets were impressed for that purpose, as well as all kinds of drays and carts. Four thousand Tennessee militia arrived by water on the 21st, and Jackson was further reinforced by the Barratarians, to whom an amnesty was granted by the general and the governor of Louisiana, on condition of their joining in the defence of the country.

The loss of the gun-boats having given the enemy command of lake Borgne, he was enabled to choose his point of attack. It became, therefore, an object of importance to obstruct the numerous bayous and canals leading from that lake to the highlands on the Mississippi. This important service was committed to major-general Villere, commanding the district between the river and the lakes, who, being a native of the country, was presumed to be best acquainted with all these passes. Unfortunately, however, a picket which the general had established at the mouth of the bayou Bienvenu, and which, notwithstanding general Jackson's orders, had been left unobstructed, was completely surprised, and the enemy penetrated through a canal leading to his farm, about two leagues below the city, and succeeded in cutting off a company of militia stationed there. This intelligence was communicated to Jackson about 12 o'clock on the 23d. His force at this time consisted of parts of the 7th and 44th regiments, not exceeding 600 together, the city militia, a part of general Coffee's brigade of mounted gun-men, and the detached militia from the western division of Tennessee, under the command of major-general Carrol. These two last corps were stationed four miles above the city. Apprehending a double attack by the way of Chef Menteur, general Carrol's force, and the militia of the city, were left posted on the Gentilly road, and at 5 o'clock, P. M. Jackson marched to meet the enemy, whom he was resolved to attack in his first position, with major Hind's dragoons, general Coffee's brigade, parts of the 7th and 44th regiments, the uniformed companies of militia, under the command of major Planche, 200 men of colour, chiefly from St. Domingo, and a detachment of artillery, under the direction of colonel M'Rea, with 2 six-pounders, under the command of lieutenant Spots, not exceeding in all 1500 men.

Jackson arrived near the enemy's encampment about 7, and immediately made his dispositions for the attack. The enemy's forces, amounting at that time on land to about 3000, extended half a mile on the river, and in the rear nearly to the wood. General Coffee was ordered to turn their right, while, with the residue of the force, Jackson attacked his strongest position on the left near the river. Commodore Patterson, having dropped down the river in the schooner Caroline, was directed to open a fire upon their camp, which he executed about half after 7. This being the signal of attack, general Coffee's men, with their usual impetuosity, rushed on the enemy's right and entered their camp, while Jackson's troops advanced with equal ardour.

Unfortunately, a thick fog, which arose about eight o'clock, caused some confusion among the different corps. Fearing the consequences, under this circumstance, of the further prosecution of a night attack with troops then acting together for the first time, Jackson contented himself with lying on the field that night; and at four in the morning assumed a stronger position about two miles nearer to the city.

In this action the American loss was 24 killed, 115 wounded, and 74 missing; the British loss amounted to 46 killed, 167 wounded, and 64 missing.

The country between New Orleans and the sea is one extensive swamp, excepting the immediate banks of the Mississippi. These banks are generally about a quarter of a mile wide, and being higher than the country behind, are dry, except in time of inundation, when the whole country would form one vast flood, were it not for the artificial banks or levees which have been erected for the preservation of the farms on this narrow, but fertile strip of land. The city of New Orleans itself is protected from the river in the same manner. At intervals there are *bayous* or outlets which pierce these banks; the water. which flows through them, however, never returns to the bed of the river, but finds its way to the Gulf of Mexico by other channels through the swamps.

From this description of the country, it will be perceived that New Orleans is extremely susceptible of defence, and that over a certain proportion, numbers are nearly unavailing. The position taken up by general Jackson occupied both banks of the river, On the left it was simply a straight line of a front of about 1000 yards, with a parapet, the right resting on the river, and the left on a wood, which communicated with the swamp, and the passage of which had been rendered impracticable for troops. This line was strengthened by flank works, and had a ditch with about four feet of water. On the right bank was a heavy battery of 15 guns, which enfiladed the whole front of the position on the left bank.

The British having erected a battery in the night of the 26th, succeeded on the following day, in blowing up the schooner Caroline, which lay becalmed a short distance above in the Mississippi. Her crew, however, had previously made their escape. Emboldened by this event, the enemy marched his whole force on the 28th up the levee, in the hope of driving the Americans from their position, and with this view opened upon them, at the distance of about half a mile, his bombs and rockets. He was repulsed, however, with the loss of 16 killed, and 38 wounded. The American loss was 7 killed, and 8 wounded.

Another attempt was made upon the American lines on the 1st of January. The enemy having the preceding night erected a battery near the works, in the morning opened a heavy fire from it, and made two bold attempts to force and turn the left wing, in both of which they were repulsed; and in the course of the night they retreated to their lines, leaving all their guns on the battery, which they had previously spiked,

VICTORY AT NEW ORLEANS.

and a considerable quantity of ammunition, working-tools, and their dead unburied. Their loss on this occasion was 32 killed, 44 wounded, and 2 missing; that of the Americans, 11 killed and 23 wounded.

General Jackson was reinforced by 2500 Kentucky militia on the 4th, and on the 6th the British were joined by general Lambert, at the head of the second part of the expedition. Serious preparations were now made for storming the American works.

On the night of the 7th, with infinite labour, the British succeeded in getting their boats into the Mississippi, by widening and deepening the channel of the bayou, from which they had about two weeks before effected their disembarkation. Though these operations were not unperceived, it was not in Jackson's power to impede them by a general attack: the nature of the troops under his command, mostly militia, rendering it too hazardous to attempt extensive offensive movements in an open country, against a numerous and well-disciplined army. Although his forces, as to number, had been increased by the arrival of the Kentucky division, his strength had received very little addition; a small portion only of that detachment being provided with arms. Compelled thus to wait the attack of the enemy, Jackson, however, took every measure to repel it when it should be made, and to defeat the object in view.

Early in the morning of the 8th, the enemy, after throwing a heavy shower of bombs and Congreve rockets, advanced their columns on the right and left, to storm the entrenchments on the left bank of the Mississippi; throwing over a considerable force in his boats at the same time to the right bank. The entrenchments on the right bank, were occupied by general Morgan, with the New Orleans contingent, the Louisiana militia, and a strong detachment of the Kentucky troops; general Jackson, with the Tennessee and the remainder of the Kentucky militia, occupied the works on the left bank.

The columns of the enemy advanced in good order towards Jackson's entrenchments, the men shouldering their muskets, and all carrying fascines, and some with ladders. The batteries now opened an incessant fire on the British columns, which continued to advance in pretty good order, until, in a few minutes, the musquetry of the militia joining their fire with that of the artillery, began to make an impression on them, which soon threw them into confusion. At this time the noise of the continued rolling fire resembled the concussion of tremendous peals of thunder. For some time the British officers succeeded in animating the courage of their troops, although every discharge from the batteries opened the columns, mowing down whole files, which were almost instantaneously replaced by new troops coming up close after the first: but these also shared the same fate, until at last, after 25 minutes continued firing, through which a few platoons advanced to the edge of the dith, the columns broke and retreated in confusion.

A second attack was received in the same manner. The British were forced to retreat, with an immense loss. But vain was the attempt of the officers to bring them up a third time. The soldiers were insensible to every thing but danger, and saw nothing but death, which had struck so many of their comrades.

Near the commencement of the attack, general Packenham, the British commander-in-chief, lost his life at the head of his troops, and soon after generals Keane and Gibbs were carried off the field dangerously wounded. A great many other officers of rank fell, and the plain between the front line of the British and the American works, a distance of 400 yards, was literally covered with the enemy's dead and wounded. At this time general Jackson's loss was only seven killed and six wounded.

The entire destruction of the British army had now been inevitable, had not an unfortunate occurrence at this moment taken place on the right bank of the river. The troops which had landed there were hardy enough to advance against the works, and at the very moment when their entire discomfiture was looked for with confidence, the Kentucky militia ingloriously fled, drawing after them, by their example, the remainder of the forces. Commodore Patterson, who commanded the batteries, was of course forced to abandon them, after spiking his guns.

This unfortunate rout totally changed the aspect of affairs. The enemy now occupied a position from which he could annoy Jackson without hazard, and by means of which he might have been enabled to defeat, in a great measure, the effects of the success of the Americans on the other side of the river. It became, therefore, an object of the first consequence to dislodge him as soon as possible. For this object, all the means which Jackson could with any safety use, were immediately put in preparation. But so great had been the loss of the British on the left bank, that they were not able to spare a sufficient number of troops to hold the position which they had gained on the right bank without jeopardizing the safety of the whole. The troops were, therefore, withdrawn, and Jackson immediately regained the lost position.

The spirit of atrocity and vengeance, which marked the conduct of the British during the campaign, was manifested even in this battle, although they suffered so signal a defeat.— After their final repulse on the left bank, numbers of the American troops, prompted merely by sentiments of humanity, went, of their own accord, in front of their lines, to assist the wounded British, to give them drink, and to carry them (as they did several of them on their backs) within the lines.— While they were thus employed, they were actually fired upon, and several killed. Yet the others, regardless of the danger, persevered in their laudable purpose. This instance of baseness may have proceeded from individuals; nor would it in common cases be presumed, that the men were ordered to fire by their officers: but if the fact be, as has been repeatedly asserted without contradiction, that the watchword of the day was the significant words " *beauty and booty*," no charge would seem too attrocious for belief against the British commanders.

The total loss of the Americans in this action, on both sides of the river, was 13 killed, 39 wounded, and 19 missing. The British acknowledge a loss of 293 killed, 1267 wounded, and 484 missing. About 100 stand of arms of different descriptions were taken by the Americans.

The British having retired to their old position, continued to occupy it till the night of the 18th, although constantly annoyed by the American artillery on both sides of the river. At midnight they precipitately decamped, and returned to their boats, leaving behind, under medical attendance, '80 wounded, including two officers. Fourteen pieces of heavy artillery, and a quantity of shot, were also abandoned, and a great deal of powder, which, however, was previously destroyed. But, such was the situation of the ground which the enemy abandoned, and of that through which he retired, protected by canals, redoubts, entrenchments, and swamps on his right, and the river on his left, that Jackson could not, without encountering a risk which true policy did not seem to require or to authorise, attempt to annoy him much on his retreat. He took only eight prisoners.

Commodore Patterson, however, dispatched five boats and a gig, manned and armed with 50 men, under the command of Mr. Thomas Shields, purser on the New-Orleans station, to annoy the retreat of the British. On the night of the 19th, a boat lying at anchor was captured by surprise, without resistance, containing 40 dragoons and 14 seamen. The prisoners exceeding the detachment in numbers, Shields returned, and placing them in charge of the army, again set out in pursuit, in the hope of intercepting some of the enemy's boats about day-light, but without success.

On the morning of the 21st, Shields once more pushed off among the transports of the enemy, and captured several, but unfortunately, owing to a strong contrary wind, he was not able to bring them off; some of them were therefore given up to the parolled prisoners, and the remainder destroyed.— Seventy-eight prisoners were brought in by this intrepid little band.

Meantime the British fleet having proceeded up the Mississippi, bombarded Fort St. Philip for eight or nine days; but not being able to make any impression, they commenced their retreat about the same time that the army above embarked in their boats, viz. on the 18th of January. The bombarding vessels were stationed most of the time out of the reach of the guns of the fort. Major Overton, the commander, lost only two killed and seven wounded.

We have never seen any official statement of the forces employed in this expedition; but the most probable calculation makes the force landed below New Orleans, about 15,000 viz. 11,000 land-troops, and 4000 sailors and marines. So confident were the British of success, that collectors of the customs and other civil officers attended the expedition, several of whom were among the prisoners taken by Shields, on the retreat of the army.

As soon as the British troops were embarked on board their shipping, the squadron made for Mobile bay, and completely invested Fort Bowyer both by land and water. A large force was landed on the 18th of February, who made regular approaches, keeping up a constant firing, until the 11th, when, the approaches being within pistol-shot of the fort, colonel Lawrence was summoned to surrender. Resistance being unavailing against the overwhelming force of the enemy, articles of capitulation were agreed to, surrendering the fort to the British, the garrison, consisting of 366 men, including officers, being considered prisoners of war. On the 10th, and 11th, general Winchester, who commanded at Mobile, threw a detachment across the bay for the relief of Fort Bowyer, but too late to effect any thing, except the capture of one of the British barges, with 17 men.

While these operations were carried on in the Gulph of Mexico, a considerable force was stationed off the coast of

South Carolina and Georgia, menacing Charleston and Savannah. They took possession of Cumberland Island, as a military station, but nothing of consequence was effected on the main, excepting the capture of St. Mary's, by a detachment under admiral Cockburn, who again returned to Cumberland island, after they effected their purpose by the destruction of the forts in the neighbourhood.

Having thus reviewed every important military event, we shall now turn our attention to the ocean, where our cruizers continued to range with unabated vigour, and where, to use the querulous language of the British journalists, " if they fight, they are sure to conquer; if they fly, they are sure to escape."

It will be recollected, that in October, 1812, the Constitution and Hornet sailed from Boston on a cruize, which proved memorable by the destruction of the Java by the former, and that of the Peacock by the latter. The Essex, captain Porter, sailed from the Delaware about the same time, under orders to join commodore Bainbridge, who commanded the squadron. Porter left the capes on the 28th of October, and steered for the Cape de Verd islands, the first appointed rendezvous, crossing the track of the homeward-bound British Indiamen, and the outward-bound West Indiamen. Without meeting any enemy's vessels, he reached St. Jago, and put into Port Praya for supplies. On the 29th of November he left the Cape de Verds for the Brazil coast. A few days after, a British packet was captured, with about $55,000 in specie, which being taken out, the vessel was dispatched with a prize-master to the United States.

The island of Fernando de Noronha, the second place of rendezvous, was reached on the 14th of December. Here Porter received a communication from the commodore, addressed to him under the fictitious title of sir James Lucas Yeo, stating that he would find him off Cape Frio. Without entering the port, therefore, the Essex stood to the southward. Near Rio de Janeiro a British schooner was captured, and after taking the prisoners out, it was discovered, that about an hour before their capture, they had parted with a small convoy of British vessels under charge of the Juniper, a three-masted schooner. All sail, therefore, was immediately made in pursuit, but every effort to reach them proved abortive. During the pursuit intelligence was received, from different vessels, first of the blockade of the Bonne Citoyenne by the Constitution and Hornet, and afterwards of the capture of an American vessel by the Montague 74, which captain Porter strongly suspected to be the Hornet, with the addition that the Montague had gone in pursuit of the frigate.

This intelligence removed all expectations of the Essex being enabled to join commodore Bainbridge; and it became
absolutely necessary, therefore, for Porter to depart from the
letter of his instructions. He accordingly determined to pursue that course which seemed best calculated to injure the
enemy, and to enable the cruize to be prolonged. This
could only be done by going into a friendly port where supplies could be obtained, without the danger of blockade; and
the most suitable place for that purpose seemed to be the port
of Conception, on the coast of Chili. The season, it being now
the end of January, was, to be sure, far advanced for doubling
Cape Horn; the stock of provisions also was short, and the
ship in other respects not well supplied with stores for so
long a cruize. But there appeared to Porter no other choice
left, except capture, starvation, or blockade. This course
seemed to him the more justifiable, also, as it accorded with
the views of the secretary of the navy, as well as those of the
commodore. Before the declaration of war, Porter had laid
before the secretary a plan of annoying the enemy's commerce
in the Pacific, which had been approved of; and prior to this
cruize, commodore Bainbridge having requested his opinion
as to the best mode of annoying the enemy, Porter had laid
the same plan before him. This had also been approved of
by the commodore, who signified his intention to pursue it,
provided supplies of provisions could be procured. Although
there was considerable responsibility attached to this proceeding, and the undertaking was greater than had yet been engaged in by any single ship in similar pursuits, yet the season
admitting of no delay, Porter, immediately on getting to sea,
stood to the southward, and the crew were put on short allowance of provisions, in order to husband them for the long voy-
age on which they were now embarked.

Cape Horn was doubled about the middle of February,
amidst tremendous storms; and the Essex surmounted all the
dangers of hurricanes, fogs, and breakers, by the intrepidity
of her commander, and the distinguished coolness and activity
of her crew, to which the uncommon degree of health they
enjoyed, from the judicious arrangements of captain Porter,
not a little contributed. In the latitude of about 40° south,
pleasant moderate weather succeeded to the incessant storms
and severe cold experienced in the passage around the stormy
cape, and on the 6th of March, the Essex came to an anchor
off an uninhabited island called Mocha, in the latitude of about
38° 15' S. about eight leagues distant from the coast of Chili.
At Mocha, a considerable supply of fresh provisions was pro-

cured by shooting the wild hogs and horses which abound in that island. The flesh of the latter was found to be the preferable food, that of the hogs being tough.

Porter again steering his course along the iron-bound coast of Chili, on the 15th of March put into the port of Valparaiso, where, contrary to his expectations, he was received with the utmost attention and hospitality. This arose from the change which had lately taken place here, the Chilians having assumed the government, though, without absolutely declaring themselves independent of old Spain. The arrival of an American frigate was considered a most happy event, and was celebrated in their capital, St. Jago, by illumination and the ringing of bells. It was generally believed in Chili, that Porter had brought proposals for a friendly alliance, and assurances of assistance in their struggle for independence; and this construction he thought it politic rather to encourage, as it suited his views of readily obtaining supplies.

The Essex remained a week at Valparaiso. During that time two Spanish vessels had sailed for Lima, which rendered his speedy departure necessary, as they would certainly communicate the intelligence of his arrival to the enemy, and as it was Porter's intention to visit that coast next, for, from all accounts, the coast of Peru, and from there to the Gallapagos islands, was the favourite fishing-ground of the British whalers. Porter accordingly run down the coast of Chili and Peru, and thence proceeded to the Gallapagos island. In this track he fell in with the Peruvian corsair, which he disarmed, and among the Gallapagos captured three British whalers.

The Essex remained six months at the Gallapagos islands, during which, however, one trip was made to Tumbez, on the coast of Peru, where a number of prisoners were landed on parole. During the cruize among those islands, the whole of the valuable British-whale vessels in the Pacific were captured, excepting one which had been laid up at Coquimbo for the want of guns, she having been disarmed by the government of Chili, in consequence of the active part she had taken in favour of the Peruvians, who adhered to Ferdinand. The value of these prizes to the enemy was estimated at two millions and a half of dollars. By this cruize, too, the whole of the American whale-ships were rescued from certain capture, and protected in those seas until the proper season for their return to the United States. The captured vessels were twelve in number, carrying, in the whole, 107 guns, and 302 men.— Two of the prizes were given up to the prisoners, three were sent to Valparaiso, where they were laid up, and three were

X

sent to the United States. Lieutenant Downes convoyed the prizes sent to Valparaiso, in another prize, which had been fitted up as a cruizer, under the name of the Essex Junior. He rejoined captain Porter at the Gallapagos on the 30th of September, and brought letters from Valparaiso, containing information that a squadron under the command of commodore James Hillyar, consisting of the frigate Phœbe, of 36 guns, the Raccoon and Cherub sloops of war, and a store-ship of 20 guns, had sailed from England in pursuit of the Essex. That the Raccoon and Cherub had been seeking her for some time on the coast of Brazil, and had then proceeded in quest of her to the Pacific.

The Essex had now been nearly a year at sea, almost without intermission, and, as may be supposed, required considerable repairs to put her in a proper state to meet the enemy. Captain Porter, therefore, determined to steer for the Washington Islands for that purpose, and, on the 2d of October, the Essex, in company with the Essex Junior, Greenwich, Seringapatam, New Zealander, and the Sir Andrew Hammond, finally left the Gallapagos, or the Enchanted Isles, as some have called them, from the difficulty of clearing them, owing to the currents and baffling winds. These islands are described by captain Porter as being all of volcanic origin, and totally devoid of running streams. There are some few springs, but the water is quickly absorbed by the loose and thirsty lava and cinders, of which these islands are principally composed.— When Porter visited them, their only inhabitants were tortoises, guanas, lizards, and snakes, but as he lost a number of goats, which were put on shore to graze, the probability is that they will soon be stocked by these useful animals. The turtles are in such abundance as to furnish plentiful supplies of fresh provision for ships stopping there.

The Marquesas, of which the Washington groupe forms a part, are situated between the latitude of 6° and 11° S. and 136° and 142° W. from London. Captain Porter, with his squadron, arrived at the island called Nooaheevah by the natives, on which Porter bestowed the name of Madison's Island, in honour of the American president. Here a fine bay was discovered, which appeared to offer every advantage that could be desired. A friendly intercourse was soon opened with the natives dwelling near the beach; but their operations on shore were threatened to be disturbed by the natives of a neighbouring valley, who were at war with those among whom Porter had landed. On the capture of one of their strong holds, however, by a party of sailors, who accompanied the friendly natives, the hostile Indians gladly accepted of the peace offered by Porter, on the condition of establishing a friendly commerce with him. The Indians now erected a little village for the reception of the articles taken out of the Essex, in order to her repairs, and the greatest harmony prevailed between the Americans and most of the tribes of the island, who brought plentiful supplies of provisions in exchange for pieces of iron, fish-hooks, and whale's teeth.

But the conduct of the Typees, one of the most numerous and warlike tribes in the island, again threatened to put a speedy stop to the useful intercourse established with the natives. They continually insulted the friendly Indians, calling them cowards for submitting to the white men, to whom they applied the most degrading epithets. In reply to a messenger whom Porter sent to their valley, to induce them to remain at peace, and to require an exchange of presents as a proof of their friendly disposition, they desired to know why they should seek his friendship, and why they should bring him hogs and fruit? If he was strong enough, they said, they knew he would come and take them: his not doing so was an acknowledgment of his weakness. Porter was extremely averse from engaging in a useless warfare with these people; but he conceived that necessity compelled him to take some steps to punish them, in order to secure the friendship of the other Indians, who made no secret of their belief that his backwardness to engage in war arose solely from cowardice. A distant day was therefore appointed for an expedition against the Typees, and in the mean while Porter practised every means to inspire them with peaceable views, by making them acquainted with the deadly effects of fire arms. But they felt too conscious of their numbers, and of the natural strength of their valley, surrounded by mountains impenetrable, as they believed, to white men, to listen to peaceable overtures; and in this disposition they were confirmed by the event of the first attempt made to enter their country. Thirty-five men, with captain Porter at their head, landed in their valley, but from the nature of the country, it was found impossible to make any impression on them with this small force; and after penetrating through marshes and thickets, through which they had to fight their way, the progress of the party was finally stopped by a strong wall, seven feet high, flanked by impenetrable thickets.

The situation of the party was at this moment peculiarly hazardous. The surrounding hills were covered by those Indians, who at present professed friendship. Great numbers also had landed with them, but they had taken little or no part

in the contest, and the appearance of a defeat, it was supposed, would bring on an attack from the tribe that had been before defeated, if not by the whole force of the island. A retreat was therefore feigned, in order to draw the Indians from
their fort, and in an instant they rushed upon the party with
hideous yells. The first and second which advanced were
killed, and those who attempted to carry them off were wounded; on seeing which, they abandoned their dead, and precipitately retreated to their fort. Porter was now suffered to retreat nearly unmolested. On arriving at the beach a messenger was again dispatched to offer peace, but they only answered by a challenge to renew the contest.

Porter now determined to embark, as the Indians had all descended the hills, and the defeat of the white men by the Typees formed the universal topic of conversation. The punishment of the hostile natives being deemed, however, more
important than ever, a large body was next day marched to
their valley across the mountains, and notwithstanding the extreme difficulties of the route, penetrated into their country,
and completely drove them out of the valley. We regret to
say, that the whole of their villages were burned and laid
waste, as, though the practice is usual in Indian warfare, we
cannot perceive that the same necessity existed that can be
urged for this measure in contests with the Indians in our own
territory.

The Typees were now glad to accept of the same terms of
peace which they had before scorned, and every tribe on the
island courted the friendship of the whites.

Previous to the Typee war, a fort had been erected in the
valley, where Porter first landed, by permission of the inhabitants, and the flag of the United States was hoisted, and the
island formally taken possession of in the name of the American government, by the title of Madison's Island, under a sa-
lute of 17 guns. The object of the ceremony being explained
to the inhabitants, they expressed much pleasure at the idea of
being adopted *Mellickees,* as they called the Americans.

The Essex being now completely repaired, and provisions
for four months laid in, she sailed for Valparaiso on the 12th
of December, in company with the Essex Junior. The three
prizes were secured under the guns of the fort, and left in
charge of lieutenant Gamble of the marines, and 21 men, with
orders to proceed to Valparaiso after a certain period.

Shortly after captain Porter reached Valparaiso, commodore
Hillyar arrived there in the Phœbe frigate, accompanied by
the Cherub sloop of war. These ships, having been sent out

expressly to seek for the Essex, were in prime order and equipment, with picked crews, and hoisted flags bearing the motto "God and country, British sailors' best rights: *traitors offend both.*" This was in opposition to Porter's motto of "Free trade and sailors' rights," and the latter part of it suggested, doubtless, by error industriously cherished, that the American crews were chiefly composed of English seamen.— In reply to this motto, Porter hoisted at his mizen, "God, our country, and liberty: tyrants offend them." On entering the harbour, the Phœbe fell foul of the Essex in such a manner as to lay her at the mercy of captain Porter; out of respect to the neutrality of the port, however, he did not take advantage of her exposed situation. This forbearance was afterwards acknowledged by commodore Hillyar, and he passed his word of honour to observe like conduct while they remained in port. They continued, therefore, while in harbour and on shore, in the mutual exchange of courtesies and kind offices, that should characterize the private intercourse between civilized and generous enemies; and the crews of the respective ships often mingled together, and passed nautical jokes and pleasantries from one to the other.

On getting their provisions on board, the Phœbe and Cherub went off the port, where they cruized for six weeks, rigorously blockading captain Porter. Their united force amounted to 81 guns and 500 men, in addition to which they took on board the crew of an English letter of marque lying in port. The force of the Essex consisted of but 46 guns, all of which, excepting six long twelves, were 32 pound carronades, only serviceable in close fighting. Her crew, having been much reduced by the manning of prizes, amounted to but 255 men. The Essex Junior being only intended as a store-ship, mounted ten 18 pound carronades and ten short sixes, with a complement of only 60 men.

This vast superiority of force on the part of the enemy prevented all chance of encounter, on any thing like equal terms, unless by express covenant between the commanders. Captain Porter, therefore, endeavoured repeatedly to provoke a challenge (the inferiority of his frigate to the Phœbe not justifying him in making the challenge himself), but without effect. He tried frequently also to bring the Phœbe into single action ; but this commodore Hillyar warily avoided, and always kept his ships so close together as to frustrate captain Porter's attempts. Finding it impossible to bring the enemy to equal combat, and fearing the arrival of additional force, which he understood was on the way, Porter determined to put to sea the first op-

portunity that should present. A rendezvous was accordingly
opened for the Essex Junior, and having ascertained by repeated trials that the Essex was a superior sailer to either of
the blockading ships, it was agreed that she should let the
enemy chase her off; thereby giving the Essex Junior an opportunity of escaping.

On the next day, the 28th of March, 1814, the wind came
on to blow fresh from the southward, and the Essex parted
her larboard cable, and dragged her starboard anchor directly
out to sea. Not a moment was lost in getting sail on the ship;
but perceiving that the enemy was close in with the point forming the west side of the bay, and that there was a possibility
of passing to windward, and escaping to sea by superior sailing, captain Porter resolved to hazard the attempt. He accordingly took in his top-gallant sails, and braced up for the
purpose, but, most unfortunately, on rounding the point, a heavy
squall struck the ship, and carried away her main top-mast,
precipitating the men who were aloft into the sea, who were
drowned. Both ships now gave chase, and the crippled state
of his ship left Porter no alternative but to endeavour to regain
the port. Finding it impossible to get back to the common
anchorage, he ran close into a small bay, about three quarters
of a mile to leeward of the battery, on the east of the harbour,
and let go his anchor within pistol shot of the shore. Supposing
the enemy would, as formerly, respect the neutrality of the
place, he considered himself secure, and thought only of repairing the damages he had sustained. The wary and menacing approach of the hostile ships, however, displaying their
motto flags, and having jacks at all their masts' heads, soon
showed him the real danger of his situation. With all possible dispatch, therefore, he got his ship ready for action, and
endeavoured to get a spring on his cable, but had not succeeded, when, at 54 minutes past 3, P. M. the enemy commenced
an attack.

At first the Phœbe placed herself under his stern, and the
Cherub on his starboard bow; but the latter soon finding herself
exposed to a hot fire, bore up and ran under his stern also,
where both ships kept up a severe and raking fire. Porter
succeeded three different times in getting springs on his cables, for the purpose of bringing his broadside to bear on the
enemy, but they were as often shot away by the excessive fire
to which he was exposed. He was obliged, therefore, to rely
for defence against this tremendous attack merely on three
long twelve-pounders, which he had run out of the stern-ports;
and which were worked with such bravery and skill, as in half

an hour to do great injury to both the enemy's ships, and induce them to haul off and repair damages. It was evidently the intention of commodore Hillyar to risk nothing from the daring courage of his antagonist, but to take the Essex at as cheap a rate as possible. All his manœuvres were deliberate and wary; he saw his antagonist completely at his mercy, and prepared to cut him up in the safest and surest manner. In the mean time the situation of the Essex was galling and provoking in the extreme; crippled and shattered, with many killed and wounded, she lay awaiting the convenience of the enemy, to renew the scene of slaughter, with scarce a hope of escape or revenge. Her brave crew, however, in place of being disheartened, were aroused to desperation, and by hoisting ensigns in their rigging, and jacks in different parts of the ship, evinced their defiance and determination to hold out to the last.

The enemy having repaired his damages, now placed himself, with both his ships, on the starboard quarter of the Essex, out of reach of her carronades, and where her stern-guns could not be brought to bear. Here he kept up a most destructive fire, which it was not in Porter's power to return; the latter, therefore, saw no hope of injuring him without getting under way and becoming the assailant. From the mangled state of his rigging, he could set no other than the flying jib; this he caused to be hoisted, cut his cable, and ran down on both ships, with an intention of laying the Phœbe on board. For a short time he was enabled to close with the enemy, and the firing on both sides was tremendous. The decks of the Essex were strewed with dead, and her cockpit filled with wounded; she had been several times on fire, and was in fact a perfect wreck; still a feeble hope sprung up that she might be saved, in consequence of the Cherub being compelled to haul off by her crippled state; she did not return to close action again, but kept up a distant firing with her long guns. The disabled state of the Essex, however, did not permit her to take advantage of this circumstance; for want of sail she was unable to keep at close quarters with the Phœbe, who, edging off, chose the distance which best suited her long guns, and kept up a tremendous fire, which made dreadful havoc among the crew of the Essex. Many of her guns were rendered useless, and many had their whole crews destroyed: they were manned from those that were disabled, and one gun in particular was three times manned; fifteen men were slain at it in the course of the action, though the captain of it escaped with only a slight wound. Captain Porter now gave up all

hopes of closing with the enemy, but finding the wind favourable, determined to run his ship on shore, land the crew, and
destroy her.   He had approached within musket-shot of the
shore, and had every prospect of succeeding, when, in an instant, the wind shifted from the land, and drove her down upon
the Phœbe, exposing her again to a dreadful raking fire. The
ship was now totally unmanageable; yet as her head was toward the enemy, and he to leeward, captain Porter again perceived a faint hope of boarding.   At this moment lieutenant
Downes of the Essex Junior came on board to receive orders,
expecting that captain Porter would soon be a prisoner.   His
services could be of no avail in the deplorable state of the Essex, and finding from the enemy's putting his helm up, that
the last attempt at boarding would not succeed, Downes was
directed to return to his own ship, to be prepared for defend-
ing and destroying her in case of attack. He took with him
several of the wounded, leaving three of his boat's crew on
board to make room for them. The Cherub kept up a hot
fire on him during his return.

The slaughter on board of the Essex now became horrible,
the enemy continuing to rake her, while she was unable to
bring a gun to bear in return.   Still her commander, with an
obstinacy that bordered on desperation, persisted in the unequal and almost hopeless conflict.   Every expedient that a fertile and inventive mind could suggest was resorted to, in the
forlorn hope that they might yet be enabled by some lucky
chance to escape from the grasp of the foe.   A halser was
bent to the sheet-anchor, and the anchor cut from the bows, to
bring the ship's head round.   This succeeded; the broadside
of the Essex was again brought to bear; and as the enemy
was much crippled, and unable to hold his own, Porter thought
she might drift out of gun-shot before she discovered that he
had anchored.   The halser, however, unfortunately parted,
and with it failed the last lingering hope of the Essex.   The
ship had taken fire several times during the action, but at this
moment her situation was awful. She was on fire both forward
and aft; the flames were bursting up each hatchway; a large
quantity of powder below exploded, and word was given that
the fire was near the magazine. Thus surrounded by horrors,
without any chance of saving the ship, Porter turned his attention to rescuing as many of his brave companions as possible. Finding his distance from the shore did not exceed three-
quarters of a mile, he hoped many would be able to save themselves should the ship blow up. His boats had been cut to
pieces by the enemy's shot, but he advised such as could swim

to jump overboard and make for shore. Some reached it, some were taken by the enemy, and some perished in the attempt; but most of this loyal and gallant crew preferred sharing the fate of their ship and their commander.

Those who remainded on board now endeavoured to extinguish the flames, and having succeeded, went again to the guns, and kept up a firing for a few minutes; but the crew had by this time become so weakened, that all further resistance was in vain. Captain Porter summoned a consultation of the officers of divisions, but was surprised to find only acting lieutenant Stephen Decatur M'Knight remaining; of the others, some had been killed, others knocked overboard, and others carried below disabled by severe wounds. The accounts from every part of the ship were deplorable in the extreme; representing her in the most shattered and crippled condition, in imminent danger of sinking, and so crowded with the wounded, that even the birth-deck could contain no more, and many were killed while under the surgeon's hands. In the mean while the enemy, in consequence of the smoothness of the water and his secure distance, was enabled to keep up a deliberate and constant fire, aiming with coolness and certainty as if firing at a target, and hitting the hull at every shot. At length, utterly despairing of saving the ship, captain Porter was compelled, at 20 minutes past 6, P. M. to give the painful order to strike the colours. It is probable that the enemy did not perceive that the ship had surrendered; for he continued firing; several men were killed and wounded in different parts of the ship, and captain Porter, thinking he intended to show no quarter, was about to rehoist his flag and to fight until he sunk, when the enemy desisted his attack ten minutes after the surrender,

The loss on board the Essex was 58 killed, 39 wounded severely, 27 slightly, and 31 missing. The loss on board the British vessels was 5 killed and 10 wounded.

Thousands of the inhabitants of Valparaiso were spectators of the battle, covering the neighbouring heights: for it was fought so near the shore, that some of the shot even struck among the citizens, who, in the eagerness of their curiosity, had ventured down upon the beach. Touched by the forlorn situation of the Essex, and filled with admiration at the unflagging spirit and persevering bravery of her commander and crew, a generous anxiety ran throughout the multitude for their fate: bursts of delight arose, when, by any vicissitude of battle, or prompt expedient, a chance seemed to turn up in their favour; and the eager spectators were seen to wring their hands, and uttered groans of sympathy, when the transient hope was defeated, and the gallant little frigate once more became an unresisting object of deliberate slaughter.

- Though, from the distance and positions which the enemy chose, this battle was chiefly fought on Porter's part by six twelve-pounders only, yet great damage was done to the assailing ships. Their masts and yards were badly crippled, their hulls much cut up; the Phœbe, especially, received 18 twelve pound shot below her water line, some three feet under water. It was with some difficulty that the Phœbe and the Essex could be kept afloat until they anchored the next morning in the port of Valparaiso.

Captain Porter and his crew were paroled, and permitted to return to the United States in the Essex Junior, her armament being previously taken out. On arriving off the port of New York, they were overhauled by the Saturn razee, the authority of commodore Hillyar to grant a passport was questioned, and the Essex Junior detained. Captain Porter then told the boarding-officer that he gave up his parole, and considered himself a prisoner of war, and as such should use all means of escape. In consequence of this threat the Essex Junior was ordered to remain all night under the lee of the Saturn, but the next morning captain Porter put off in his boat, though thirty miles from shore; and, notwithstanding he was pursued by the Saturn, effected his escape, and landed safely on Long Island. The Essex Junior was, however, released, and arrived shortly after at New York.

The small party left with lieutenant Gamble in charge of the prizes at Madison's island, met with a series of misfortunes, which eventuated in the loss of all the vessels, and the breaking up of the establishment. Hardly had the Essex got clear of the Islands, before a hostile disposition was discovered in the natives; and in a few days they became so insolent, that Gamble conceived it to be absolutely necessary to land his men to recover by force of arms the articles they had stolen from his encampment, and to deter them from putting their threats into execution. Fortunately this was accomplished without the firing of a musket, and a perfect amity was kept up for several months afterwards.

On the 9th of May, while Gamble was preparing to depart for Valparaiso, an attack was made on his ship by the natives. His numbers had been previously reduced by desertion, and by a mutiny, which ended in the escape of the mutineers in one of the prizes. After suffering a severe loss in the scuffle with the natives, a breeze fortunately sprung up, which enabled the party to leave the bay. It being now reduced to eight souls, not more than three of whom were effective, it was impracticable to reach Valparaiso, which lay to windward. Gamble therefore steered for the Sandwich islands, where he was captured by the Cherub sloop of war.

The cruize of the Essex in the Pacific ocean will ever form one of the most memorable events in the history of our country; and posterity will hesitate whether most to admire the wisdom which devised, or the energy which carried it into execution. With a single ship, ill appointed for such a cruize, Porter boldly braved the terrors of the tempestuous cape, and by his successful intrepidity cut off the whole of the valuable commerce of the enemy in those waters, where Great Britain never dreamt that an American frigate would dare to make her appearance. For twelve months Porter lorded it over the Pacific, at the head of a little squadron of his own formation, without any expense to his country, his ships being fitted out and furnishd with provisions and stores solely from the fruits, of his enterprise. Numerous ships were sent to the Pacific in pursuit of him, others were ordered to cruize in the China seas, off New Zealand, Timor, and New Holland, and a frigate sent to the river La Plata. These vessels, it is said, were ordered to effect his destruction without respect to the neutrality of any port in which he might have taken shelter, an order which was faithfully executed by commodore Hillyar, notwithstanding the honourable example set him by captain Porter. The gallant defence of the Essex adds another laurel to the wreath which encircles our seamen, and, as was officially acknowledged by commodore Hillyar, " did honour to her brave defenders, and most fully evinced the courage of captain Porter, and those under his command."

Meanwhile the remainder of our little navy continued to make every sea the theatre of their exploits. No more frigates, it is true were added to the list of our naval triumphs, for, taught by sad experience, strict orders were issued by the British admiralty to their frigates, to avoid encounters with those of the United States, and indeed they were seldom allowed to put to sea alone. Six sloops of war, however were captured; the Epervier by the Peacock, the Reindeer and Avon by the Wasp, the Penguin by the Hornet, and the Cyane and Levant by the Constitution frigate. The loss of the American navy at sea was two sloops of war and the President frigate, each of them by an overwhelming force.

The blockade of the American coast, which nominally extended from Rhode Island to the Mississippi, was on the 25th

of April, 1814, extended to every port of the United States.—
But neither our public nor our private cruizers were to be deterred from proceeding to sea by those paper blockades. An
astonishing havoc was committed upon the English commerce,
not only in the high seas, but on the coast of Great Britain,
in her channels, and even in the very mouths of her harbours.
Such was the uneasiness and alarm created by the numerous
captures by the Amercans, that for a while insurance could
not be effected at all to distant ports, and even from England to Ireland, a few hours sail, a premium of five guineas
per cent was demanded.

The admiralty were besieged with memorials from the mer-
cantile cities, and from the insurance offices: but they acknowledged the remedy to be beyond their power. In answer to
numerous remonstances on this subject, it was officially stated
by Mr. Croker, that an ample force had been under the orders
of the admirals on the different stations, and that during the
time when the American depredations were stated to have
taken place in St. George's channel, not fewer then three frigates and fourteen sloops of war were actually at sea for its
protection.

The achievments of the American privateers have in many
instances rivalled those of our public vessels; and we regret
that our limits have hitherto prevented us from paying them
the attention they deserve. It would be improper, however,
to pass over the gallant defence of the Generel Armstrong, by
captain Reid and his brave crew, in the port of Fayal. This action forms but one out of the many instances in which the British commanders have set at nought the rights of neutrality,
by the capture of American vessels in friendly ports; but in
none has it been effected at such an expense of blood to the
violators.

On the the 26th of September, about dusk, while the General Armstrong lay at anchor in Fayal harbour the British brig
Carnation hove in sight within gun-shot, and no sooner did she
understand the character of the privateer, than she hauled
close in and let go her anchor within pistol shot of her. At the
same time the Plantagenet 74, and the frigate Rota hove in
sight, and after an interchange of signals between them and the
Carnation, the latter threw out all her boats, and appeared to
be making unusual exertion. The moon being near its full
enabled captain Reid to observe these movements, which determined him to haul in nearer to the shore. Accordingly after
clearing for action, he got under way, and began to sweep in.
The moment this was perceived by the Carnation, she cut her

cable, made sail, and dispatched four boats in pursuit well manned and armed. On approaching the Armstrong, the boats were repeatedly hailed by captain Reid, but they made no answer, and only pulled with the greater speed. A fire was therefore opened upon them, which was immediately returned; but the boats soon cried for quarter, and hauled off. They then fled to their ships, and prepared for a second and more formidable attack: the privateer, in the mean time, was anchored within half cable's length of the shore, and within half pistol shot of the castle.

At 9 o'clock the Carnation was observed towing in a fleet of boats from the 74 and frigate. They soon after left her, and took their station in three divisions, under cover of a small reef of rocks, within about musket shot of the General Armstrong, where they continued to manœuvre for some time, the Carnation keeping under way to act with the boats, in case the privateer should attempt to escape. At length, about midnight, the boats were observed in motion, coming on in one direct line, in close order, to the number of 12 or 14, manned as was afterwards learnt, by 400 men. A severe conflict ensued, which lasted near forty-minutes, and terminated in the total defeat and partial destruction of the boats, with an immense slaughter on the part of the British.

During these attacks the shores were lined with inhabitants, who, from the brightness of the moon, had a favourable view of the scene. The governor, with most of the first people of the place, stood by, and saw the whole affair. After the second attack a note was sent from the governor to captain Lloyd, of the Plantagenet, who commanded the British squadron, begging him to desist from further hostilities; but Lloyd answered, that he was now determined to have the privateer, at the risk fo knocking down the whole town; and that if the governor suffered the Americans to injure the privateer in any manner, he should consider the place an enemy's port, and treat it accordingly. Information to this effect being conveyed to captain Reid by the American consul, the wounded and dead were carried on shore, and the crew ordered to save their effects as fast as possible.

About day-light the Carnation stood close in to the Armstrong, and commenced a heavy fire; but after several broadsides, she hauled off, having received a shot in her hull, her rigging much cut, and her fore-top-mast wounded. She soon after came in again, however, and anchored close to the privateer, when captain Reid ordered his crew to scuttle and abandon the vessel, to prevent the enemy from getting her off.

Y

She was soon afterwards boarded by the enemy's boats, and set fire to.

The loss of the Americans in this affair was only two killed and seven wounded; the British had 120 killed and 130 wounded. Several houses in the town were destroyed by the enemy's shot, and some of the inhabitants wounded. Two British sloops of war arrived a few days after, which were immediately taken into requisition to carry the wounded to England.

In this situation stood affairs when a treaty of peace was agreed upon by the commissioners of the two nations at Ghent. After a tedious procrastination on the part of the British government, the negociation was commenced by the British commissioners bringing forward demands which could only have been acceded to by a degraded and conquered people, one of which was declared to be a *sine qua non;* and that, after finding that the only effect produced by these demands was the union of the whole American people to resist them, they were all withdrawn, and a treaty agreed on, simply placing the political rights and territories of the two nations on the same footing as previous to the war. It was signed at Ghent on the 24th of December, and soon after ratified by the prince regent. It received its final ratification by the president on the 18th of February, 1815.

This treaty was generally satisfactory to the American people, for, though it left the great questions of impressment and illegal blockades, unsettled, it was believed, that the respect which the victories of the navy had inspired towards the American flag, would prevent a repetition of those outrages which preceded the war. The mighty changes which had taken place in Europe were believed to have the same tendency, by removing many of the pretexts on which these outrages were founded.

But although the peace with America was also a general subject of joy in Great Britain, much dissatisfaction was excited on the publication of the terms. The treaty formed, indeed, a deplorable contrast with the high-sounding threats and boasts of the ministry but a few months before; and after the demands which had been brought forward, it was conceived that it consummated the humiliation of the British ministry.*

---

* *The public stocks experienced a considerable depression on the publication of the treaty, it being conceived, that nothing but the probability of a new war in Europe could have occasioned the disgraceful compromise, as the treaty was called by the government papers.*

On an address being moved in the house of commons congratulating the prince regent on the re-establishment of peace, an amendment was moved, which, though it was not carried, shows in a striking manner the sentiments of a great part of the nation. The amendment proposed that the following should be substituted for the original address.

" To assure his royal highness that we contemplate with great satisfaction the restoration of a state of peace and amity between his majesty and the United States of North America; but we should deem ourselves highly deficient in the discharge of our duty towards his majesty and his people, were we not to express to his royal highness our deepest regret, that a measure so necessary to the welfare and prosperity of his majesty's dominions, was not sooner accomplished: that in reviewing the terms of the treaty which his royal highness has been graciously pleased to lay before us, we are at a loss to discover what were the causes which so long retarded its conclusion; that, in our opinion, the honour of his majesty's crown, and the interests of his people, both required that as soon as the peace of Europe had been established by the treaty signed at Paris, on the 8th day of May, in the last year, the speediest and most effectual measures should have been adopted for the negociation of a treaty of peace with the United States of North America; that the complete and entire cessation of hostilities in Europe had removed or suspended the operation of the causes, which had occasioned or accompanied the late war between his majesty and the United States; that the elevated and commanding station which the united kingdom then held amongst the nations of the world would have rendered the manifestation of a sincere wish for the restoration of the blessings of peace with the United States highly honourable to his majesty's counsels; and would have afforded the government and people of America the most unequivocal proofs of the generosity and magnanimity of the British nation; of a sincere desire to bury in lasting oblivion the recollection of that hostility which then unhappily subsisted, and of its anxious wish for the re-establishment of peace upon terms honourable and advantageous to both countries, and likely to insure its own permanancy by the justice and liberality of its conditions; that we are the more deeply afflicted by the long and (as we deem it) unnecessary delay in the conclusion of peace, when we reflect upon the great and incomparable injury his majesty and his people have sustained, by the unnecessary and unprofitable waste of treasure, by the loss of so many distinguished and heroic officers, and of such numbers of brave, loyal, and expe-

rienced troops; and we most deeply lament that these calamities should be aggravated by mortifying reflections, that the
fame of the British arms may appear to be diminished by the
failure of the latest military enterprizes of the war.   That it
affords us, however, consolation to find, that peace is at length
re-established; and to assure his royal highness, that it is the
earnest wish and desire of this house to cultivate and maintain
the most cordial and intimate union with the government and
people of the United States.

   " That we rely upon his royal highness's wisdom and good-
ness to cherish and preserve the most friendly relations between them and his majesty's subjects; and we confidently
trust, that a corresponding disposition in the government and
the people of the United States, will enable his royal highness
to continue unimpaired, and undisturbed, the harmony now so
happily restored between them; and that the two freest nations
in the world may exhibit to mankind the grateful spectacle of
mutual confidence and lasting peace."

   The experience of the war has taught us many useful les-
sons, which it is to be hoped our statesmen will not suffer to
pass without profit.   We have learnt that a large and efficient
revenue, not vulnerable from abroad, is essential to its successful conduct; and that a dependence on loans for the extra expenses of war is fatal and ruinous.

   We have learnt that a navy is not only the best and cheapest,
but the only effectual defence against the invasion of a coast
so extensive as that of the United States; that a navy is peculiarly suited to the genius of our country; and, that, as it
cannot possibly endanger our republican institutions, its size
ought to keep pace with our means of supporting it.

   We have also seen the advantages and defects of our militia
system; and the necessity that exists for more clearly determining the powers of the general government on this and on
other important questions.   It is to be hoped that the present
period of unexampled harmony will not be suffered to pass
unimproved.*

---

   * By the articles of confederation, the states appointed the
regimental officers, the general government the field and general officers.   Is there any solid objections to this plan?